# CODE NAME:
# JOHNNY WALKER

# THE EXTRAORDINARY STORY OF THE IRAQI WHO RISKED EVERYTHING TO FIGHT WITH THE U.S. NAVY SEALs

# CODE NAME: JOHNNY WALKER

## "JOHNNY WALKER"
### WITH JIM DeFELICE

*Wm*

WILLIAM MORROW
An Imprint of HarperCollins*Publishers*

*Designed by Richard Oriolo*

Library of Congress Cataloging-in-Publication Data has been applied for.

ISBN 978-0-06-226755-9

14 15 16 17 18   OV/RRD   10 9 8 7 6 5 4 3

To my wife and children, the great loves of my life

Livin' the dream . . .

# CONTENTS

# A NOTE TO THE READER

Though many people know me as Johnny Walker, it is not my real name. It's actually a nickname the SEALs gave me while I served with them in Iraq.

In order to protect my family, both here and in Iraq, I have decided to use *only* that name. I have also found it necessary to omit and generally obscure the identities of those closest to me in Iraq, along with other identifying characteristics, so that their lives will not be endangered. I have done the same for security reasons involving some of the missions I undertook with American and Iraqi forces, as well as changed or otherwise used my own nicknames for all former and active-duty SEALs important to the story.

The incidents recounted here are from my own memory. Admit-

tedly, time blurs much, but I and my cowriter have tried to corrobo-
rate everything possible. The dialogue has been reconstructed and
in many cases translated from Arabic; it is not meant to be verbatim
but rather representative of what was said and what happened at
the time.

# INTRODUCTION

## INDOMITABLE SPIRIT

Johnny's ingenuity, indomitable spirit, and utter fearlessness not only protected the lives of many SEALs, but also saved the lives of countless innocent Iraqis. He is a true hero to all of us.

Some of my most memorable moments in Iraq took place while hanging out with Johnny and the Iraqi commandos, marveling at Johnny's ability to unite Shias, Sunnis, and Kurds as we discussed challenging topics like religion and ethnic conflict. This continues to be Johnny's contribution—his monklike, thoughtful appreciation of how life works and how to lead it well.

Seeing Johnny and his family living safely in the United States, embracing life as patriotic Americans, is something I will cherish forever.

—CAPTAIN X, SEAL TEAM COMMANDING OFFICER

## GOOD FROM EVIL

The war in Iraq: No issue has divided our country more since Vietnam. The soldiers, sailors, airmen, Marines, and their families have paid an incredibly high psychological and physical toll. The same can be said for the Iraqis. Economists decry the amount of money spent with little return on investment. Parents lost children. Husbands and wives lost spouses. Children lost parents. Warriors lost brothers and sisters. The question I have been asked many times, by others and even myself, is: Was it worth it?

While deployed to Iraq, that answer changed many times. When a suicide bomber detonated himself at Checkpoint 12 in the Green Zone, killing a young National Guardsman, the answer was no. But when we decimated an al-Qaeda cell responsible for training and equipping suicide bombers, then it was absolutely yes.

When an IED detonated and killed not only American soldiers but also a mother and her children, it was a resounding no. But when our snipers killed a mujahideen fighter placing an IED, it was a resounding yes.

Of course, without the war, or without any war for that matter, those situations would never present themselves. War is worth it only for those who don't have to fight it or live with the consequences. But make no mistake, there are some horrific people in the world who will stop at nothing to impose their twisted vision on all those who won't fight or fight back. They need to be dealt with viciously, yet surgically.

I have come to realize lately that perhaps the better question to ask is whether any good came from the war. I will allow the historians and politicians to debate endlessly on the strategic impact. I, like every other person who fought there, can only answer on the personal level.

My answer is yes.

For me, the little things made all the difference. Conducting a direct-action mission in al-Dora to capture an al-Qaeda member may have had little strategic significance. But it meant that the California National Guardsmen and -women who controlled that jewel of a neighborhood would not get hit with an IED for a week.

Lives were saved; others found a moment of respite from horror.

There were many similar tactical victories that did much good. For me, the most surreal and decisive came during the trial of Saddam Hussein. At the time, I had two of our new interpreters living in my room. We had a satellite television hookup, and it quickly became the hangout for all the linguists, better known to us as "terps." The day the verdict was to be read, representatives from every demographic in Iraq crowded into my room. One was a Shia who had fled to the States after the first Iraq war when he and the other Shia were systematically wiped out following their unsuccessful uprising. Another was a Kurd who had escaped with his family to America following the extermination of his village from a gas attack by Saddam; he and his wife had carried their children to safety by trekking fifty kilometers in the winter to the Turkish border. One gentleman was a Christian who had had the misfortune of taking care of Uday and Qusay—Saddam's sons—when they were children; he'd left the country after the first Gulf war and moved to Pasadena. And, of course, Johnny Walker, still an Iraqi citizen, was there.

It is impossible for me to describe the emotion and elation when the verdict of "guilty" came across the TV. They were all dancing, hugging, shouting in celebration. I could literally feel the yoke of tyranny being lifted off their collective shoulders. It was good.

For all of them except Johnny, it was closure. They could do their time in Iraq and return to the new lives they had made for themselves in America.

Not Johnny.

This was when the gravity of the situation really hit me. Johnny Walker would have to live with the aftermath.

Shortly thereafter, I hit up Johnny to see if he wanted us to work on a path to citizenship for him and his family. He responded, "Brother, this is my country. I am going to see it through."

I kind of figured he would say that, but I could tell that I'd blown oxygen on a flame that was lit in the room on the day of the verdict.

Over the course of the next month, I hoped in vain that Johnny would come and take me up on the offer. Finally, in October 2005, the day came for me to depart Iraq and head home. It goes without question that I could not wait to see my family. But I had a huge pit in my stomach. I knew the danger Johnny was in. (He understates it in this book).

When we said good-bye, I feared he wouldn't survive the war. He risked so much to help us and there was no way to repay him if the U.S. pulled out of Iraq. It felt wrong not having him come to the States, but I respected his dedication to his country. Still, upon my return to the safety of my country and the love of my family, I felt a lingering guilt.

That changed months later when I got the call from the CO of SEAL Team 1 telling me that things had gotten too bad for Johnny and family and he wanted to come to the States. The concern and guilt now had an outlet. Over the next three and a half years, countless SEALs played a part in moving the painstakingly slow immigration process forward. It is a testament to Johnny's incredible character when I look at the time and energy put into this endeavor by so many warriors.

I must pause here and thank George, the lawyer, for all his help. He managed the process with incredible patience and a tireless work ethic. Without his benevolence and skill, Johnny's story may not have been told.

On July 8, 2009, I was out in the desert conducting training prior to a return trip to Iraq. I knew Johnny and family were inbound to San Diego, but until I had confirmation I couldn't be at ease. Finally I get a text from George: "He made it. They are all here."

Instantly, nearly four years of stress disappeared. My eyes welled up. Next to my marriage and the birth of my kids, I have never been happier.

Only a psychopath or someone with no skin in the game wants war. But good can come out of any terrible situation and war is no exception. Because of war, Johnny and his family, whom I love like my own, live in the United States: safe, free, and at peace.

These days, I can't help but smile every time I see Johnny Walker. He still has that cool swagger he had in Iraq, but he looks genuinely happy and at ease. We talk about the mundane things in life instead of targets or the history of the rift between Sunni and Shia.

Johnny and his family are living proof that the American Dream still exists. I hope, no *I know,* his incredible children will grow up to be wildly successful. After all, they inherited the genes of a warrior, of a hero, of a true American.

—"TATT," SEAL CHIEF PETTY OFFICER

# PROLOGUE: FREEDOM

**M**Y AMERICA IS your America, and your America is mine. It is a refuge and a dream, a place of freedom and respite, responsibility and wonder. To have arrived here, after the journey I took, after the bombs and gunfire and killings, the beheadings and kidnappings, the dangers, after everything that has happened in my life: the idea that I am free now, and the knowledge of everything it means, fills me with gratitude. I am thankful for every moment and every breath. I am grateful to the SEALs who risked their lives for my family, grateful for the sacrifices of other servicemen and -women, grateful to my neighbors and new friends who have welcomed me to this land of large dreams and open skies.

Every day, I live a dream. My dream. But unlike most, my dream began amid a nightmare—a murderous war in Iraq that destroyed not only the lives of many of my friends and relatives, but an entire country and culture. That destruction began long before the war I fought in. Long before that conflict began, Iraq was a broken country, a place ruled more by fear than law, a place where making a decent living was for many an impossible dream.

The American war brought hope to the disenfranchised Iraqis. But soon that hope evaporated, replaced by violence and bloodshed. The Americans were an excuse but not the cause of this nightmare. The hatred and villainy it engendered tore what had been my country apart; its effects continue to this day.

I am far away from that now.

Today, on a cool morning in San Diego, I walk out on the pier at Imperial Beach and feel the wind push against my body, tearing at my clothes and sandpapering my face. It's a wonderful feeling.

At six in the morning, the beach is nearly always deserted. It is as if I have the edge of the world completely to myself.

I wait a little while. The fishermen come and cast their lines into the surf. Someone once told me that fishing is a great act of faith—to fish one must be incredibly patient, but one must also believe. He waits in the water and the wind, casting and standing, believing that eventually his persistence will pay off. He dreams of landing a fish. He rehearses for it in his head; he hopes; he waits.

That sort of dreaming is familiar to me. That is how I came to America, an immigrant before I even knew I could travel, a citizen in my hopes before the wish could even be spoken. A fisherman.

America is a land of immigrants. Every family here has its own unique story of travel, of hardship in many cases, of triumph and sadness. Many of these stories are filled with tears; a few are marked by blood. My story has both.

I have debated how much to say about the war and my role in it. I thought of not telling about these things, but in the end, I decided that people should know the real story. I think a lot of people will say that what happened was very savage. Perhaps they will think that I am a savage as well, though in my mind I did what I had to do and killed only to survive.

Some people, including some of the bravest warriors America has produced—the SEALs—have called me a hero.

That is not a word I use to describe myself. I am only a man who did what I thought I needed to do, what I felt I had to do. I was a man doing a job, one I was happy to have, for it meant I could support my family at a time and place when it was difficult to do so.

And for a while at least, a job I thought meant I was changing my country for the better.

People ask how many missions I went on, how many times I faced death. I don't know. I went on at least hundreds and more likely thousands of operations with just the SEALs alone, sometimes two or three in a single night. American military units rotated in and out of the country every few months, taking a rest back in the States for months and even years. For me, there was no rotation, and the rests were not only very short, but in a war zone. IEDs and stray bullets were as much a danger as actual combat or "direct action," often more so.

It all seemed like a normal life then. Perhaps that itself is a measure of the war's insanity.

If I have courage or fear or even savagery, it is because I am human. These things are in all of us; war only brings them out. We are all capable of the worst possible crimes. We can all kill; we can all destroy. These are far easier to do than build, or help someone live. I have found to my horror that it does not take much to become a monster.

I didn't always think this way. Maybe like most people—I *hope* most people think this way—I thought at one time that the world was basically good. I believed, and still believe, that we can all live together in peace, and by working together make our communities and the world a better place. I feel, I know, that it is better to make and to build than to tear down and destroy.

I thought all people around me believed that, too.

Little by little, I saw this wasn't true.

I fought it; I tried to change it; eventually I saw my only course was to escape it. But before I was able to call America my home, I had to denounce America. Before I could taste freedom I had to taste death itself.


**IT WAS THE** late summer of 2004. I'd been working for a number of different American organizations, civilian and military, for more than a year. The liberation of Iraq had been a glorious moment, a triumph that nearly all of us in Mosul shared. When I got my first job as a translator, everyone on my street celebrated with me. "Way to go, Johnny," they said. "Now you are made."

"What a wonderful thing."

But in barely a year, all of that changed. Things turned murderously bad. My job went from a thing to be celebrated to a thing to be hidden. Any association with Americans was a death sentence. If Navy SEALs loved me for helping them, mujahedeen terrorists hated me for the same thing.

One morning on my way to the SEAL base, a car pulled up behind me as I approached a traffic circle in western Mosul. Instinctively I knew what would happen. As I looked for an escape route, the car drew close and the man in the passenger seat began firing.

I was lucky. The bullets missed.

I veered off the road, then gunned the engine and managed to hit the other car as it turned. I jumped out, AK-47 in my hands.

How many rounds I fired, I have no idea. Both men in the car died, either because of the crash or because of my bullets, I'll never know—and it makes no difference.

People ran to us. As the crowd gathered, I could feel their hatred. "What is it?" they demanded. "What are you doing?"

There was only one way to escape.

"They worked with the Americans," I said loudly. "They had to die."

The crowd began to cheer. A few pelted the car with rocks. Suddenly, the car was in flames.

I quickly made my getaway.

It was one of the worst days of my life, the day that I denounced America. But it was also the day that my escape to the United States began.

# 1

# BEFORE THE DREAM

**THE IRAQ YOU** know is not the Iraq of my youth. The Iraq I know now is not the place where I grew up. Its location on earth may be the same, its essential geography identical. But it is a very different place.

I do not wish to paint a portrait of paradise, for Iraq even then was far from a perfect land. Everyone puts a sheen on their past, their childhood especially; we almost always see it through a window that blocks out the darkness and enhances the light. Looking back, we remember the smiles of our fathers and mothers, our triumphs and successes. The failures seem smaller, the disappointments faded to the margins where they belong.

Eons before the Roman Empire was conceived, the region that is now Iraq gave birth to the civilization of Sumer. The cities that made up Sumer were among the earliest known to us today. Cradled along the rivers, the southern Mesopotamian civilization thrived starting sometime before the twenty-ninth century B.C. Archaeologists credit the people with many inventions, from the simple but radical concept of the wheel, to mathematics that used the number 10 as its base—the same system we use today. Sites related to the Sumerian people dot Iraq, and despite the violence of the country's recent history, important archaeological discoveries continue to be made.

That past is literally buried by the sands of time. Alexander conquered what is now Iraq in the fourth century B.C.; the Parthians and the Romans followed. Christianity came to the land between the first and third centuries A.D. Assyria—northern Iraq between the Euphrates and Tigris—was an important center for the early Eastern Christian church. In the seventh century, Khālid ibn al-Walīd, one of history's greatest generals, helped bring Islam to Iraq; it has been the dominant religion ever since.

For the next thousand years, Iraq was part of various kingdoms, settling under Ottoman rule in the sixteenth century and then, following World War I, becoming a League of Nations "mandate" under British control. Though Iraq was formally granted independence in 1932, British influence remained strong until after World War II.

Through much of this time, the most important allegiance a man had was not to the distant emperor or sultan, or even to the local governor or consul, but to his family and tribe. Even today, tribal identity is very important. Experts say there are over one hundred and fifty tribes in the country.

Iraqis are related to tribes in two ways: birth and marriage. If a man marries outside his tribe, as a general rule, his children belong to the tribe he comes from. My own tribe is small but important. (I still have many relatives in Iraq, and mentioning its name will give them troubles they do not need.) Our ancestors and current members include many successful people. My own grandfather was a prominent leader; he had a private militia and was hired by the Turks to fight against the British.

I was born December 4, 1964, in Mosul. The city straddles the Tigris River about 225 miles north of Baghdad. It's a sprawling city, with parts that date back to the early Mesopotamian civilizations and areas that were among the most modern in Iraq before the war. Some 1.8 million people live in the city, many in densely packed areas of small homes often shared by many adult members of a family.

Americans often don't realize how urban Iraq really is. The government estimates that more than three-quarters of Iraq's 31 million people live in cities. More than 7 million of them live in Baghdad. Imagine a country the size of California, but with most of its population clustered into a handful of cities. The vast desert that many Americans think of when they picture Iraq lies west of Baghdad. Lightly populated, it is not the environment most Iraqis experience day to day.

Mosul is a case in point. When I was born it was a large, flat city, a collection of khaki-brown brick and concrete buildings spreading as far as the eye could see. Lush parks with tropical green trees and large lawns added color, while the curved roofs of mosques and minaret towers gave the city depth. Newer buildings in the city center pushed against the old but didn't obliterate the place's history, much less imply the frantic pace of Western metropolises. A Westerner might imagine a Mediterranean city without the Mediterranean; a little slower, a little older, not quite as romantic.

For me, Mosul was a wonderful city. The nearby mountains are beautiful. The streets were clean. My family was respected. We lived in an apartment roughly a thousand square feet, cramped for a large family but typical of our street, a dense residential area a block from one of Mosul's main thoroughfares. The houses were cement and brick, khaki tan, neatly kept but far from fancy or ostentatious. I had an older brother, Hamid, born in 1957; a younger brother, Saif, came in 1973. I have three sisters, all older than me: Samaa, who was born in 1953; Hana, born in 1954, and Muna, born in 1962.

There was one other child in our immediate family, another brother, Ali, a few years older than I was. He was outside the house one day when he was eight, playing near an open cooking fire. Suddenly his clothes somehow caught fire. By the time the flames were extinguished, his body was badly burnt; he died of his injuries.

I was very young at the time, three or four maybe, but I can clearly remember how horribly my mother cried. Her tears came for days and days. The pain in her heart never left her.

After Ali's death, my mother became very protective of her children, all of us, but most especially me. I couldn't play near a heater, whether it was outside or in, even if it was electric and didn't have flames. She watched us all very closely—I felt at times that I had a chain around my leg. As I got older, I pulled at that chain, and soon left it far behind.

Admittedly, I had an adventurous streak. I was far from a delinquent and certainly not a bully, but I never shied from a fight or a confrontation. Mine was a rough-and-tumble childhood

Living in tiny, cramped houses with lots of relatives, we kids spent most of our time outside on the streets. Unspoken rules governed where you could go and what you could do. It was best not to stray from your own neighborhood, but if you had to for some reason, an errand or something, you had to act a certain way or pay the consequences. You had to be humble in other neighborhoods and kowtow to the kids who lived there. If you acted like you were too tough or looking for a fight, watch out.

Naturally, I went against these rules. I went into other neighborhoods a lot, looking for trouble. It was a challenge, a way to prove myself not to the kids in those neighborhoods, but to the ones where I lived.

Looking back now, I know much of this was silly if not stupid, but as a kid I felt as if I had to prove myself. And I did pretty well in the fights. Not that I won all or even most of the time. Winning and losing wasn't as important as making a good show of yourself. Not quitting, not giving up, just plain being tough—that was how you got respect.

Word would get back quickly after an encounter. The other kids would nod and smile.

"He's tough," they'd say.

"Yeah, he's a leader."

Things didn't always go very smoothly. I remember quite a few beatings at the hands of larger bunches of kids. One day I found myself in another neighborhood, surrounded by seven or eight kids, all around my age. I would have tried fighting them, maybe all at one time, but they were too smart for that. Instead, they formed a loose circle and kept their distance while pelting me with rocks. As soon as I'd get close to one I'd be hit with a couple of stones and have to duck away. Finally I found an opening and was able to run off.

The encounter had brought me nothing but bruises. It demanded revenge—an important concept in Iraq, even today. Whether you're a kid who's been surrounded and humiliated by others or an adult whose family has been wronged, avenging your honor is critical. If you let a slight go unanswered, it's hard to hold your head up on the street, even if you're the only one who knows what happened.

Feeling wronged because I'd been outnumbered and hit by rocks, I decided I needed to do something to restore my honor. So later that night, I took my trusty slingshot and went back to the street where I'd been pelted. The kids were nowhere to be seen, of course, but I found the house where one of them lived.

There was a white light outside the house . . .

*Ping!*

A smooth stone from my slingshot broke the light. I had my revenge. I went home a happy boy. I knew the kids would know exactly who broke the light. I hoped they'd venture into my neighborhood, where they would get a proper beating from *my* gang of friends; we'd use our fists, not rocks. But they never did.

Looking back, it seems silly and petty, but that was the law of kids and the neighborhood. And worse: in time, the insignificant posturing by boys not yet mature would become something more sinister. If you grow up needing to revenge any and all slights, you can't help but think that way as an adult. If there is no antidote to this—if the government is weak, if education is lacking—then violence surely begets more violence.

Not that I was philosophical as a child. Life was much more immediate and visceral. Truth was what you held in your hand— like my slingshot.

I was pretty good with slingshots. I would carve them from wood I found, shaving them smooth and carving them until they felt just right gripped between my fingers. Then I would soak them in salt and water, which made them tougher—or at least that was our neighborhood theory. I got so good that I made slingshots for all my friends.

I revived my slingshot skills years later while working with the SEALs. When we were operating in cities, we generally went on missions at night. Darkness helped conceal us and offered some protection. Streetlights were therefore an enemy. Rather than shooting them with guns, which of course made noise, I volunteered to ping them with a slingshot. With a little practice, my skills returned, and I was able to hit a lightbulb-sized target fairly regularly from thirty yards. The SEALs got me a high-tech slingshot made of metal, but the real secret to my success was the judicious choice of ammunition: only the roundest, most aerodynamic stones would do. I took to scouring the camps for them, and even naming my favorites. The SEALs may have had a chuckle, but "Fireball" and "Lightning" served them well.


**MY FATHER WAS** a good man, solid, loving, not a hero and not exceptional. He was also a *nice* guy, who seemed to get along with everyone. He could be tough when he needed to be—he wasn't soft—but mostly I remember him being kind to people. He wasn't a big fan of tribal things, let alone government; he cared about his own wife and kids, and took care of us. If there was an average male in Mosul, he was it.

I remember tagging along with him to his friends' houses many times. He would show me off proudly, even though looking back I had no special talents. I guess he saw me through a father's loving eyes.

"Here is my son," he would say. "Look at him—what a smart boy."

I was smart, though in all honesty you couldn't prove it by my grades as I got older.

In Iraq, children start elementary school at age six and spend six years there. Middle school and high school follow; usually students spend three years in each. At the end of high school, exams are held to see if you can qualify for college.

Attitudes toward education were a lot different than they are in the United States. Not that school wasn't considered important at all, but there certainly wasn't the sort of emphasis on getting good grades and doing well that there is here.

Even considering that context, my own attitude was not very good. I surely did not value my education as much as I could and should have. Because of this, I spent four years in middle school and another five in high school. Lack of effort, not intelligence, held me back as a young teenager.

And yet I remember high school as an exciting time for learning. I liked science and math, and on my own studied a wide range of subjects from American history to Karl Marx. It was during this time that I began learning about America. I remember reading *The Old Man and the Sea,* by Ernest Hemingway—a book I can still recall and occasionally cite to my friends.

Hemingway was a genius. He moves you, from emotion to emotion—wave to wave. *The Old Man and the Sea* has no fat, no wasted words or parts; everything works together to construct a perfect story of a fisherman fighting against the elements—of a simple man fighting to survive against all odds, of a people triumphing just by breathing.

I wish I could write like that.

I read Hemingway in English, but many Western writers' works were translated into Arabic, which is where I encountered most of them. I still remember a handful of teachers who influenced me, mostly for the better. Ziad, who taught English, and Waad, who instructed Arabic and literature, were the sort of teachers every student should have. Waad in particular was a very forgiving and understanding teacher. He gave you a chance, then a chance and a chance. He was a kind man, and I learned a lot from him. The same was true of Ziad, and I remember both men fondly.

Then there was my math teacher, whom I'll call Edmund. He was a Christian, unlike the others, but religion had nothing to do with his teaching style. He had a darker nature than the other men, more typical of the teachers in my school, and I would imagine throughout Iraq. Physical punishment was very much accepted at the time, and Edmund regularly delivered beatings in class, even for the smallest offense. I personally don't object to punishment any more than anyone else, but if a teacher was unfair, that bothered me. Edmund's punishments were out of proportion to the crime. Years later, I don't remember the infractions I was beaten for, but I do remember the lack of justice.

I remember one time a friend was late to school. As punishment, the teacher—none of the men I've named, though I can't remember who it was—had my friend hold out his hand so he could smack it with a cane. He hit him so hard I thought his hand was broken.

I decided to get even for him. After we were dismissed, I went home and got my slingshot. Walking back to the school lot, I found my teacher's green Volvo, stepped back, and took up position.

*Fsssshew . . . thwack, crash!*

The first stone broke the window. I kept up the bombardment, breaking another window and inflicting a few nice dents until all my ammo was gone. They say justice is sweet, and I have to admit it felt pretty good to mete it out.

To me things had to be balanced. It wasn't that my friend had been in the right. The problem was, his punishment was out of proportion to his crime. My assault evened the ledger.

The next day, the teacher asked if anyone knew what had happened to his car. My friend immediately figured out what had happened, but he didn't rat on me. Others may have suspected, but the teacher never caught me, and I certainly wasn't going to confess.

Corporal punishment was one reason, I guess, that I tried to be good—not because I was afraid of getting hit, but because I knew I couldn't control myself if someone hit me. I was sure that I would go crazy and fight to the end. One of us would have died, and I'm sure at that age I thought it would be the teacher.

**THERE WAS ONE** thing besides justice that I deeply cared about in school: sports.

I discovered basketball as a middle school student. I lucked into a gym teacher who would eventually become a good friend—Mr.

Yas. At first he seemed very harsh and tough. But I soon learned the method behind his strictness. He was being tough for a good reason. He saw that I had a lot of potential, and by demanding that I do my best, he was pushing me to achieve. And he was tough but not unfair; strict, yet with a good nature. It was no surprise that he became my favorite teacher.

Mr. Yas taught us many sports, but basketball was my best. I learned to shoot, to rebound, to play defense. Dribbling became second nature. Basic concepts blossomed into complex patterns in the paint.

I got better as I grew, and by the time I got to high school I made captain as a freshman. From that year on, I played what we called *bifet,* the equivalent of a center/power forward in American basketball. The team jelled around me. In my second year we had the best high school team in the entire city, and dominated regional competitions. The team's success made me something of a celebrity. It was heady stuff.

In America, a standout high school basketball player might dream of the NBA, and would certainly be recruited for college. Unfortunately for me, basketball in Iraq was nowhere near as developed. There was little chance of me making a living at it, and it had no bearing on my going to college. But it was certainly fun while it lasted.

I grew to over six feet tall in high school, eventually reaching six-four. My height gave me an advantage in another sport: track. I learned to high-jump.

Running at a bar and hoisting yourself over it isn't exactly natural; you can't do it without a great deal of practice. It was even more difficult for me because I didn't have experienced coaches, and there weren't even videos around to show us how it should be done. I learned from pictures and some verbal instructions that one of my coaches gave me. Once I was able to imagine how it should go, I worked on getting my body to do what my brain saw. My body eventually complied—so well, in fact, that I became the best high jumper in the city. By the time I graduated high school, I had the best high school high jump in the entire country—1.95 meters, or just under six and a half feet.

I should say that, while that was a *great* jump in Iraq, American high school athletes routinely approach seven feet, and most state records are higher.

For a short time—a very short time—I thought that maybe I might compete for the Olympics as a high jumper. I entered some regional matches and did fairly well. But I was never serious enough about training to get to the level I would have needed to join the national team.

I was easily disillusioned when I found there weren't immediate payoffs. As a teenager I couldn't see where all the hard work might get me. I remember winning a pair of shoes at a national meet for my performance, finishing first among all athletes under twenty years old. Rather than being happy, my only thought was, What kind of sport is this where all the winner gets are lousy shoes?

Not exactly the Olympic spirit, I know. But how to be selfless or even a good sportsman were not lessons I had learned. I was immature, and my ambitions centered around money. In my mind, I equated wealth with success. If I were a star—whether it was at track or basketball or something else—I thought surely I would be given a vast house with a swimming pool and beautiful gardens. I would have many fancy cars, BMWs and the like. My house would be on a lake. My family would spend days fishing and hunting.

More than luxury, more than wealth, the thing success would buy was true freedom. Only money would bring that in Iraq.

What sort of dreams does a teenage Iraqi boy have? Very similar dreams, I would guess, to the dreams boys all over the world have. We see ourselves as heroes. We want to be important. We want success, though what we know as success is what we are already familiar with. If we know war, we want to be war heroes. If we know sports, we want to be sports heroes.

My first dream was to be a pilot, flying at the speed of sound. What a dream that was: to be on top of the world, looking down. To be able to travel anywhere in the world. It would have been fantastic.

As my basketball skills improved, I dreamed of being a great star in Iraq, and the world. I didn't know much about the United States, so it wasn't really part of the dream yet. It was too distant, and maybe too perfect, even for a dream.

Sports brought me local fame and new friends throughout the city. We started spending time in bars, getting into a little trouble— the occasional fight. I was less aggressive than I had been when I was younger, more sure of myself, maybe. Still, if you pushed me the wrong way I would certainly stand up for myself. What's the American saying? I didn't start fights, but I certainly finished them.

Naturally, this was the time I discovered girls. A lot of them want to talk to you when you are a local hero, even in a society where boys and girls are not supposed to mingle. What we did as teenagers wouldn't raise an eyebrow in America, but in Iraq, simply talking to a girl could cause a scandal. I did my share of talking, with the occasional stolen kiss when no one else was looking.

To graduate high school and go on to college, I needed to pass a special exam. Math was my downfall. I missed a lot of my math classes because of basketball and other activities in school. As I said, my heart really wasn't into studying. I stayed in high school for five years, but never did well enough to pass. As a consequence, like all Iraqi men not going on to college or able to buy their way out of service, I had to go into the military.

Before I left Mosul, though, I made one last, very important discovery: a girl named Soheila. She changed my life.

# 2

# LOVE
# AND WAR

**O**NE HOT AUGUST day in 1987, just before I joined the army, I spotted a pretty girl going into a house near when my cousin lived. She was the most beautiful thing I had ever seen. Ever. At that very moment, I felt something I had never felt before. Her name was Soheila.

How do I describe that feeling? Even in Arabic, I struggle to find the right words. My tongue is not capable of describing my emotion in that moment. There is no way to describe how my heart boiled inside my chest.

I couldn't keep my feelings to myself. I told my sister, who told Soheila. She seemed unimpressed. Fifteen or sixteen at the time, she brushed off my interest. She was concentrating on her schoolwork, hoping to go into medicine when she got older. She was hoping to be a doctor or something else important—she had a flare for writing. She had no time for boys, let alone me.

I'm not one to take no for an answer, especially in something so important as love. My sister tried to let me down gently, but I paid no attention: I knew what I wanted. I called Soheila a few days later.

"Hey, Soheila," I told her. "I don't want anything from you. I just want to be friends."

That was apparently the right thing to say, because she didn't just blow me off. Soon, we were talking to each other practically every day.

Though I'd never taken much notice of her, in fact our families had once been very close. Soheila's great-grandparents had come to Mosul in 1937 from Basra, the large Shiite-dominated city far to the south of Iraq. They had relocated to save Soheila's great-grandfather's life. He'd been in a conflict there that resulted in someone's death. Though the actual circumstances now are obscure, it seems obvious enough that he was blamed; in order to escape retribution the family fled north, looking for a city where they weren't known.

They found their way to Mosul. Without family, they had no one really to rely on. My grandfather happened to befriend the family and helped them get established; for a time they even lived in the same house. The two families grew close enough that my mother and her sisters considered Soheila's mother and aunts to be cousins.

Some of that connection was lost as the offspring grew. The girls moved out on their own to various places, and by the time I was in high school I personally had only a slight acquaintance with the family. But the women in the families remembered their friends, and my mother and Soheila's mother would occasionally share tea when they saw each other. That family connection turned out to be important to helping me fulfill my growing desire.

I haven't talked about religion to this point because it hasn't been a critical part of the story. Our family was Sunni, the largest branch of Islam in the world, and the most numerous in Mosul by far. We weren't overly observant, which was pretty much the norm when I was growing up. I might have gone to a mosque once or twice a year, if that. Soheila's family was from the Shia branch of the religion. Today, there is much animosity between Shia and Sunni in Iraq. This wasn't true at the time. And since her family had been in the city for decades, most people had no idea that they were Shia. Religion simply wasn't as important as it would become later on, and for most people it wasn't a divider. It certainly didn't keep us apart.

Iraqi culture was a different story. A boy phoning a girl is frowned on at best, forbidden at worst—*especially* if there is a love interest.

Because of the closeness of our families in the past, I could claim to be a quasi-relative, which makes seeing someone from the other sex a little easier. And in theory, I was only interested in being Soheila's friend. But of course friendship wasn't what I was after, and I couldn't keep up that pretense very long.

Soheila was a true beauty, and there were plenty of men in Mosul who wanted to marry her. Most were older and more accomplished than I was, with better prospects for giving her a happy and comfortable life in Saddam's Iraq. But while it had taken her a little longer to love me the way I loved her, I think the more she knew me, the more she saw that we were made for each other.

Ordinarily, I would have gone to Soheila's father and told him that I wanted to marry his daughter. But Soheila's mother and father had divorced when she was young. Her father had gone back down south; Soheila lived with her mother. So it was her mother I really had to persuade.

After some months, I decided to tell my mother that I wanted to marry her. My mother agreed to tell Soheila's mom.

Soheila's mother said no.

*No!*

"Soheila is the smartest one in our family," said her mother. "I want her to be a doctor. I want her to be a famous woman. I am sure that she will be something special."

I thought she was already someone special, but that didn't seem to count for much.

Soheila found out about my proposal and argued with her mother, saying that she would continue going to school and become a doctor after she was married. But that didn't change her mother's mind. Part of my offense may have been my boldness—it wasn't considered proper to be obviously in love—but I also had lesser prospects and accomplishments than other suitors. In any event, the love of my life was forbidden to me. I went into the army a bachelor, though not a committed one.

**IF YOU WERE** rich in Iraq, you could pay money to avoid having to serve in the military. It was one of the many things that helped make the society unfair. Needless to say, I didn't have the money to pay, and since I had not done well enough on my tests to be admitted to college, the army was my future—at least for two years, the mandatory enlistment. I reported for duty in early 1988.

By accident, my timing happened to be perfect. The war with Iran, which had been going on since 1980, was petering out and would soon be officially over. Though inconclusive, the war claimed the lives of untold thousands of Iraqis; casualty estimates range as high as half a million. Countless civilians on both sides died, and the war caused considerable financial hardship in Iraq. It was my great fortune to miss having to fight in the conflict.

If you're thinking that my experience as a soldier was anything like joining the American military, you're greatly mistaken. The

Iraqi army was about as similar to the U.S. Army as a plastic toy tank is to the real thing.

Say, instead, a *broken* toy tank.

Basic training wasn't very arduous. Nor did anyone make much of an effort to figure out what I was good at, let alone ask what I wanted to do. I was "volunteered" to become a radioman, then assigned to an anti-aircraft unit.

It worked like this: There were a bunch of us in a room. An officer divided us up with an arbitrary wave of his hand.

"You men over here," he said, "you are now going to become communications specialists." And a similar process decided I was working in an anti-aircraft unit.

It didn't make all that much difference to me. I looked at my service just as an obligation, something to get through before real life began. I did manage to make a few friends; some of them remained quite close after our service. We slept in barracks, a dozen or so of us together. Our equipment was ancient, laughable by American standards. Much of it was Russian, though its age was a bigger drawback than who had manufactured it.

My anti-aircraft artillery group was stationed in Baiji, 160 kilometers or roughly a hundred miles south of Mosul on the road to Baghdad. The unit was part of the "sky protection service," though I'm not sure how much protection we really offered. My crew manned a Russian-made 37 mm gun. The gun had been a reasonably decent weapon when it was first fielded by the Soviet Union—which would have been in 1939. It was obsolete well before the end of World War II. By the time my unit operated it, it was old even by Iraqi standards, outclassed not only by missiles but by weapons such as the ZSU-57-2, which fired larger shells greater distances, and the ZSU-23-4, whose four-barrel guns could be aimed with radar.

Not that any of that mattered. We were close to the lowest rung of the ladder when it came to the army. If there was a war, our job was likely to be bomb fodder.

Life in the military was dull, duller, and dullest. I can hardly remember any of it, but let me assure you, I was never Iraq's stand-out soldier. I did my job, followed orders, and got along with the other men in the unit. For me, that was enough of an accomplishment. I became familiar with an AK-47 assault rifle, but was far from a marksman with it. As for the radio, I could turn the knobs and work the switches, but that was hardly rocket science.

At the very end of July 1990, I went on leave and returned to Mosul. While I was there, I went to the hospital to visit a friend. On August 2, I happened to be waiting in the hospital when I heard on the radio that Kuwait had just become the nineteenth province of Iraq.

Shit, I thought. Now there will be big trouble.

SADDAM HUSSEIN HAD been our country's dictator since my childhood. Technically, he was the president and the head of the Ba'ath Party. In reality, he was close to a god, with the power of life and death over us all.

He hadn't been elected to either position. A member of the al-Begat tribe—which itself was part of the al-Bu Nasir tribe—he had joined the Ba'ath Party as a young man and rose through the ranks during a period of turmoil and revolts in the late 1950s and '60s. When the Ba'athists took control of the government in 1968, he became an important power behind the scenes. He consolidated his hold on the government and took formal power in 1979. Within weeks he completed a purge of that Ba'ath Party, eliminating anyone who might be able to challenge him.

Saddam, as a Sunni and as a Ba'athist, was a member of the minority in Iraq. To rule the country, he divided his enemies, often violently. He built up an internal security system, enforcing his will through spies and common people willing to rat on their neighbors and in some cases even their family members. Criticizing Saddam was treason; claiming someone had done so was an easy way to get back at someone you didn't like.

From what I have heard, Saddam started out as a fairly benign ruler. The older people told me he did the country much good when he first came to power. He built schools and hospitals, and seemed to be working for the people. But if that was true, his thinking changed as his rule went on. He started working for himself and his friends. Perhaps the circle around him grew tighter and greedier. With less people to tell him the truth about things, maybe he thought it was fine to take what he wanted for himself, rather than using his power to make things better for the country as whole. Whatever the reason, the results were devastating for Iraq.

With Saddam's rise, the Ba'ath Party was in effective control of the country. In most areas, especially in Mosul and other places in the north where Saddam's party was strong, you had to be a member of the Ba'ath Party if you wanted to work. It wasn't optional. Most people who were members of the party didn't like Saddam, but they needed to support their families.

Even I was a member of the party, though only at the most basic level. I joined when I was in middle school. We all did. It wasn't voluntary; on the other hand, the requirements weren't the most onerous. I spent three or four months going to meetings, which to me were just another set of classes I had to attend, though these were held after school. The lessons were little more than indoctrination sessions, and shallow ones at that. Supposedly we were being taught about Iraqi history and the like, but the classes were really designed to convince us that Saddam was godlike and that we should follow all that he and the Ba'ath Party dictated.

The instructor was not very good. He had a lot of his basic facts about Iraq wrong. For someone like me, a bit of a smart aleck and a showoff, this was a real temptation. I could show how tough and quick I was with something other than my fists.

I was wise enough not to contradict him directly in class, which would have brought me a swift cuff or some other punishment. Instead, I started asking him questions. He got embarrassed, because he really didn't know the answers and wasn't very good at camouflaging his ignorance. He'd fumble around, the other kids would give me knowing looks, and I'd do my best not to smirk.

The secret of my success was a book on our country's history. The instructor was supposed to be working from the book, but was too lazy to read it. I was simply looking through the book for arcane details and then asking about them. He grew more and more embarrassed as the classes went on, until finally he told me I didn't have to attend anymore.

That was the most valuable thing I learned from the Ba'ath Party—if you were enough of a smart-ass, they would leave you alone.

There was a line, of course. If you were *too* much of a smart-ass, especially when you got older, they had ways of dealing with you which were not very pleasant. But I was able to walk the line.

LIKE MOST IRAQIS, I'd had no idea that Saddam was planning an invasion of Kuwait. Anyone paying attention in the outside world knew that tensions had been building between the two countries at Saddam's instigation for months, but most Iraqis had no clue what was going on, even if they were in the military.

In the U.S. Army, soldiers hear plenty of rumors and can piece information together from different things like mobilizations and news reports. But in Iraq, no one trusted anyone, and rank-and-file soldiers certainly weren't to be trusted with any information. The isolation of our unit, along with its distance from Baghdad and the front lines, meant that little information, even of the rumor variety, made it to me.

And of course the general public found out only what Saddam wanted them to find out. He wasn't about to publicize his intentions to take over Kuwait until he was ready to do so. Once the invasion started, all of the information the government-supported media spread reinforced his contention that the Kuwaitis were in the wrong and that their country rightfully belonged to us. Within twenty-four hours, Kuwait was suppressed and Saddam presented the country with a fait accompli.

The history of Kuwait and Iraq was a complicated one, but not in the ways that Saddam and his regime implied. According to most sources, Kuwait City was only settled in the eighteenth century; the area was mostly empty before then. By the nineteenth century it was an important trading metropolis. That importance grew as oil became a critical export in the region.

Like most of the Middle East and all of Iraq, Kuwait was part of the Ottoman Empire. But in the mid-eighteenth century, Sabah I bin Jaber established himself as the emir of Kuwait. (Sabah I bin Jaber was the leader of a tribe that originated in Iraq; among the reasons they are said to have gone to Kuwait was persecution by the ruling Turks.) Though still owing allegiance to the Ottomans, Sabah I bin Jaber was granted a certain amount of autonomy and independence over the region. Some of that independence continued after the arrival of the British, who also ended up formalizing Kuwait's borders with Saudi Arabia and Iraq.

In 1961, Kuwait became independent. At no time in the modern era had Kuwait been part of Iraq.

Nor had it been hostile. Kuwait was a close ally of Iraq during the Iran-Iraq War of 1980–1988. The country gave or loaned Iraq a great deal of money as well as strategic support. Leftover debts from the war were one of the reasons for friction with Saddam's government at the end of the 1980s. But these were never more than a pretext for Saddam. He saw an opportunity to do many things by annexing Kuwait besides skipping out on money owed.

Kuwait had oil revenues that he coveted. Kuwait City was a modern trading port, which would give Iraq much more access to world trade and, not coincidentally, bring the regime additional money. Conquering Kuwait would make Saddam appear grand and accomplished to his people. It would also take their minds off the long and senseless war that had dwindled down to an inconclusive close a few years before. And what would the world care about Kuwait?

While I knew there would be trouble as soon as I heard the news, a lot of my neighbors saw things differently. Kuwait was an opportunity. To them, the invasion was a chance to rip off Kuwait. I remember seeing cars loaded down with loot: televisions, household items. There were suddenly a lot of new cars in the neighborhood— even a Chevy Caprice. The classic American automobile became a status symbol for a short while in some parts of Iraq.

Let me not say that everything was stolen. I don't know. Maybe some were purchased. But certainly the prices must have been very low compared to what they would have been before the invasion.

Meanwhile, Saddam filled our airwaves with proclamations that Kuwait belonged to Iraq, and that it was only just that we reclaim our territory. The actual history didn't matter to Saddam.

"We took our rightful lands back," he claimed again and again. "It was always ours, and now it is again."

I felt about Kuwait the same way I felt when I heard about break-ins or robberies—it wasn't right.

I wasn't surprised when I heard that America's President Bush was getting together a coalition to free the annexed country. It wasn't hard to figure out what would happen—Iraq would lose. I remember having many conversations with friends in the army. A surprising number thought that Iraq would defeat the United States and other coalition members because our religion was better and that God would inevitably be on our side.

"It's not about religion," I told them. "It's about technology. And we have no right to be in that country."

Of course, I could only have such conversations with people I truly trusted. Talking about the war—or saying anything that could be interpreted as criticism of Saddam—would have been suicidal. At best I would have ended up in jail.

I came back from Mosul and rejoined my anti-aircraft unit, waiting for the inevitable. It took several months for the Western nations to organize and group for an attack. The fall passed into winter. The conflict didn't seem real. There were negotiations, deadlines—nothing that remotely affected me and my tiny anti-aircraft installation deep in northern Iraq.

Finally, on January 17, 1991, the air war began. The Americans and their allies took out key Iraqi air force installations in the first few hours of the campaign—we weren't touched, which gives you some idea of how important we were. In fact, the war remained distant until U.S. bombers blew out a bridge in Mosul and I heard about the attack from friends and family. Shortly afterward, I saw a division of Iraqi army soldiers walking up from Baghdad. It was a strange sight, thousands of men walking along the road.

To this day, I have no idea what they were doing. Retreating from a nonexistent (at that point) enemy? Heading north to reinforce the border with Turkey? Mobilizing to the Kurdish area to prevent a rebellion? Whatever it was, they were in no hurry to get where they were going.

Power went out in much of the country, including Baiji. The city was home to an oil refinery, and eventually the plant was targeted by the allies as they attempted to cut supplies of fuel to the Iraqi military. Our anti-aircraft battery was attacked by one or more allied planes. I'm not sure whether they were British or American, though from what I remember I think the aircraft was a Tornado, which was flown by Britain's Royal Air Force as well as the Italians and Saudis. In any event, the plane was too far for me to get a positive identification myself, and frankly I had good reason to stay in our bunker: the aircraft dropped cluster bombs on us.

I am happy to report that we didn't fire at them, and there were no casualties on the ground. None as the result of the bombing, that is. There was one loss due to stupidity. Which, in war, is more dangerous than explosives.

After the attack, we found an unexploded cluster bomb lying on the ground near one of the batteries. One of our officers approached the bomb and for some unknown reason drew his pistol and fired. He was a good enough shot to hit the bomb—which then exploded, killing him.

What is the American saying? You can't fix stupid?

The officer's idiocy was typical not just of our leadership, but of the army in general. The last thing Saddam wanted was an army that was so highly trained and capable that it might challenge him. Dumb officers who were loyal were preferable to smart officers who might want to be dictator themselves someday. We'd been at war for years with Iran, yet our leaders didn't know that much about advanced Western weapons. They had no idea of the firepower Americans possessed.

Nor did they understand America. The coalition allies used strategies that they hoped would limit civilian casualties and collateral damage. From the Iraqi point of view, these limited attacks seemed like the sum total of American capabilities. It was hard for our leaders to understand that the allies were pulling their punches. That made no sense to them.

Our guns, useless as they were, remained intact. But the raid on the refinery was successful enough to put the plant out of opera-tion for the duration of the war. It was a scene repeated over and over again in Iraq, as the Americans and their allies overwhelmed pitifully antiquated defenses and poorly trained men. The coali-tion made quick work of the Iraqi army in Kuwait. The route used to retreat became known as the Highway of Death, as our escap-ing troops were easy targets for allied planes. Frontline Iraqi units that didn't surrender were destroyed as the coalition executed what became known following the war as the "left hook," sweeping into Iraq and cutting off the south with an attack from the western desert along the Saudi border.

Sometimes I think it would have been better if the Americans had kept up their attack, gone on to Baghdad and chased Saddam from power. But if they'd made the attack without much of a plan for what to do afterward—as they did in 2003—the end result would have been chaos and eventual bloodshed among Iraqis. The misery would have been the same, just sooner.

As soon as the coalition ended its attack, the cities in southern Iraq began rebelling against the dictator. Iran helped both encour-age the rebellion and then support the people who were trying to take over. But as soon as he knew that the Americans wouldn't attack him in Baghdad, Saddam pushed what was left of his forces south to end the rebellions. The rebellions were quickly crushed.

My unit stayed put. There wasn't too much call for anti-aircraft guns to fight poorly armed civilians.

I don't know what I would have done had I been ordered to join an attack. I hope I would have been brave and done the right thing: not harmed innocent civilians. But at that time, it's very likely I would have followed orders.

Thank God I was never faced with that situation.

The people couldn't do anything about the dictator. I'm sure a lot of Iraqis farther north wanted to be rid of Saddam, too. He had brought terrible times to the country. But he still had much power. Though defeated, the army remained loyal to him. The Fedayeen Saddam—a special paramilitary group aligned with the Ba'ath Party and loyal to Saddam personally—enforced discipline. (*Fedayeen* means, roughly, "man who sacrifices"; in theory these thugs were supposed to sacrifice their lives for Saddam. In reality, they generally sacrificed others for their own benefit.) The Ba'ath Party was the only viable political organization in the country. Saddam had everyone's arm, everyone's leg, tied to his.

It was not simply a matter of threats or violence. Saddam's dictatorship was the only thing the people had ever known. For many, imagining an Iraq free from him was unimaginable.

Except in the south, where there had been a lot of destruction, things quickly returned to normal. Within a few weeks, life was about the same as it had been before the invasion.

Don't take that to mean things were perfect, or even good. Prices had been climbing slowly before the war. They continued to do that after the conflict. It was a classic situation of supply and demand. With less and less available, things became more precious. The price of beef escalated from roughly fifteen hundred dinar (between two and three dollars at the time) a kilo to twelve thousand dinar. Anything that had to be imported became very expensive. Gasoline, regulated by the state and refined in Iraq, was an exception, but even things like electricity increased greatly in price.

This didn't happen overnight. Things got worse gradually, then accelerated as the United Nations clamped down because Saddam didn't comply with its stipulations following the war. UN sanctions squeezed imports and made it difficult to export anything. Little by little, jobs began to disappear. Each day, things got a little worse. You didn't notice it until you thought back to the previous month.

The electrical shortages became worse and worse. Power was cut for two hours each day in Mosul. Then, after some time passed, three hours, then four. Finally, power might be cut for ten or twelve hours, turned on for two, then cut off for another long stretch.

Why didn't Saddam comply with the UN? Why did he let the sanctions get worse and the economy shrivel?

In retrospect, it seems ridiculous. He had to know that the Americans were not fooling around. And he had no serious nuclear program; even if he had, it would have been a foolish waste of money and resources.

I can't read the mind of a crazed dictator. I can only make guesses.

I think perhaps he didn't want the rest of the world to know that he'd been bluffing about weapons of mass destruction. I think he thought if other nations—Iran in particular—found that out, we would be attacked. Or that people in Iraq would rise up against him.

Or maybe it had nothing to do with protecting either himself or the country. Maybe it was more his pride. Pretending to have weapons meant he could pretend to be strong. If others thought he was strong, then in his mind maybe he was strong.

But the reality was that he and Iraq were really very weak. Defying the UN was foolish. It hurt only Iraqis—and ultimately led to Saddam's downfall.

But it took a few years for things to get desperately bad. We were sliding down the hill but didn't really know it.

THE GULF WAR ended in February 1991. My military service finished a few months later. I was released from the army and returned to Mosul, where my sister's husband gave me a job in his construction business operating heavy machinery—bulldozers, earthmovers, and my favorite of all, graders.

Construction may not be a glamorous job, but to me there's

something important in building things, whether they're roads or skyscrapers. Creating is a critical human activity. It's being positive; it's doing something. It's the opposite of war, where the goal is to tear things down.

I wasn't particularly philosophical as I worked. I wanted to make a living. I wanted to earn money and have a good life, one where I fulfilled my dreams.

Those dreams had been modified by reality. Lessened. I wouldn't be king. But I was going to be successful. Maybe not rich, but well off, with enough money to have a nice house, nice cars, and a nice family.

And I definitely had someone in mind to start that family with.

**SOHEILA AND I HAD** kept in touch while I was in the army. Now I saw my chance to spend more time with her—and to make her my wife. I told her I would do anything and everything to convince her mother to let her marry me.

But now there was competition, serious competition. A cousin of hers had a very important job in the government and had been nominated to be a high-ranking minister in Saddam's government. He was single, and needed a pretty wife in order to hold that position with respect.

Even though he was the same age as Soheila's mother, he told the family that he wanted to marry Soheila.

"I'm very important now," he told Soheila's mom. "I will let Soheila live an amazing life with my money . . ."

*Blah-blah-blah.* You can imagine the things he said. Not that they were lies: I am sure that he was sincere, and would have given Soheila many things.

Except true love.

Soheila's mother agreed to let him marry her. When I heard,

I went wild. Angry? I was beyond angry. Fury doesn't begin to describe how I felt.

But I was calm, too. I was not going to be beaten in this.

I gathered up some friends and relatives and went to pay Soheila's family a visit. As Soheila remembers it, a few of us had had something to drink before we came over. She also remembers that I had a pistol.

My memory is vague on both counts.

"Hey," I told her mother as soon as I saw her outside the house. "I will marry Soheila. No one can touch her. I am her cousin."

(The claim about our being cousins may sound strange to Americans. In Iraqi culture, cousins have what might be called the right of first refusal—they can say that they have the right to marry a girl and no one else can object.)

Technically, I was not her cousin. Our families were close, and at times the women used words like *aunt* and *cousin* to signify this. But there was no actual blood relation, and my claiming there was wouldn't make it so.

But all is fair in love and war, yes? I may not have fought in the war that had just passed, but this was an entirely different matter.

"I'm her cousin, and I will marry her!"

"You are not her cousin!" her mother screamed back. "You don't have that right."

"I am!" I insisted. "I have this right, and no one else will marry her but me. If anyone gets close to Soheila or tries to take her, I will kill them. She is mine. Nobody can take her."

By now, I had created quite a scene, both inside and outside the house. Neighbors came over and tried to calm me down. Even my own friends were concerned. I stayed for five hours, arguing my case and letting other people do so. Finally no one had any energy left even to talk. I went home, still determined that I was going to win.

Soheila's cousin heard what had happened and soon changed his mind about wanting to marry her. But Soheila's mother was still reluctant to give Soheila permission to marry me.

I kept working on Soheila. It was clear that she loved me—she was writing me love poems regularly. The words went straight from her pen to my heart, kisses that could penetrate all the way to my soul. Our love burned so deeply that every day I could not be with her was like living in hell.

One day, I convinced the brother-in-law I worked for to speak to the family for me. He and some of his friends went to Soheila's house and spoke to her mother, trying to convince her that we loved each other and should be allowed to marry.

He was a respected man, well off and influential, but even his pleas didn't move her.

A short time later, Soheila came down with a mysterious illness that kept her in bed for days. Maybe it was the flu; she certainly had all the symptoms. But as Soheila tells the story, it was something else: lovesickness. According to her version, her mother's refusal to let us marry had caused her illness.

I think I like her version best.

Whatever the cause of her fever, her mother's sister found her in bed one day and had a long talk with her. Soheila poured out her heart, confessing her deep love for me—which by then was no secret to her aunt.

"I will talk to your mother," her aunt said finally. "You are getting married. And in the meantime, you will get better."

Soheila's aunt and some of her cousins went to her mother. They succeeded where I and an army of my friends had not: her mother finally gave in and gave her approval for us to wed.

It wasn't the heartiest endorsement: "If it is her choice, I will not block it."

She added that if Soheila changed her mind, that would be

fine with her. But that was all we needed. I knew Soheila wouldn't change her mind, and I wouldn't either.

Soheila also had to get the approval from her father, who was down in Basra. That was easy—he told her he only wanted her to be happy, and it didn't take much for him to see what I meant to her.

We were married in the summer of 1993: August 2, to be exact.

It seemed like we had waited forever, though in Iraq and certainly at that time, a wait of several years was not considered unusual. Our ceremony was traditional and stretched over two days—and then further with our honeymoon.

Traditional Iraqi engagements and weddings consist of several different parts. The first is the Mashaya, where customarily the leader of the groom's family goes to the bride's family and discusses things such as what presents will be given to the bride and her family, and what sort of prospects the groom and his family have. This is done completely among the men; our society is extremely male oriented. Assuming that all find the match satisfactory, there are special drinks and rounds of celebration. The day before the ceremony, the bride's family holds an elaborate party known as Nishan. Tradition calls for the bride to change her dress seven times, with each color she wears signifying something different, from innocence to sophistication, from happiness to mystery.

The actual ceremony is even more elaborate. There is a section where the imam questions the bride about whether she really wants to marry the man. This can be somewhat humorous, as the bride has the option of extending the process as long as she wants—though it's a bad sign if it goes on too long.

Fortunately, Soheila took pity on me and did not drag this part out.

I'd saved up money from my job to pay for as much food and drink as I could. I bought Soheila many presents—jewelry, clothes, furniture. We rented two large halls and had two different parties:

one for men and one for women. Some Iraqi families follow the strict tradition of separation of the genders, and we had to accommodate them and make them feel welcome. Hospitality is important to Iraqis in general, and certainly to me. I want my guests always to feel like they are my guests, honored, and having a good time. If you are in my house, you are the king. There is nothing I cannot do for you.

The halls were quite a distance from each other. Following Iraqi tradition, Soheila stayed with the women and I stayed with the men.

That night—it was probably the next day by then—many of our friends took their cars and escorted us to a tourist spot in the northwestern part of the country, complete with a lake and a private villa. This wasn't a small procession; Soheila counted thirty-five cars in the line behind us. But they left soon after our arrival: just like Americans, Iraqis like to start their married lives with private time, so they can get to know each other.

Soheila and I got to know each other many times in those three days. We enjoyed ourselves immensely. And then it was back to reality.

**WHEN WE RETURNED** to Mosul, we went to live with my mother and two brothers, one of whom was married and had two children. It was a medium-sized house by our standards, with six rooms. Soheila and I took one of the rooms downstairs, which gave us a little privacy.

By this time, the country was straining. It was difficult to make a living, and even harder to dream. With both my brother and myself working, our family was one of the luckier ones, able to depend on each other and pull together. Many Iraqis were poorer, without skills or the cleverness one needs to survive in hard times.

My older brother, Hamid, was a car mechanic, and while his work often didn't pay much, he was generally employed. I continued working for my brother-in-law, though we started to have small squabbles and conflicts. His business was starting to dry up, though by comparison with others he was still doing well.

I soon had every incentive to work as hard and as often as I could. My first daughter was born in May 1994; two years later, my first son was born. Another daughter followed a few years after that, and eventually another son. (I am not naming them, to preserve their privacy as they grow older.)

The problems of the country inevitably strained the family. Then one of my sisters ran into debt; to help her, we decided we had to sell the house. The place we rented was smaller, but the sale gave us breathing room financially.

Things became even more difficult for us when Hamid, my older brother, was jailed because of a dispute with a member of the Fedayeen Saddam, the paramilitary organization headed by Saddam's son Uday Saddam Hussein and then his younger brother Qusay Saddam.

Years later, after Saddam was pushed out, the Fedayeen Saddam became one of the focal points of the insurgency attacking Iraqis and Americans. Before the war it was more like an informal militia or paramilitary group along the lines of the Black Shirts under Mussolini during the fascist regime in prewar Italy. It was said that the Fedayeen were responsible for smuggling and other crimes; they were also said to threaten and even attack political opponents of the regime. Tangling with its members was like tangling with mobsters. If you went against them, you invited all kinds of problems.

My brother's difficulties began when a member of the organization tried to take money from him. Like me, my brother didn't appreciate being pushed around, let alone robbed—so he beat the man up. In revenge, the man and his friends trumped up charges against him and had him put in Badush, the notorious regional prison. He was sentenced to five years.

Not only did we now have one less wage earner in the family, we had the added expense of trying to feed my brother, who would have starved on the rations they gave out at the jail. My mother and his wife visited as often as they could; it was never a pleasant experience. Even in America, I would imagine, prisons are not hospitable places, but those in the States are probably like hotels compared to the desolate, cramped, and filthy places in Iraq. It is one thing to keep common criminals locked up in such hellholes, and another to keep political prisoners and people like my brother, whose only offense was to stand up for himself against bullies. He was kept there for a year and half, until a general amnesty and his own good behavior won his release.

I didn't help by having a conflict with my brother-in-law. I'd been chafing at some of his directions, disagreeing with the jobs he gave me, and feeling that I could do better on my own. I felt he was taking advantage of me, not paying me what I was worth or what my family needed to survive. Finally one day I had enough and told him, "I'm done."

I walked out and started working for myself as a truck driver, driving loads of goods from Mosul to the south, and from the south back north. At first I did very well, or at least better than I had been doing working for my brother-in-law.

The hours were long; I would usually go from five in the morning until five or six at night. Most times I would come home so exhausted I just shut everything else out. What was happening in the wide world outside of Iraq made no difference to me. I was lucky just to get a shower, eat a bit, and go to sleep.

As time went on, the amount of money people were willing to pay to ship items became less and less. They just didn't have it. Once I transported some sheep from Mosul to Basra. I made the equivalent of forty dollars. It took me a day and half to get down to the city and back, partly because of the poor roads and partly because the truck I'd leased was old and slow. Once I got to Basra, I had to wait to find a load to take north, another long ordeal. Even after finding a somewhat steady gig transporting chlorine south and fertilizer north, I made only seventy dollars a round-trip after expenses.

Besides legitimate costs for fuel, there were also bribes that had to be paid. These didn't amount to much individually—the equivalent of a dollar could get you very far with a policeman. But the idea of having to participate in the corruption was galling.

The struggle to keep working and feed my family wore me down. I felt like a donkey, with more and more weight piled on my back. My spirit certainly sagged. If I'd ever felt any loyalty to Iraq as a whole, it was gone.

As time went on, I came to believe I would do anything to feed my family. Anything: if someone gave me money to kill someone, I would take the money and do it, without hesitating.

I look back in horror. It's a terrible thing to have thought. But it is what I thought.

A terrible truth.

Desperation robs a man of his soul as well as his best intentions. How can a person live in misery and be happy about the place where he lives? How can a person be optimistic for the future? How can he dream in the face of bleakness?

Strapped for money, we moved from the house to a small apartment. There were only three rooms for all of us—myself, my wife, and our children; my brother, his wife, and their two children; and my mom. Soheila was often sad, worried sick about the children's future as well as ours. It was as if we inhabited a graveyard, without hope for the future.

In 1997, I was called back to army duty for two months. It at least brought a little pay without much work. Since I was a heavy-machine operator, my skills were in demand. I volunteered to grade the airport, an important job—but one that only took a single day.

They were so happy they gave me a month off.

When I reported back, my superiors told me that they wanted me to "volunteer" to represent the unit in a large track-and-field competition. They knew I'd been a high jumper when I was younger and thought I might do well.

Naturally, I accepted. That earned me another month's vacation. A strange way to run an army, but it worked for me.

I actually won the military competition, with a jump around 1.65 meters. Not bad for a heavy-machine operator who hadn't competed in years.

IRAQ MIGHT HAVE continued on that downward slide for many more years before hitting the absolute rock bottom. Or maybe not. Maybe Saddam would have come to his senses as pressure increased. Maybe there would have been a revolt that overthrew him, an uprising similar to the so-called Arab Spring. Maybe, maybe, maybe . . .

If any of those impossible scenarios had occurred, my life would have been radically different. What exactly I would have done I cannot say, but surely you wouldn't know of me. My life would have remained mostly ordinary and not of interest to anyone in America. My dreams would have been irrelevant to the wider world, and maybe even to me.

But fate stepped in.

I WAS HOME in Mosul on September 11, 2001. It was the afternoon. I'd come home from driving my truck and was relaxing, when suddenly someone said to turn on the TV.

The attack on the World Trade Center in Manhattan was being replayed on Iraqi national television.

*Holy shit.*

I knew that there would be trouble. And somehow I knew it would come to Iraq. I was filled with a strange, desolate feeling, not because I thought there would be a war—that I didn't know. It was more despair about the world.

Many Muslims were celebrating the attacks. Their glee appalled me.

Why destroy things? Why celebrate hate and death?

Many questions occurred to me as I sorted through my feelings. It was clear to me that violence and destruction were not right, and that killing innocent people was not condoned by any religion, let alone Islam.

So what should a person do?

Build things.

The energy and intellect that it took to plan such horrible mass murder—could not that have been used to make something important? Instead of hijacking an airplane to kill people, why not build an airplane to help people?

If we just want to destroy something, how long will it take? A few minutes? What is the use of that? What is the use of any destruction?

Making things, building, learning—that is what we all should be doing, Iraqis, Muslims, Americans. That is what people were created for. That is our highest achievement. Why do some of us insist on debasing the race by following creeds of destruction?

I had no answers at that time; I didn't even have all the questions. While I didn't know it then, they would multiply and deepen over the next ten years, until they completely shaped my life.

Questions about destruction, about religion, about our responsibility to each other—they're not just philosophical or hypothetical for me. I know firsthand what destruction feels like and what happens in its wake. I have walked down its streets. I know what desolation looks like, how it feels on your skin. I know how depression tightens like a noose around your neck until you can't breathe.

I have been fortunate to see the opposite, to see the hope that education brings and feel the difference that freedom can make.

But in Iraq after 9/11, the predominant emotion favored destruction and all the dark forces that hinder mankind. You heard all sorts of conspiracies about the attacks and all kinds of justifications about why it should have happened.

*Oh, those terrible Americans, they did this to justify killing Muslims . . .*

*The Jews, they did that . . .*

Mass murder can never be justified. That is something all people should know in their hearts, no matter where they come from or what religion they follow. But with the state-controlled media blaring these rumors and misinformation, many Iraqis were swayed from their honest opinions and feelings. They didn't know what to think, and more than a few lost the ability to tell right from wrong.

Rationally, I suspected that America would start hunting the men who had blown up the towers. It was a matter of American pride.

I also knew that the whole world outside the Middle East would support the United States.

What I didn't know was what this would mean for Iraq.

Iraq was not involved in the attack, and before it happened there was not much regard for Osama bin Laden in the country.

Immediately after 9/11, however, Iraqi television began calling him a hero. The media fed people stories to reinforce that. It was clearly Saddam's doing. He hated the U.S., so any enemy of America's was by his definition a hero or a friend of his. The dictator himself called the attack a victory and celebrated it as if he had personally been the one who blew up the towers. More importantly, he celebrated the destruction not as an attack on civilians, but as if the towers were military weapons destroyed in a fierce land battle.

Saddam's sudden decision to champion Osama bin Laden was just his latest ploy to try to remain popular with Iraqis. He'd been using religion in the same way for several years, trying to portray himself as a defender of Islam. It was pure sham. He stepped up his claims after 9/11, proclaiming he was "God's slave" and making sure there were plenty of pictures and films of him "proving" he was religious.

I doubt many people believed it, but of course openly questioning Saddam's sincerity, let alone mocking him, was an easy way to get yourself imprisoned.

FOR WESTERN READERS not familiar with the religion, I'd like to present a few facts about Islam to help explain some of the events that follow. This is not religious instruction, only a bit of background to help people make sense of some things. I am not a scholar or a religious teacher, and my words are only meant to point people in the proper direction. There are certainly many texts available to explain Islam in depth, and anyone with true interest should seek them out.

The faith of Islam began fourteen hundred years ago, inspired by the word of Allah, the one true God, and exemplified by Abū al-Qāsim Muhammad ibn 'Abd Allāh ibn 'Abd al-Muttalib ibn Hāshim—Muhammad—the last prophet sent to restore the faith of Adam, Noah, Abraham, and the other prophets.

All Muslims accept these facts.

All Muslims agree with the basic tenets of the faith, which include the five pillars of Islam: belief, worship, charity, fasting, and the pilgrimage to Mecca, known as the *hajj*. These pillars are at the core of our religion; they are like the vital organs in the human body, all the same and all present in every living person.

But just as living people vary in size, shape, and personality, our great religion has some subtle variations among its believers. One of the most important distinctions is between Sunnis and Shiites. This is a division that has marked Muslims for hundreds of years; it is a complicated distinction that has come to involve culture as well as faith.

The simplest way to think of the division is through its history: after the death of Muhammad, one branch of Islam accepted Abu Bakr as their leader or caliph; these people were Sunni. Another group accepted Hazrat Ali; they were Shia. From this seemingly simple split, the two main branches of Islam developed different though related traditions. Though at times their disagreements have been violent, for much of Muslim history individuals aligned with these two branches have lived in peace and harmony. The way I see things, Sunni and Shia have much in common and little in dispute, but many disagree

It is estimated that Sunnis, such as myself, make up 75 percent of all Muslims. Shiites account for the next largest percent of Muslims, around 20 percent. Other branches of Islam include Sufism, whose adherents believe very strongly in the mystical aspects of the faith.

There are differences of practice and faith within each group of Muslims. And of course there are extremists who pervert the central ideas of the religion for their own evil purposes. Sunni traditions count several important schools, each with different interpretations of Islam. The differences can seem very subtle to an outsider, but they are nonetheless important to those of us who believe.

Osama bin Laden was part of a radical faction of Sunni Muslims who believe that very strict interpretations of Sharia, or Islamic law, must be imposed on the people or Islam will cease to exist. They also preach violence against the West and Jews, and look upon Shiites as enemies. Needless to say, this is not the philosophy followed by most Sunnis.

While the Sunni branch of Islam predominates throughout the world, Iraq has more Shiite Muslims; it has been estimated that 60 to 65 percent of the population are Shia. Many live in the south and east, near Iran. By contrast, the north and west are predominately Sunni.

Saddam was Sunni. His strongest supporters were members of his tribe and people from the region where he was born, Tikrit, who were also predominantly Sunni.

Many Shia believed that the dictator strongly discriminated against them on the basis of religion, and with good reason. Though Shiites were the majority in the country, most of the better government jobs went to Sunni Muslims—more precisely, to Sunnis who were related to Saddam, members of his tribe, or otherwise somehow connected to him, even if only in a distant way. And being a member of the party was essential, at even the lowest level.

In other words, Shia were discriminated against, but so were Sunnis like myself who had no connection with Saddam or his tribe.

Mosul at the time of 9/11 was about 90 percent Sunni; the rest of the people were mostly Shia, with a small community of Christians. (The few Christians I knew in those days were among the most peaceful people I have ever met.)

As I mentioned earlier, there was very little religious animosity between the different branches of Islam when I was young. Even during the Iran-Iraq war, when our enemy was a nation ruled by Shiites, attitudes were not very extreme. For most people, religion was a family matter, private, and not something that the person had much choice in anyway—they followed their parents, as was their duty. At least as I remember it, religion was never an issue for fighting.

One of my best friends growing up was a Christian. There was no religious pressure on him to convert. Nor did he suffer from more discrimination than the rest of us.

For myself, the distinctions are not very important. I have my own relationship with God, and I understand how I should act and behave.

As for our children, when they were small, my kids didn't even know there was a difference. In 2003, as the fighting among Iraqis intensified along religious lines, Soheila and I gathered our children in a room.

"Okay, guys," I told them after we explained a little about our faith and beliefs. "Who's going to be Shia and who's going to be Sunni?"

All of them chose Shia. A disappointment maybe for me.

More seriously, I feel that when they are each old enough, they will make their own decision about how to honor God and live correctly. Religion is a choice. Whatever you want, whatever you believe, that is what you should follow. Who am I to impose my faith and religion on others, even my children?

**SADDAM'S ATTEMPTS AT** drumming up support by using religion after 9/11 mostly failed. But it was more dangerous than ever to talk against him, even with family and friends—you could never tell who might say something about you, either directly to the authorities or to someone who would go to them. Being critical of Saddam had always been forbidden, but now saying anything derogatory about Iraq could also land you in trouble. I heard a story about a man jailed for proclaiming that the French would win a soccer match against Iraq. Whether the story is true or not, I have no idea, but it shows the level of paranoia in the country as we came closer to war in 2002.

We all knew it was coming. The United Nations demanded to be allowed to inspect Iraqi facilities involved in the construction of atomic weapons. Saddam wouldn't let them. Some of us thought

Saddam was hoping to use the conflict to divert people's attention from the fact that people were starving. But the only thing that would have diverted attention from that would have been full bellies.

Things became steadily worse as 2002 turned to 2003. The country slid further into a black hole. Knowing war was inevitable, Soheila and I began stocking up on as much food as we could. We put away rice and canned soup. We had small freezers where we stocked meat. We stockpiled water. We stacked whatever we could in our small apartment, knowing there would soon be shortages. We had lived through two wars already, so we had a rough idea of what might happen.

We were no longer daring to dream. We were simply hoping to get past the nightmare we knew was coming.

And then, the war was upon us: not as the violent jolt we feared, but, instead, as a distant shriek in the night.

# 3

# UP FROM THE DEPTHS

**THE START OF** a war is a mysterious thing, an event simultaneously momentous and nebulous. If you are on the front line when the troops cross, or maybe beneath the targeting pipper of an aircraft, things are finite, clear, and terrible.

Absolutely horrible, but black and white, with great clarity and finality.

Farther away, nothing is clear. Miles from the front you hear explosions and see flashes. You feel rumbles. But if the fighting remains distant, you can close off your mind to these things and pretend there is no war, that nothing has happened.

Even if you don't close your mind, you may not understand war until you actually see it. The conflict might not make sense to you, even if you have seen war before. A man can never fully imagine the reality of war, even if he's lived it already.

For us, the war with America seemed far away for the first few days, very nebulous. We could see it on television, but that was as close as we got. American airplanes and missiles attacked first, hitting Saddam's Baghdad palace and striking military targets near the southern border and Baghdad early on March 19, 2003. The next day, American troops came across the border, attacking in the south. Within days they stormed Nasiriya, then continued north toward Baghdad. In the meantime, they secured the southern oil fields and Basra, and hooked up with Kurdish rebels in Kurdistan, in the northern precincts.

Mosul, far from Baghdad, could almost have been in a different country. But a few nights after the start of the war, I was woken by the rumble of an explosion somewhere nearby. Even as the ground was still shaking, I rose and made sure my family was all right, then waited, sleeplessly, until dawn to find out what had happened.

As soon as it was light, a friend and I drove toward the center of the city. Eventually we found the source of the explosion: a Tomahawk missile had struck a building used as a telecommunications center. The facility had housed phone-switching equipment handling the local exchanges. The missile or missiles had struck in the exact center of the building, cratering it and obliterating phone service in the area.

It was an odd sight: The fence that bordered the property was intact, and most of the building's walls were still standing. But the roof was gone, and from up close the structure looked like a scorched box filled with rubble. The dust from the explosion lingered in the air, scratching my eyes.

From that moment on, the war felt very real, even in Mosul. The city was spared destruction on a grand scale—the business areas were largely untouched by American bombs, as far as I can remember—but there was no longer any way to deny the reality of the war. We were going to lose, badly. It was just a matter of time before the Americans came.

There was no hope for Iraq, or Saddam. The Kuwait war had shown us that the dictator's military might was a complete fiction. A dozen years had passed, and it was inconceivable to anyone that the military had gotten any better. Iraq itself had gotten worse.

But even if most of us wished Saddam were gone, it was still a depressing feeling to be caught in a country at war. We had grave doubts about the future.

And as much as I hated Saddam, I wasn't a fan of the Americans. I wasn't a *hater* of Americans; my attitude would be closer to neutral, I guess. I admired the culture, or what I'd seen of it— basketball, the movies. I knew the U.S.A. was a great military power. But I wasn't looking forward to having Iraq ruled by Americans. Nor did I have any dreams or illusions about going to America or, even more extreme, turning Iraq into a Middle Eastern version of America.

Democracy? It was too lofty a concept to consider. What most of us thought about was simple: What things did we have to do to get through the day?

Sometimes we thought about the next day, and the day after that, but that was the extent of our future. Those thoughts were always in the barest terms: How will we survive?

We stayed in our houses mostly, gathering what news we could from the state-run television channels, deciphering the truth from the bullshit. The same day I saw what the Tomahawk had done to the phone building, the Americans launched an attack against the airport on the southwestern side of town. This was a much larger attack, and the explosions seemed louder by a factor of ten.

I saw the attack from a friend's house near the airport. While we were far enough away to be safe, the waves of bombs or missiles that struck the base were clearly visible. I saw an F/A-18 or similar aircraft fly over the area as the bombs struck.

When the raid died down, we went to the airport grounds to see what had happened. As we got close, I saw a single man, not a soldier but a civilian, handling a Russian-made machine gun on the roof of a one-story house. He was firing into the air, as if his lone gun might drive off the unseen planes.

"Why are you doing that?" I asked. "You're not shooting at anything."

The man looked at me blankly.

"You can't reach the airplanes with that," I told him. "And truly, if a pilot sees your gunfire, he'll come back and hit you with a missile that will blow you into a million pieces. For what?"

He stopped shooting, though whether I had convinced him or he simply had run out of bullets, I have no idea.

The American attack had struck the anti-air defenses and some of the military facilities at the airport and camp. But it missed the Iraqi army. The units that had been headquartered in Mosul had already disappeared, the men either ordered away or simply deserting. No one in the city seemed to know where they had gone.

Shortly after the attack on the airport, members of the Peshmerga arrived in town from Kurdistan. The Peshmerga were Kurdish militia, paramilitary forces that in some cases were working with U.S. Special Forces and the CIA to fight against Saddam during the early stages of the war. Whether these men were one of those units or not, I have no idea. I wasn't about to ask; it was obvious that the best way to deal with them was to keep our distance.

The Peshmerga and the Kurds in general had a long history with Saddam, none of it pleasant. First of all, to explain: The Kurds are a separate people who have lived in the areas of Turkey, Syria, Iran, and Iraq for hundreds of years. During that time, they've had varying degrees of autonomy over the region they call Kurdistan. In the 1880s, they attempted to rebel against the Ottoman Empire but were unsuccessful. Other nationalistic movements followed, but so far none have successfully established Kurdistan as an independent nation.

The three provinces in Iraq that are predominantly Kurdish

are Erbil, Dahuk, and Sulaymaniyah. Years of Kurdish rebellions against Iraqi governments resulted in a pledge in March 1970 to establish autonomy for the Kurdish areas in northern Iraq, but those plans were never realized. Saddam's repression provoked a Kurdish rebellion in the 1980s; the dictator responded ferociously, murdering countless Kurds, civilians as well as freedom fighters. He destroyed whole villages and sent Kurds to other parts of Iraq, hoping to dilute their hold on the north. It was during this time as well that he is said to have used chemical gases on the people.

Mosul is south and west of these areas, and ethnically separate. Still, it is very close—if you drew a straight line from the Kurdish city of Dahuk to Mosul, it would measure roughly thirty-seven miles. A significant number of Kurds lived in Mosul before the war, and there were lingering ethnic rivalries and prejudices, though for the most part everyone got along. I myself have had different relationships with Kurds in general and in particular. I have several good friends who are Kurds; I've known Kurds who were jerks. If I were to make a general statement, I would say that most Kurds are very hardworking and honest, but I could easily come up with exceptions.

Following the first American Gulf War and Desert Storm in 1991, the United States and its allies tried to help the Kurds, including their territory in a northern no-fly zone and extending humanitarian aid. Saddam's air force, already battered by the war, could not operate in that area, making it more difficult for him to oppress the Kurds. With encouragement from the United States, the government inside the Kurdish area of Iraq became more autonomous.

At the same time, internal conflicts rose. Two different factions rose to prominence and then fought with each other. Iran encouraged both factions at different points and took a clandestine but active role encouraging the fighting and backing its own favored group. In 1996, after an Iranian assault into Iraqi territory ostensibly aimed at rebels planning an attack into Iran, Saddam Hussein sent forces north. The United States bombed Iraqi bases and tightened the no-fly zone, and in the end Iraq withdrew most of its troops from the region, but not before helping the Kurdish Democratic Party, its temporary ally against the Iranians, to win control of the region.

Once the war with America started, the Kurdish factions worked in parallel to rid themselves of the dictator. Both cooperated with the United States, as did their militias. Their goal was to carve out a permanent Kurdish state, their longtime dream. And this was obvious in their actions both inside and outside Kurdistan.

The first thing the Peshmerga and the Kurdish militia did when they arrived in Mosul was open the banks and take most of the money. They blew the safes and made off with the contents. Were they robbing it or, as was later claimed, securing it against Saddam's forces?

It certainly looked like robbery to me. Just enough was left for local people to help themselves and not feel left out.

Then the Kurdish troops ransacked the army barracks at the airport, taking the weapons and other equipment for their own. They grabbed anything they could move, including artillery pieces and tanks. Large flatbeds came and hauled vehicles away for days.

With the place ransacked, the Kurds left Mosul. By then, order in the city had broken down. The police seemed to be in hiding. People were looting government buildings, taking things they wanted or needed. The rest of us huddled in our houses, gathering to watch the news on our generator-powered TVs and discuss whatever rumors we'd heard.

Every so often a small group would surge past the house, heading to loot one place or another. I remember a friend shouting to me to come downtown with him; he and the others were going to see if they could find any money left in one of the banks.

"No way," I told him. "I'm not a thief."

"Come on," he insisted.

"No."

"Fuck you, then."

"Fuck you."

My friends thought I was an idiot for not joining in.

Al Jazeera, the Arabic news station, became something of an information lifeline for us in the early days of the war. Its reports helped us track what was going on. I spent hours and hours with my friends in small, cramped apartments, smoking cigarettes nonstop and listening to the news, trying to interpret each small tidbit, no matter how trivial.

The British reached Basra, the major Iraqi city in the south, on March 22. U.S. Marines battled the Iraqi army near Nasiriya the next day. These early battles set what would be the pattern for the rest of the war: opposed first by the regular Iraqi army, the U.S.-led coalition forces quickly defeated their conventional enemies. But once the Iraqi army retreated or disintegrated, guerrilla fighters appeared. Some had been in the army, some were from the Fedayeen Sadaam, some were radical Islamists. The last group was less discriminating in its choice of targets; its tactics often included hiding among civilians or even using them as shields. The conventional fighting was quick; gaining actual control of the urban areas was more difficult and time consuming.

Basra was not declared under control by the British until April 6, due largely to the allies' attempts to limit civilian casualties and damage. It was the first major city declared completely under allied control.

By March 27, a week after the start of the war, U.S. forces had reached the area of Samawah, the city midway between Basra and Baghdad. In the days that followed, the Americans prepared for a drive on Baghdad itself. The assault on the capital began in the outskirts on April 2; the next day U.S. forces took the airport. A week later, on April 9, Baghdad was declared under U.S. control.

In Mosul, we waited for the inevitable arrival of the American army. A few people were optimistic that they would bring change for the better. My wife, Soheila, was one.

"Maybe we will have a democratic government," said Soheila. "Maybe when it is all over, we will be better off."

I kept my darker opinions about the future to myself.

"We have to change," said Soheila. "Life has to change—we will go through this and things will be better."

She had a few tangible things on her side of the argument—oil, the creativity of the Iraqi people. The country, after all, has the potential to do much that is very good. But even at that time, hoping for a better future could not erase the tension we all felt, nor the sense that we might die in the crossfire between the United States and the last defenders of the regime.


**AND THEN SUDDENLY,** the atmosphere changed. U.S. soldiers arrived in Mosul, and it was like a holiday. People were excited— and *happy*.

Kids swarmed around the procession of army vehicles, waving. Soldiers threw them candy and a few gave them toys. There was suddenly a feeling of celebration and liberation. People were over-joyed that Saddam was no longer in charge. The surge of relief made us dizzy.


**I DON'T KNOW** what we all expected to follow. I don't know what I expected. Things were better in many ways. I no longer feared being bombed or getting caught in the crossfire between the Americans and Saddam's troops. But conditions in the city did not miraculously improve. Work was still hard to come by. The store of food and other supplies Soheila and I had put away slowly but steadily dwindled.

Days passed. The electricity came back. But life was far from normal and in no way easy. Few businesses were functioning; there was no government to speak of. I divided my time between asking around for work and hanging out with friends trying to get an idea of what was going on and what would happen next.

One day some American soldiers pulled up in a Humvee on a street where I and a friend were standing. They got out and entered the nearby store. The men were wearing full combat gear, and they reminded me of the heroes I'd seen in American movies. I'd never been this close to Americans, and I wondered what they were like.

For whatever reason, I felt as if I had to talk to them. So I convinced my friend to come with me. We walked over to the men who were waiting outside the store. With not very good English, I asked them for some MREs—Meals Ready to Eat, the standard American military food ration, usually eaten when in the field.

One of the soldiers, who by that time had probably had enough MREs to last a lifetime, handed over a small box.

I took it back to our apartment as if it were a trophy.

"What is this?" asked my mother as I set it down on our kitchen table

"American food."

"Let me see."

We opened the package. Even I was surprised by what we found—chicken, fruit, gum, napkins.

"You know what?" said my mother. "An army with food like this? They will never lose."

The food was surprisingly good, and not just because we were skimping on our own. And my mother was right—there was no comparison to the rations the Iraqi army typically had. In our military, it was not unusual to go completely without army-supplied food for three or four or even five days. If you couldn't buy something on your own or get it somehow from home, you would starve. But here was a country that gave its soldiers so much food that they grew tired of it and even gave it away.

From that moment on, I wanted to work with the Americans. I realized they had money and food, two things in very short supply in Mosul, and if I worked with them, I could take care of my family.

I began seeking out American soldiers, asking who I could talk to about getting a job. Finally I found an officer who was relatively friendly. Mack—I forget his real name and even his rank, though I think he was a captain—couldn't give me a job, but he was respectful and encouraging in other ways. When we met, he was overseeing a work unit building and repairing playgrounds around the city. I started hanging around and helping when I could, digging the holes for swing sets and then helping get them up.

My English was very, very limited. But there were no translators with Mack's unit, and that occasionally made me useful. I helped communicate a few simple phrases from fellow Iraqis, and slowly I gained his confidence by answering questions he had about the area and different customs.

One day, I noticed a man walking toward the plot of land where the Americans were working. I recognized him right away; he was well known locally as someone soft in the head, often under the influence of drugs. No one in Mosul who knew him took him seriously.

He could, however, be very belligerent some days, and even from a distance it was obvious this was going to be one of those days. He walked up to the soldiers and tried starting a fight. I rushed over and intervened.

"He's not in his right mind," I told the Americans, who were bewildered by his rants. "Don't pay attention to him. He doesn't know what he's saying."

I pushed him away. He retreated—then returned a few minutes later, holding a hand grenade.

The grenade was ancient; I doubt it would have exploded no matter what the circumstances were. But you can imagine the reaction. I ran over and grabbed him before he got too close to the soldiers. I took the grenade away and gave it to one of the soldiers, then pulled the idiot down the street. I found his home and told his family what had happened. They saw to it that he never bothered the Americans again.

It seems remarkable now that an incident like that could have passed without grave repercussions for the man, but it did. This was a calm period of time in Mosul—there may have been some animosity toward the Americans, but if so it hadn't been expressed in violent terms. A year or two later, a man with a grenade, no matter how old it was, no matter how crazy he was, would surely have been shot on sight. But at this point it was unusual and bizarre, very much out of the ordinary, and fortunately not taken as a real threat.

Grateful for my help, Mack gave me advice on how to find a job. He told me that the army was looking for translators and that the best way to get a position was to apply at the U.S. base at the airfield outside the city. The airport—the same one I'd seen bombed—had been turned into a large American complex, and units from all different service branches were locating there.

Mack went further than just giving me advice. He managed to get me an appointment for an interview at eight o'clock one morning. I'm still grateful for his help.


THE AIRPORT WAS six or seven kilometers from my house—roughly four and a half miles away. The only way to get there early in the morning was to walk. And so I did.

When I got there, I saw there was already a crowd of other men outside the fence. We waited awhile, maybe a half hour, maybe an hour, until finally an American soldier came and shouted to the small crowd.

"Nothing today!" he yelled from the other side of the fence. "Nothing. No interviews."

That was the extent of the explanation. I hung around as the others left, and spoke to the man, asking for more information. He was vague. I persisted.

"Tell you what," he told me finally. "Come back next week. We'll give you a test, and maybe an interview. Then we'll see."

Maybe he was just trying to get rid of me, but I interpreted it as a promise of success. I went home, practiced my English, and waited every day for my chance to go back.

"I am going to get a job with the Americans," I told my family.

They were overjoyed. We would have money, food—everything we needed.

I practiced harder, as much as I could. I got up early the day of the appointment and walked back to the airport. The guard at the first gate recognized my name, and I was sent to a second spot on the base to wait for my interview.

Ten others were already there, standing against a chain-link fence, waiting. I heard them talking as I walked over, each practicing English. Every one of them spoke better English than I did.

Oh my God, I thought. I have no chance.

I waited, dreading and yet hoping at the same time. A Kurdish civilian came out and began calling names. I soon realized that he was in charge of getting people in and out; he might have been a translator himself. Whatever he was, it was clear that he didn't come from Mosul. His accent was pretty heavily Kurdish; his Arabic seemed spotty.

It didn't take long to see that he was favoring the Kurds who were waiting, rather than the Arab Iraqis. Just in case there was any doubt, a few men came out and were ushered inside without having to wait. As if to underline the reason for the favoritism, they joked with the man in Kurdish on the way in.

After waiting for an hour or maybe more, I finally went over and asked what was going on.

"We have been waiting a long time," I told the Kurd as politely as I could. "What is going on?"

"Oh, nothing. You just have to wait."

"What about these other people you are letting in? Why are they cutting in line?"

"Oh, no, no, they have appointments."

"I have an appointment, too," I told him. I doubt I concealed my anger.

"You will be let in soon. I promise."

I went back to the others. Another hour passed. I asked again when we would be seen. My Kurdish "friend" gave me the same sort of blow-off. Once more I sat with the others. Finally, I could take it no longer.

"Listen," I told him, "this isn't fair. All of us have families. You have to give us all a chance. We want to work."

"I know what I am doing," he insisted. "Just be quiet or I'm kicking you out of here."

"Hey, I'm being respectful. Don't tell me that you're kicking me out."

I could feel my anger rising inside. The man was a petty dictator, a punk with a tiny bit of power, which he was using to favor his friends. It was all I could do not to punch him through the fence.

By one o'clock, I was out of cigarettes—and had no money to buy any others. We still hadn't been seen.

I felt my chance slipping away. I walked over to the fence and called to the Kurd.

"Hey. Give me my chance. Let me in. I'll take the test. If I fail, then I fail, but at least let me have my chance."

"You talk a lot," said the Kurd, no longer even pretending to be polite. "I will tell you—you are not going to get a job with us."

"Okay. So I have nothing to lose!"

I grabbed hold of the fence and pulled myself over in a flash. Jumping to the ground before he could react, I raced over and grabbed him. He tried to jerk away. I spun him back and gave him a head butt.

I was a wild man, as angry as I'd ever been in my life. My entire chance for a job—survival even—had been completely destroyed by this petty bastard. All my frustration went into my fists.

Blood spurted from his nose. He fell to the ground. The American guards began moving in my direction. I jumped back over the fence. I'm guessing they didn't like the Kurd too much either, because they let me go without any trouble.

Still, in my mind, my big chance, my plum American job, had just vanished.

I sank to the bottom of a black ocean, devastated, as I went home.


HAVE YOU EVER played old-fashioned pinball? You might get five balls for your quarter. You play the first, then the second, the third . . . finally you are on the very last chance, the very last ball, and the machine tilts.

You're out of chances, out of money, out of luck. Done.

That is how I felt.

I spent a few days making the rounds in Mosul, visiting places and people I'd visited before, looking for work. Of course there was none. I kept asking—not for charity, not for a handout, just for a chance to work.

With no luck, I found myself one night at my cousin's house. We talked, drank tea, smoked; finally, it got very late, time to go home. His house was far from mine. Under ordinary circumstances, I would have called a taxi to get home. But when I stuck my hand in my pocket, I realized I had only a few coins left to my name.

I took them out and counted. I had enough for a taxi.

Or lunch money for my kids.

Or cigarettes.

Not all three, or even two.

I felt incredibly poor. I *was* incredibly poor. I considered my choices. The Americans patrolled at night. No one really knew what they might do if they saw a lone Iraqi walking on the streets. It was said by many that they would they think he was a terrorist and shoot him.

I wasn't sure whether I would look like a terrorist to them or not. I didn't have a long beard and wore Western-style clothing, but at night these things might not be distinctive. And they couldn't see in my heart. From a distance all I would look like was a shadow, a dark and potentially ominous shadow.

"Screw it," I said aloud, to no one in particular. "I'll take my chances and walk. I'll buy half a pack of cigarettes and give the rest of the money to my kids."

I got the cigarettes and started on my way. I was surprised to find people out here and there. I walked at a nonchalant pace; too fast might be dangerous.

I hadn't gone all that far when I spotted some American vehicles parked on the street ahead, in front of a government building I had to pass to get home. I slowed my pace a little more, keeping my body erect and my hands at my side—I didn't want even my shadow to cast any suspicion.

Up ahead on the street, some women were talking loudly and complaining in Arabic. They were saying bad things about the

American troops, calling them occupiers and worse. I'm sure the Americans didn't understand most of what they were saying, but the women's voices had an angry tone, so the general gist of their displeasure was surely evident.

Just what I need, I thought. Trouble.

The Americans started moving toward the women. I couldn't let them beat the women—no Iraqi man could allow that, not and retain his honor.

Interfering might easily be a death sentence. But to live without honor would be worse.

I crossed the street and hurried to the women. I hardly said anything before they started to complain to me.

"The Americans are kicking out all the families," said one, excited. "They are cruel bastards!"

I gathered from what they were saying that the American troops were evicting squatters from the government building. People had taken up residence in the offices after the invasion, most because they had no other place to live. It may not have been the best place for them, and perhaps they had no legal right to live there, but for them it was a practical solution to a difficult problem.

The Americans didn't really understand. All they knew was that the government didn't want the people there, and they were to get them out. Certainly these troops, who would have been given orders with little real explanation of the situation, had no way of knowing how needy the residents of Mosul were.

I talked to the women for a few minutes. One or two of them recognized me from my days as a high school sports hero. They also knew my family, still deeply respected in Mosul.

"Tell me and explain the problem," I said. "One at a time."

"The soldiers won't let us in, the bastards," they complained. "If they don't, we will force our way in. What will they do? Shoot us? Beat us? Let them!"

I put my hand in my pocket, feeling the coins I'd left for my kids. Would I even have a chance to see them in the morning?

"Let me talk to the soldiers," I told the women. "Calm down and stay here."

"But—"

"Don't say anything. Let me handle this."

"They are bastards!"

"Hey guys, let me help you," I pleaded. "Just be calm. I will help you. I will talk to them in English."

I took a deep breath, then went to the soldiers and found the man in charge, a Sergeant Byrd. The women gathered up close behind me.

"Sergeant, you have a problem here," I told him. "With these women."

The sergeant had apparently already dealt with them, and knew their anger well.

"They need to calm down and move away," said the sergeant, who was with the 108th Military Police Company, a storied U.S. Army airborne unit. "We can't let them in."

"Do you speak Arabic?" I asked him.

"No."

"Then let me talk to them and see if I can help you," I said.

I turned to the women and started talking to them, making them explain the entire story as I translated as best I could. From their point of view, they had just been kicked out of their homes: they'd been living in the building since the invasion.

The sergeant gave his side of the situation—he had orders not to let anyone in without permission from the government.

"You know that the building is not your house," I told the women. "It's the government building. And these soldiers—they have no idea what the conflict is. They don't know about the government or the orders."

The women grumbled, but of course I was telling them the truth.

"What you have to do is go to the government," I told them. "You have to go in the morning and get a house. Tell them that the Americans took the house. They will have to find you a new one."

"The government will do this?" one of the women asked.

"They will have to."

"Okay."

It was like a miracle—they turned and left. There was no further trouble.

Sergeant Byrd was impressed.

"Do you want to work with us?" he asked.

"Sure," I said.

"Come Saturday to the police station."

I showed up that Saturday, talked for a few minutes with some officers and others connected with the MP unit, and I was in. Without a plan, without an idea—I suddenly had the job I'd been dreaming of.

THIS TIME, I WAITED until I *officially* had the job to brag about it. When I was finally positive that I had been hired, I rushed home to Soheila, feeling as dizzy as a school kid in love.

"This is going to change our lives," I told her. "This is going to make it possible for us to live again."

She didn't understand at first, or maybe she was just skeptical.

"I got a job with the Americans," I told her. "Real work. Money."

Soheila smiled. It is the sort of smile she gives me a lot—an indulgent wife smile. It is sometimes hard for husbands to interpret what wives are thinking—a good thing, probably!—but I can guess what this one means easily: *Johnny is being Johnny, and that is one reason I love him.*

Wives.

In the context of everything that has happened since, it may seem odd to people when I say that everyone I knew congratulated me when they heard I had gotten the job. But at that point, America and Americans in general, were largely still popular in Mosul. The city was not a dangerous place for anyone, not even Americans. The incidents like the one with the nut and his grenade were few. People were hopeful that the Americans would bring genuine and positive change.

Many of my friends, in fact, were jealous. The job paid well by Iraqi standards and was something to be bragged about, not hidden. On my first day at work, the Americans drove me home to my apartment. I walked through the street like a conquering hero— everyone who knew me respected me even more than they had before. Associating with the Americans was considered an honor and matter of prestige.

That was something that would soon change.


UDAY HUSSEIN AND his brother Qusay were cornered by American forces as they hid in Mosul in July 2003, right around the time that I got my first job. They resisted and were killed in a gunfight.

Our house was on the other side of the city, far from where they were killed. Their deaths had no effect on us, and if it meant something to the majority of residents in Mosul I never noticed. I would guess that the main concerns of most Iraqis that summer, inside Mosul and out, had to do with supporting their families. Jobs were scarce. The economy, thoroughly battered by Saddam and sanctions, had been nearly obliterated by the war. Civil order was only being fitfully restored. Americans were helping the Iraqi government and police reconstitute themselves, but even by prewar standards the society was badly broken.

Sergeant Byrd's company was primarily responsible for training the local police and helping them when needed. They undertook two patrols a night and went on operations with the locals. My main job was to act as a translator and liaison, helping the Americans and Iraqis understand each other.

As a rule, the American patrols were peaceful, and we quickly settled into a routine. I worked the night shift, from about 8 P.M. to 6 A.M. We would meet with the Iraqi officer in charge at the main police station where we were assigned. We'd check on the prisoners and get an idea of what was going on, asking the Iraqi police about rumors and criminal activity. Then we'd leave for a patrol, usually around 8:30 or 9 P.M. We'd make the rounds of the city. By midnight we would head over to the airport and the American base for food and a break.

That was a special bonus—American chow.

We'd go back to the station, handle whatever business had come up, then do another patrol in the early-morning hours.

It was very easy work. The MPs were especially concerned about the status of the Iraqi prisoners, making sure they weren't abused. Iraqi standards for dealing with accused criminals were *much* different than American standards, and the Americans kept emphasizing that the prisoners could not be physically harmed or bullied.

They'd have me translate for them as they questioned the prisoners about how they were being treated. The Americans kept asking if the prisoners were being beaten or otherwise mistreated, which as far as I know wasn't happening. Admittedly, Iraqi methods of arrest and interrogation were far harsher than the Americans were used to, but it seemed that the police had throttled back under the direction of the MPs.

As I became more comfortable with the job and the Americans, I started to trust them more. They told me they were trying to rebuild

Iraq, trying to help common people by bringing justice to their lives. Everything I saw them do reinforced this, and finally I decided not just to take them at their word, but to help them do just that.

"You should cut down on the corruption," I told Sergeant Byrd. "The criminals who are stealing the people's bread—if you want to go after thugs and bring justice, that's what you should do."

The problem was well known to Iraqis in town. The government had a large storehouse of wheat and flour at the edge of the city. The grain was supposed to go to the residents. Instead, thieves were taking it and selling it or the bread they made from it on the black market.

The Iraqi police were too scared to do anything about the thieves. I'm sure they felt that they had nothing to gain but grief— even if they arrested the black marketeers, the bastards would soon bribe their way out of trouble. And then undoubtedly they'd come back and revenge themselves.

Byrd and the other Americans seemed interested in doing something, though it was hard really to tell. My English was still a little weak.

One night not long after I'd told them about the black market operation, one of the American officers asked if I was interested in seeing some action.

"Sure. Okay," I told him, not really knowing what to expect. "It's good for me."

The MPs got ready to roll. I soon realized we were headed for the grain warehouse.

Even during Saddam's time, the storage facility had been a prime target for thieves. Large bins were buried in the ground, storing wheat until it could be ground into flour and distributed. The bins looked like large graves in the center of the complex. Thieves would drive in at night, pull off the bin covers, and take the grain.

The MPs arrived at the site in a number of Humvees. No one

seemed to be at the site at first. The military vehicles were loud, their engines distinctive; undoubtedly the thieves had taken the chance to hide as we approached. I could see several trucks used to transport the stolen goods parked near the bins. They were empty.

The army sent a helicopter to help with the operation. As its beam played over the grounds, I told one of the MPs to follow me through the property.

I walked through the lot to a truck that looked new. I jumped behind the wheel—the keys were in the ignition.

"Watch," I said. I turned the ignition and started the vehicle.

As soon as they heard the motor, several thieves climbed out of the bin nearby where they'd been hiding and started to run. While the MPs gave chase, I got the truck moving forward, then jumped out, leaving it in low gear. It rolled down into the vacant bin with a thud and crash. It wouldn't be used to steal from anyone anymore.

I did the same to two or three other trucks nearby, ruining them as well.

Most of the thieves managed to escape, and it's doubtful that the operation put much of a dent into Mosul's black market. But it was a success in one way: it told the thieves they couldn't just take what they wanted.

It was also important for me: I had become something more than just a translator. I was no longer working for the Americans, but with them. They wanted to bring justice to Iraq, and so did I.

Somehow, I had adopted Soheila's optimism for our country. I suddenly saw that there was a chance for real change. I was nearly forty years old, a mature man, and yet I was as hopeful as a teenager starting a new family. Maybe Iraq *could* be a good place to live.

If we got rid of the corruption, if people kept working together, if we made things rather than destroyed them—what greatness could we achieve?

# 4

# FIGHTING FOR A BETTER IRAQ

**I WORKED WITH THE** U.S. Army for several more months, into 2004. Most of my work was routine. The city remained relatively peaceful—wary, increasingly frustrated, but calm on the surface.

Underneath, things were changing little by little. Insurgents were moving in and natives were starting to vent the resentments they felt. Life hadn't improved much since Saddam had been chased away, and it grated. Still, while the rest of the country was becoming increasingly violent, in Mosul actions against the Americans were the exception, relatively isolated and insignificant.

The Americans weren't completely blind to increasing dissatisfaction, but they were limited in how to deal with it. Gradually, the MP units began dealing with more counterinsurgency issues, even as their focus remained mostly on the Iraqi police force and law enforcement in general.

My first real experience with a major counterinsurgency operation came early in 2004 when my company loaned me to another unit that wanted to help an agent infiltrate a terrorist cell in the city. The operation was complex—they intended to arrest a man who was already working with them as an informer. That would boast his bona fides with the insurgents, who would believe he had every reason to hate the Americans and would continue to share information with him.

I didn't know the intricacies of the plan; all I was told was that his arrest had to look good. It had to be clear that he was an enemy of the U.S. Army and that he had every reason to hate Americans and to want them dead.

How do you do that, except by giving him a good beating in front of the neighbors?

I grabbed him as they took him out of the house, and threw him to the ground. He was clearly expecting something, but had enough of a surprised look on his face to sell the whole act. I hammed it up, yelling at him and throwing a few kicks and punches in his direction—not *too* hard, but enough to make it clear I thought he was the son of a foul dog with murder in his heart.

The Americans rushed over to pull me off. That was my signal to go at my victim in a frenzy, pushing against them and trying to get more slaps and punches in.

I had to make it look real. There was a good bit of groaning and probably a few bruises before I was down.

The American soldiers were shocked. They thought I'd lost my mind. I got a good dressing-down from the officer in charge when we returned to the police station.

Why had I hit the man? Why had I put up such a fuss?

"Hey, this is my culture," I told him. "I know what I am doing. If you just take him out the way you were going to, people will think it is a setup. People will not believe you. You have to beat him—you have to make it look real."

"That's not the way we do things."

"That is the way you have to do things, if you want to succeed. This is my country. My rules."

"No."

"You guys are not allowed to beat him," I said. "And everyone knows, American rights, no bullshit, yes? But I can beat him. And that is what would happen if he really was bad. Iraqi police—Iraqis—we don't expect the arrest to be soft. So if you do not want him to be killed by these guys as a spy, you have to act as if he is bad. Do you understand? My country, my rules."

That phrase became kind of a joke with me as time went on. *My country, my rules.* But at the heart of it was a great truth. Without understanding the culture of a place, it is next to impossible to have the effect you want. What to one culture seems a sign of strength, to another may be a billboard of weakness. And that was often true in Iraq.

Americans value restraint as a worthy trait. That makes completely no sense in my native country. Our logic is very simple: Why did this person not hit back? Because he can't. He is weak. He is a fool. Hit him again. Get what you want. He is weak and will give in.

I didn't convince the soldiers at the time, and they were wary of me for a while. Still, that mission was a success, the man we arrested was accepted by the insurgents. Maybe you can't give my fists much if any credit, but I know that what I did made the arrest look real.


I KNOW THERE are stories about Americans mistreating prisoners at other places in Iraq, but from what I saw in Mosul, they erred on the side of being too careful, if anything. Iraqi culture is very rough and emphatic. Someone who is arrested is a disgrace to others in the community, and he can't be handled as if he is an angel. A man who is a traitor—the insurgents were traitors to the new Iraq—should be treated even worse. If you are serious about the charge, that is.

The Americans were too lenient in many ways. They didn't understand our culture—if you want results, you can't just *be* strong, you have to *act* strong. People have to see you being strong. What good is a watchdog that sits quietly in the corner of a yard when an intruder is at the fence? Yes, if the robber comes over, he might chase him or even bite, but isn't it better if the dog leaps to his feet and warns the robber away before he even tries to do anything?

**A FEW DAYS** later, we went on another mission with the Iraqi police to locate a man believed to be a cell leader. The house he was said to be staying at was in a crime-ridden area of town, a place that before the war would have been dangerous to walk in alone if you weren't known. Now it was even worse.

The arresting force consisted of seven or eight American MPs and five local policemen. We drove into the neighborhood in a small train of Humvees. The suspect's house was down an alley; it was so narrow we had to park the vehicles at the end and walk in. We split into two teams—the Americans were in one group, assigned to make the actual arrest, and the Iraqi police in the other. Their job was to keep civilians out of the way and watch the back of the target house in case the man tried to escape.

I went with the Iraqis so I could relay information back and forth. As the Americans set up a perimeter around the target house, the Iraqi police and I went next door. I knocked on the door and asked the owner for permission to come through to his backyard.

"Hey," I told him. "We are looking for someone. We need to come through your house and go to the back."

He started hemming and hawing, asking questions and protesting. All of a sudden I realized why.

The intel had been wrong. The cell leader wasn't next door; he was here.

"Fuck you," I said, pushing the door open. I ran in, glancing left and right in the empty room before heading to the stairs. I leapt up in a few bounds, then found a bedroom.

The suspect was lying in bed, snoring away. A gun peeked out from under his pillow.

I grabbed the gun, then put my hand over his mouth.

"Hey, brother," I told him as he woke. "We need you to go to the police station. We have some questions for you."

"Wha?" he mumbled. "What is going on?"

"I have your pistol in my pocket for my safety and your safety," I said. "My friends here will take you without trouble. Come on."

He stared at me. I glanced over my shoulder, expecting to see the Iraqi police squad fanning out behind me. But there was no one there.

In fact, not only had the Iraqis *not* followed me in, but they hadn't bothered to come in the house at all. For some bizarre reason, they had pulled back to the alley and met the MPs. Apparently, learning that they had the wrong house—and not knowing that I was in the right one—the Americans decided to call off the operation and go back to the police station. The Iraqis didn't question them or mention that I had run into the house, let alone why. Apparently the Americans didn't notice me missing. They walked back to their vehicles and started to leave.

I didn't know any of this. I waited for a few minutes, wondering what was going on. Finally I realized that the police and the Americans had left me on my own. I was in the room with a suspected terrorist cell leader; downstairs, there was at least one man who probably sympathized with the man and was more than likely armed.

For just a moment, I considered taking the suspect with me. But that would have been foolhardy: it was daylight, and there were far too many people likely to object.

On the other hand, leaving him alone and running off would have been crazy, too. If he or the man downstairs grabbed a gun, I wouldn't make it back to the alley alive.

"Up, out of the bed," I told the suspect.

He got up cautiously. I was bigger than him, but he didn't look like a weakling either.

"Here," I told him, moving near the window. "Come here."

He came and stood in front of me.

"Nothing personal," I told him. "But I can't take a chance. I don't trust you with my life. And so—"

I pushed him out the window. He fell awkwardly amid a shower of curses. It wasn't a long fall and I knew it wouldn't be fatal, though I did hear later that he had broken his arm.

There were other things on my mind at the moment besides his health. I walked down the stairs as calmly as I could, acting as if nothing at all had happened. I still had the pistol in my pocket, my hand inches away. The homeowner stared at me but said nothing as I left.

Swiftly as possible, without looking like I was in a panic, I walked down the alley and then out of the neighborhood. No matter how calm I looked on the outside, my heart was in overdrive.

"What the hell happened to you?" asked the head of the MP unit when I got back. "Where were you?"

"Where was I?" I told him. It was an interesting conversation.

The Americans thought they had lost their suspect—until he showed up at the police station a few days later to complain about me. Unluckily for him, the man was not only a suspected insurgent but a wanted criminal, whose crimes according to the police included assault. He was arrested; I'm not sure what happened to him after that.

**WAS I WRONG** to push him? Should I have left him free to attack me?

I was learning that these are the sorts of decisions you have to make in war. It's not a matter of being desperate—it's a matter of preventing yourself from being desperate.

In this case, I knew he wouldn't die from the fall. I'm sorry that he broke his arm—that I didn't intend—but in the small room and the narrow confines of the slum I was in, pushing him was the best decision I could make.

It was either my safety or a terrorist's. I chose to protect myself.

I didn't apologize to the MPs for it, and I don't apologize now. I wish the circumstances were different—but if I am *really* going to make a wish, I would wish that Saddam had never existed, that there was no need for war, and that there would always be peace.

I would wish that there was no insurgency. I would wish that rather than resisting American help, the entire country had come together and taken advantage of it.

**THE INCIDENT HELPED** give me a reputation as someone not to mess with. Some of the Iraqis were probably afraid of me. Some of the Americans may have thought I was a little crazy. Both were mixed blessings.

I did my best to stay quiet and calm on the rest of the missions they took me on. They trusted me and knew I was on their side, but I think they were wary that I might do something they didn't want.

While the insurgency was starting to become active, there was still a lot of goodwill toward Americans in Mosul. Things were fairly calm, and most of what the MP unit was dealing with were routine police matters.

Elsewhere in Iraq, things were very different.

Immediately after the invasion, the main opposition to the Americans and the new Iraqi government came from the Fedayeen Saddam, the organization Saddam had created before being chased from power. As the opposition intensified, the American command concentrated on rounding up the ringleaders, including Saddam Hussein, who as the former dictator was seen as a key figure. But Saddam's capture in December of 2003 near Tikrit did nothing to lessen the insurgency. By that time, Saddam had little credence with anyone. He was a broken man and probably more of an embarrassment to the fighters than an inspiration.

Meanwhile, the forces fighting against Americans and Iraqis in favor of a democratically elected government had grown. Most significantly, the Fedayeen fighters had been joined by militants fighting under the banner of al-Qaeda in Iraq. These were radical Sunnis, who besides hating Americans began focusing their attacks on Shiites.

Al-Qaeda in Iraq and its affiliated groups grew rapidly in 2004. Among other tactics, it encouraged suicide bombings against civilian targets—in other words, terrorists targeted innocent civilians as a normal course of business. Many of the fighters involved in al-Qaeda in Iraq were foreigners, who came because they thought they were fighting jihad against infidels and nonbelievers. But certainly not all were. Young men from poor rural families were especially easy to recruit. While some were committed to the cause for religious and ideological reasons, in many cases money and sheer boredom were their real motivators.

There was a flipside to the insurgency among radical Shiites, who for convenience's sake I'll call Shia militias, as the best known of these groups were formed and run as small private armies. The most famous was the Mahdi Army led by Moqtada al-Sadr. Himself an imam, Sadr was descended from a line of famous clerics; he was a fiery speaker and an effective politician. He had very large support around Baghdad, most especially in Sadr City, a poor area dominated by public housing projects. The Shia militias battled the government and the Americans, and occasionally Sunnis.

Significant backing for the militias came from Iran. Although this fact was not widely publicized in the United States, Iran supplied money, weapons, and know-how to the Shia insurgency. Iran's ultimate aim was to dominate Iraq, its traditional enemy. It was a long-term goal, and the campaign was waged on many fronts. Today, any Iraqi can point to a dozen things that prove the immense influence Iran has achieved over the current government, starting with the way the Iranian flag is flown in the capital.

As you might expect, the Shiite insurgents and the Sunni insurgents were strongest in the areas where other members of their faith dominated. As the insurgencies grew, so did the tension between the two branches of Islam.

There were many permutations in the civil war that raged during the occupation, alliances of convenience and longer-lasting ones of blood. We weren't interested in the politics or the religion of the terrorists we were assigned to arrest, but in dealing with the people on the ground it was helpful to know what their overall allegiance and background was. Realizing that you were looking for a Shiite meant you didn't have to waste your time with a suspect who was Sunni, for example. But otherwise, the subtleties of who reported to whom and who prayed a certain way were irrelevant to anyone dealing on the street level with the problem. You don't ask how a man ties his turban when he's pointing a machine gun at you.

**IN THE SPRING** of 2004, the Mahdi Army began an open revolt, seizing swaths of Baghdad and some small towns in the south where

Shiites had the majority population. Al-Qaeda and the associated mujahideen associated with it—*mujahideen* means Islamic fighters in general, but in Iraq it was usually used to refer to Sunni insurgents—stepped up their attacks. It was during this time that four Blackwater contractors were killed and hung from a bridge in Fallujah, an incident that inflamed many Americans and became emblematic of the insurgency's hatred for Americans.

By now, I was one of five interpreters, or "terps," working with the MP company. With tensions increasing every day and the police now a popular target for the insurgents, the job became more stressful—and, perversely, more interesting.

Mosul, farther north than either Baghdad or Fallujah, gradually saw more and more violence. Police stations were attacked with IEDs (improvised explosive devices). Individual policemen were targeted and attacked. It wasn't only rank-and-file policemen, nor were the small, isolated stations the only ones targeted. The Sheik Fatihi police station, a major installation, was attacked with a bomb and a drive-by shooting in March. Within days, the terrorists tried to kill Major General Mohammed Khairi al-Barhawi, the chief of police for the Nineveh governorate (the province of which Mosul is the capital). Al-Barhawi escaped, but four policemen were injured, as were several civilians. The same day, insurgents lobbed four mortar shells at one of the city police stations, and two foreign contractors were killed in a drive-by shooting.

Car bombs soon became the terror weapon of choice. A quartet of bombings in June killed 62 people and injured another 220. Western analysts and news media speculated that the increase in violence was due to the pending turnover of authority from the United States to the new Iraqi government. According to that theory, the attacks would wind down once the elections were held. It was a nice theory, but facts didn't back it up; the attacks continued.

Most of these were isolated, affecting only a few people. I don't remember most of them, and what I do recall are mostly snatches of things here and there, attacks where the MPs responded and I went along.

In the fall, two American army engineers went to a police station to handle some business. As they arrived, a man in a white SUV nearby detonated the explosives in his vehicle, killing one of the Americans as well as himself.

I was with the MPs at their airport base when the call came in. We loaded into the Humvees and drove over. I jumped out as soon as we pulled up, and began gathering information. There was a crowd already, and newspeople seemingly everywhere—I ended up being in one of the video reports of the incident.

Looking at the bodies of the dead men—both the American and the insurgent—I had a terrible sense that much worse was to come. The new Iraqi government had done little to clamp down on the violence; it was impotent, and that impotence would encourage even greater violence. On top of that, there was plenty of desperation and corruption, the twin enablers of the insurgency. Not every policeman in the city we worked with would take money to look the other way or tell al-Qaeda about our plans, but there were certainly plenty who would do both. Many government officials were even worse. And people who weren't corrupt were fearful, afraid for their lives. Just doing their jobs put them in danger. The fact that the police did nothing after the IED attack was hardly surprising.

Americans tended to look at the violence in terms of the attacks on their soldiers and other citizens, which was understandable. But many more Iraqis were targeted and killed than Americans as the insurgency continued. What happened to Mosul in 2004 was shocking. The previous fall, the city was peaceful, with most people living more or less as they had before the war—Sunni and Shia side by side. Even during winter, insurgents elsewhere labeled the city a "white chicken"—a place of cowards—because things were relatively calm and religious animosity almost nonexistent.

By the summer, all of that was over. If you were to make a comparison involving a chicken when talking about Mosul, it was to one that had had its head cut off.

The new government and the police that supported them were targets not just because they were allied with the Americans, but because the central government was seen as being dominated by Shiites. Al-Qaeda deliberately targeted Shiites to "purify" the religion. Adding to the chaos was a power struggle between al-Qaeda, former Ba'ath Party members, and the remnants of the Fedayeen, all trying to assert their will.

Desperation fed desperation, which in turn fed violence. There were few jobs and food was often scarce. Even winter clothes were hard to get that year; when you could find them, the prices were too much for many to afford. People lived in very bad conditions; most were depressed or angry, or both. I'd returned home to a hero's welcome when I got my job with the Americans. Now that was a sure way to invite trouble, if not death.

Stubbornly, I refused to recognize the danger I was in. I didn't think anything could happen to my family or myself. Partly this was because the people around me had no desire to join the mujahideen. Nor did they have any trouble with me. They knew I was a fair and honest man; no one, I thought, would hurt such a person, let alone his family.

One of my cousins had given me a colorful jacket woven in India as a gift. It was unique and I liked it a lot. I wore it on my rounds with the MPs—Soheila recognized it immediately when we saw the news video from the car bomb.

It was a bright marker, something that made me stand out. But for some reason, though I saw what was happening to my country, I didn't yet understand that standing out made you a target for all the evil around you.

SHORTLY AFTER THE SUV bombing, the MPs loaned me to another American unit working with the Iraqi police. With American help and prodding, the police had launched an undercover investigation aimed at closing a black-market operation selling guns out of a coffee shop. The investigation had reached the point where they were ready to make an arrest.

Once again I was a translator and a liaison for the Americans. I went inside with the Iraqi police, who made the actual arrest. As I was watching what they were doing, I noticed a customer stuffing a pistol under his belt. I grabbed it from him—it was a Browning semiautomatic, a nice one with wooden furniture—and turned him over to the cops. They continued going about their business, questioning the suspect and a few men who'd been dealing with him before herding them all out of the shop.

We were still a good distance from the Hummers when we were ambushed by two or three men with AKs who were across the way, crouched on a hill nearby. At that point, I wasn't authorized to carry a weapon—another thing Americans were very sticky about. I'd given the Browning to the police and was therefore unarmed.

Instinctively, I grabbed a rifle from the cop next to me and started firing. The men with the guns, probably black marketeers angry about getting their favorite shopping spot busted, ran off. Whether I hit any or not I'm not sure, but I definitely did my best to get them.

In my mind's eye, I see blood spurting everywhere when I look back. I know logically that they were too far and it was too dark for me to see, but emotionally I want to have gotten my revenge for their attack.

The Hummers raced up and I jumped in with the Iraqi cops. I still had a few bullets in the gun, and I kept it ready. I was alone with the police in the truck, and, not knowing them, it suddenly occurred to me that one or more might shoot me. I didn't know any of them, since I'd never worked with them before, and while it may seem paranoid now, at the time it felt like a very rational fear. The short encounter had changed me dramatically. I'd gone from having no fear at all for my life to being suspicious of everything and everyone around me.

Back at the base, the MPs' commander announced loudly that one of the Iraqi policemen had done an excellent job and should be commended. Then he asked that the man who had provided the covering fire step forward.

It took me a few seconds to realize he was talking about me. I was the only Iraqi who had fired back.

I stepped forward, a bit shy—I didn't 100 percent trust that I was going to be commended rather than bawled out.

The commander was surprised that the interpreter, not the police, had been the one taking the fight to the insurgents. But he praised me nonetheless.

Sergeant Byrd and the MPs who knew me said they weren't surprised at all. They'd already seen me change from a man of words to a man who was fighting as hard as they were.

After that fight, I realized I was fighting for Iraq, or at least my vision of what it could be: a safe place for family, a country with a future.

It sounds almost grandiose, like I came to a major conclusion and decision. But I didn't. It just naturally happened. To that point, the job was about making money for my family. Now it was something more.

It didn't have to be. I could have quit. Or I could have stayed back and still done my job. Most interpreters did just that.

Yet it wouldn't have felt right: I would have felt not like a quitter but a coward. Staying back as a translator in the shadows, behind others, just doing the letter of my job: that would have been even worse. That would have made me a ghost, skittering along at the edges of life. It would have been just as cowardly as running away.

Don't misunderstand. I wasn't crazy. I didn't look for a fight. I wouldn't take on a tank or go "Rambo" against hordes of better-armed insurgents. But I wouldn't let myself be pushed around. I gravitated toward the action, and once there, I did what I had to do. A kind of primitive animal instinct took over:

*Motherfucker, you want to take my life? Well, fuck you, I will take yours.*

That was the sensation I felt at the moment. And after the adrenaline faded, after things calmed down, it was joined by another, deeper feeling:

*Motherfucker, you aren't going to take my country away. You aren't going to win.*

*Fuck you. This is my country. This is my Iraq.*

ONE MORNING IN the fall of 2004, I reported to work as usual. When I came in, an American sergeant—I'll call him Sergeant East—greeted me and motioned me into a room for a private conversation. He asked if I'd be willing to change jobs and work with a different group of Americans. He didn't give many details, but he hinted that the work would be very important, and probably more exciting than what I was doing now. It would also pay more—two and a half times more, as a matter of fact.

The money alone made it worthwhile. I was a little surprised, though, that I had been asked. From his description, the job entailed a lot of missions, something the Americans generally preferred to leave to younger men. And not only was I the oldest of the interpreters at forty, but I had the worst English language skills among them.

Admittedly, interpreting on a mission was often easier than interpreting on a routine police patrol. The vocabulary was much more limited, and you could get through most of what had to be done without speaking English at all, at least until you were needed to talk to a subject or target. But youth was a real asset during an operation. Even the ones I'd been on with the MPs required the ability to move quickly, climb, jump, and simply stay working for a long period of time.

Forty doesn't seem that old now, and I suspect fifty won't seem very old in a few years either. But to be honest, my body was showing all the signs you'd expect it to show as it aged. It had been quite a long time since I'd wowed Mosul on the basketball court or represented the region in the high jump. Truthfully, there were plenty of times I felt like an old man.

Still, I was flattered to be asked, and I could tell from the way Sergeant East spoke that he thought the new job would be an honor, or at least something of a promotion.

"So who are these guys?" I asked.

"SEALs."

"Okay." I nodded, but in truth I had no idea what *SEALs* meant, let alone who these guys were or what they did. The sergeant clearly held them in high esteem, but beyond that, they were a mystery.

SEALs? *Seals?* Aquatic animals?

It's a good thing that my English wasn't any better, because then I would have been truly confused. As it was, I just decided to do as I was told and see what happened.

Sergeant East sent me over to a compound on the air base to talk to the SEALs. As soon as I walked into their common room and saw their gear setup, I realized these guys meant serious business. These weren't just warriors, they were first-class warriors. They had much better equipment than the MPs. They were all in excellent shape, real athletes. And they had a certain way of talking and walking that seemed commanding and very professional.

I was interviewed by one of the chief petty officers, Neal. He asked me a few questions about what I had done with the MPs and some other background things. The questions all seemed pretty easy. In fact, they felt *too* easy, as if I should be telling him more or have some sort of elaborate explanation. I went into detail about what I had done with the MPs and the Iraqi police, and still felt as if I wasn't giving him enough information to impress him.

The interview didn't take too long. When it was over, the chief got up to go.

"Do you think I have a chance to work with you?" I asked, sure I had done a terrible job in the interview.

"Definitely," said Neal.

*Definitely* was a word I hadn't heard before. It didn't sound positive. But I was too embarrassed to ask what it meant, so I just nodded and left.

Back with the MPs, Sergeant East asked how I had done.

"I don't know," I confessed. "Not well, I think."

"No?" he was surprised.

"No. I asked if I had a chance."

"Well, what did he say?"

"He said 'definitely.'"

The sergeant laughed and began congratulating me. It was only then that I understood that *definitely* was a good thing.

I got the job and started a few days later.

I QUICKLY LEARNED that working with the SEALs was very different than working with the MPs, and not just because they weren't training or working with the Iraqi police. While the MPs had gone on missions to pick up subjects, that had never been their main focus. The SEALs were all about apprehending insurgents, both suspected and confirmed.

Most of their assignments involved going to find a suspect and bringing him back for questioning by the authorities. These weren't always arrests, but in most cases the people who were being picked up were pretty high-ranking insurgents suspected of serious terror-ist activities. The SEALs always had to assume that the people they were going after—the "jackpot," we called them—would put up a fight. They took many steps to minimize the risk, and in most cases there was no gunfire, but there was *never* a time on a mission that they could relax.

Because of that, they planned exhaustively for each mission. I wasn't invited to these sessions at first; I probably wouldn't have understood enough English to be useful anyway. Once the planning was done, they carefully briefed the different members of the unit, making sure everyone knew what he had to do. I was briefed on only my role at first; I'd have to win their trust before I was invited to make deeper contributions. Once an operation kicked off, the SEALs tended to follow their planning to the letter. They might excel at improvisation—I can attest that they did—but they did everything in their power to not have to improvise.

Because they operated almost exclusively at night—and prob-ably because they didn't completely trust me—the SEALs gave me a little trailer to stay in when not working. This was a major change; until now I'd been free to come and go after work as I pleased. But there was no sense in arguing, and in fact the arrangement was not only convenient but probably safer for me and my family. Plus, the trailer was spacious, though empty except for a bed and a few pieces of furniture. There was no TV, computer, or even radio.

The first day I reported for work, the chief introduced me to Percy, another translator. He was a short, chubby fellow, very friendly and full of advice. He invited me into his trailer, fixed up an impromptu meal, and gave me a long rundown on what to expect. He also told me about America—he was an American citizen—and he gave me a lecture about money. I should save as much as I could, he told me.

"You'll work hard," he said, "but you can save for the future. And you can have a good future."

He was right about all of it, the money especially. I wasn't getting rich, but by the standards I'd been used to before the war, I was suddenly doing very well. I'd been making two hundred dollars a month working for the MPs. The SEALs paid me five hundred. My first paycheck made me feel like I was a king. I bought my family presents, a TV, clothes. It was a heady feeling.

Others have pointed out that American citizens—like Percy—made considerably more than native Iraqis for the same kind of work—ten times as much, and in some cases even more. That was true for interpreters as well as just about everyone else. I don't know what Percy was being paid, and I don't begrudge him it either. I'm not even complaining about my pay. To me, it seemed a fortune.

The SEALs didn't trust me yet. In fact, they kept a very close eye on me. If I wanted to go anywhere, I had to have an escort, even to the latrine, or "head," as the navy people called it. The escort would be at the next stall while I did my business.

THE SEALs ARE organized differently than any other military unit I'd known. They are grouped in different "teams," each of which generally has three troops, each with two platoons. Platoon size is around twenty men, sometimes a little less. There are West Coast teams and East Coast teams, a distinction that refers to where they are based in the United States. Odd-numbered teams are based on the West Coast, even numbers on the East. During the time I was working with them, the teams usually rotated platoons into Iraq for deployments that lasted several months—six, more or less, seemed to be the average. I started with Team 7 and ended up working with nearly all of the teams that came to Iraq. (The one exception was Team 6, which I was never assigned to.)

While the team structure forms a backbone for the administration of the units, SEALs are extremely flexible in practice. During my time with them, there were various task groups that worked with conventional soldiers and Marines for a variety of periods and missions. At different times, elements from different teams worked together as one.

The SEALs made no effort to explain their organization to me, and I don't blame them. I'm sure part of the reason had to do with security; the less I knew about them, the less I could tell the enemy if I were captured. Besides, there was no real need for me to know whether the task group I was working with was composed of men from Team 1 or Team 5 or both. It made no difference to me whether the platoon I was helping was based in the eastern or western United States.

To a large extent, the distinctions that the SEALs observed between teams or even platoons were meaningless to me. While each man had his own personality, taken as a group the SEALs were remarkably similar in the way they did things and the way they were equipped. There were always individual wrinkles, but their overall approach never varied from one unit to another. It was always professional; it was always results oriented. To a man, they were the fiercest warriors I have ever known.

Like all military units, the SEAL teams were led by officers and answered to a "head shed" of senior commanders. My personal dealings were mostly with the senior enlisted men, usually chief petty officers, who were tasked to deal with interpreters. Most of them were a cross between a dad and the most demanding but fair sports coach you can imagine. These guys were usually my direct bosses; they took care of me, and I did my best for them.

THE MISSIONS WITH the SEALs would soon blur together, but I remember my first one vividly. I went in with them to the room they used to gear up, watching them don their combat gear and ready their weapons. Night vision, machine guns—everything was differ-ent, everything was bigger, everything was better, than I had seen with the military police.

Holy crap, I thought. These guys are serious. What have I gotten myself into?

I wasn't allowed in on the brief, but when we were ready to leave, one of the SEALs gave me the name of the jackpot—our target—and told me that we were going to apprehend him.

Then he tried to give me some body armor.

"No, thank you," I told him. "I don't want to die in your clothes."

"No, no, it's for your protection," said the SEAL, who later became a good friend.

"If I am going to die, I want to die in my clothes. And I am not going to die."

We went back and forth for a bit. Finally, Neal came over and told me in no uncertain terms that I was gearing up. The platoon chief told me I had no option—they were keeping me safe, and they were making all the judgments. So I put on a vest and a helmet.

The SEALs didn't know what to expect from me. It wasn't solely a matter of trust. I'm sure the MPs had vouched for me, and the SEALs had certainly done their own checking. But you never know how someone is going to act under stress until they are actually *under stress*. Combat stress and its consequences are unpredictable.

I'd already seen that and knew that interpreters in Iraq were a mixed lot. Looking back, I can say pretty definitively that everyone the SEALs had already worked with preferred to stay way back and out of danger, something that wasn't always possible.

Neal and the others didn't yet have a good feel for how I would react. Even so, I have to say they were way overprotective. Not only did they have me bundled up in armor, they had one of their mem-bers stay with me at all times, governing my every move: *stay down,* go *here, down, up, get down.* I don't think a baby could have been better protected.

It made me a little crazy.

Just before we were going to leave, I asked the SEAL who'd been assigned as my escort—minder would be a better word—if I could bring a gun along for protection.

The SEAL—I'll call him Wolf—told me in no uncertain terms that I could not.

"You're an Iraqi," said Wolf. "You're not getting a gun."

"I need protection."

"We'll protect you."

There were probably some four-letter words thrown in as well to emphasize the point.

So I didn't bring a gun. But I wasn't about to go on an operation unarmed. I went back to my trailer and got the longest knife I had, a twelve-inch combat knife that some of the SEALs said later looked like a machete or a small sword. They'd told me I couldn't bring a gun; they said nothing about a knife.

We drove in the direction of the target house, stopping far enough away that the Hummers wouldn't tip off any lookouts or the people in the house. The military vehicles were very loud, especially at night when nothing else was going on, and any lookout with half a brain would know we were coming from a few blocks away. Out of the trucks, we formed up in a loose line and began walking in the direction of the target. The streets were dark and deserted. At this point, my job was to keep up and keep quiet.

I stayed next to Wolf as we walked to a spot a short distance from the jackpot's house. Suddenly, he motioned for me to crouch.

Unsure what was going on, I obeyed.

Light flashed.

*Ba-boom!*

The explosion shook the ground. My first reaction, my instinct, was to get the hell out of there. I was scared beyond belief. I probably would have run off if it hadn't been for the SEAL next to me.

"This is how we open doors," Wolf said, calmly rising and nudging me to my feet. "Come on."

We got up and ran to the house. The assaulters had blown open the door and secured the building by the time we got there. I went in and found the SEALs standing with a man who was looking pretty bewildered.

I'm not sure that my expression wasn't exactly the same.

My babysitter and the other SEALs looked at me expectantly.

"What is your name?" I asked the man, who'd been sleeping when the door blew open.

I forget the answer now, but whatever it was, it matched the name of the man we were looking for. I turned and nodded at Neal. He'd already heard the name and motioned to the others. They took the suspect away.

In the meantime, a search of the house turned up some bomb-making equipment. The gear was taken away with him, to be handed over to the authorities.

And that was the night. Except for panicking and nearly running away, it had been a breeze.

**I SHOULD POINT OUT** that using explosives on doors was unusual. The SEALs had various ways of getting into the houses—among them was a nifty pneumatic tool that opened them as easily as popping the lid on a can of tuna—but often they simply turned the knob. You'd be surprised how many doors weren't locked. Those that were generally gave way with a firm nudge. On many other missions, they'd simply knock.

That's not to say that missions against high-level and risky targets didn't involve force, or that SEALs never used the devices you see in movies like flash-bang grenades to surprise armed defenders. It depended on what the situation called for. But much of the showy drama captured in movies or other works of fiction was the exception. The only thing that was constant was the knowledge that a gun or an explosive might be behind the door, or in the next room. Danger was always present; it just wasn't flashy about it.

The majority of the missions I did with the SEALs, not only with this unit but over the course of several teams and nearly a half-dozen years, were similar and simple in outline:

We were given the name of a suspect to apprehend, along with the details on where he lived and some way of identifying him. We would go to the house or the apartment—it was almost always a residential building of some type—usually arriving very late at night when everyone was asleep. We'd go in, find him, take him back to the base, and turn him over to whatever agency was looking for him.

The trick for me was figuring whether we got the right person or not. Only occasionally—maybe two or three times in total, as I look back—did we get photographs before the start of the mission. So making a positive identification was often tricky—not only did we have to worry about whether the person was telling the truth, but there was often a question about whether the intel we had was correct or not.

I say *we* because as time went on the SEALs relied on me more and more to do that part of the job. And as time went on, I learned different ways of finding out the true identity of the person we were questioning.

Naturally, things like bomb-making gear in the attic or heavy machine guns under the bed were pretty much a tipoff; even if the guy wasn't the suspect, he would be taken in. But in a lot of cases, that sort of obvious evidence was missing.

Less people than you would think resisted, and even less resisted effectively. Maybe you might get resistance two times out of ten, or four out of ten later in the war—but in most cases suspects quickly realized they were surrounded by well-armed men and that physically resisting was pointless. Firefights were the exception rather than the rule.

Passive resistance was a different story. Many jackpots simply denied they were the person we were looking for. It was easy to do: the intelligence we started with was often less than perfect. If the names had been processed by a non-Arabic speaker, or even one who spoke Arabic with a different accent than what the locals used, it could take quite a bit to decipher the actual identities—the name "Tariq," for example, might be written as "Tah," because that's what the English speaker heard.

I quickly learned not to ask for a name I wasn't 100 percent sure of; I let the person I was questioning tell me who they were. It was always better to look for secondary intelligence—papers in the house, for example—before talking to anyone, so I'd at least know the proper names of the people who lived there.

Suspects who claimed to be someone other than whom we were looking for often had phony identity papers "proving" they were that person. Part of my job was separating the bullshit from the truth and the truth from the bullshit. I had to learn how to get people to talk to me without lying.

There's been a lot of controversy in the United States about torture. Not that I ever asked for permission, but I wasn't allowed to torture people to get information. What I could do was trick them, sometimes with threats that I knew I couldn't carry out, sometimes with misdirection and lies.

I learned to use clues from around the house, from other people, and from the suspects themselves to confirm their identities. I got better at it as I went. It helped greatly that I was Iraqi. I could tell where people came from, what their general religious beliefs were, and usually a little bit about their station in life. That helped a lot when I was trying to get a sense of how truthful they were— someone with an Egyptian accent who claimed to be from Kurdistan had better have a good explanation if they wanted me to believe them.

Fear was a good weapon, and there were plenty of things I could do to ratchet up someone's fear without touching them. First of all, when people appear suddenly in your house in the middle of the night, you're not going to be entirely comfortable. When those people are wearing combat gear and yelling commands, your stress level elevates. So most subjects started off intimidated, and it was just a matter of pushing a few buttons to get them fearful enough to cooperate.

"If you don't tell me who you are," I might say, "I'm going to have to take your entire family with me."

That may not sound like much of a threat in the United States, but in Iraq, it represented an enormous loss of honor, since the male head of the household ordinarily dealt with all formal matters. Taking the family to headquarters—not even to jail, just to an American base—was a slap at the man of the house's status.

The goal wasn't to get him to lie about who he was—if it had been, we could have simply arrested him and I wouldn't have had to bother asking any questions at all. What I discovered was that stress made truth and lies more obvious. Denials became much more sincere and easier to read. Even a man who lied and said he *was* the jackpot to get his family off the hook (rare, but it happened) would give himself away with his eyes or some mannerism.

The truth is, I would never have taken the man's family, and I'm sure the SEALs wouldn't have permitted it if I had suggested doing so. But most people didn't realize that.

Iraq was not the United States, where the concept of "innocent until proven guilty" is ingrained in the culture. On the contrary, the long years of the dictatorship had pretty much led us to believe *everyone* was guilty of something. But with the Americans I had to work from the premise that the people I was talking to were innocent, and only if I was sure that they were the jackpot did I identify them.

The SEALs emphasized this all the time, but it was just common sense. Even if the man was just interviewed and then released—a very common occurrence—taking the wrong person meant more than a little inconvenience for them. Hassle a man enough, and even someone who supported the new government and liked Americans would eventually turn and side with the mujahideen.

**WORKING WITH THE SEALs**, I became a connoisseur of truth and a sorter of names. But at least at the beginning, I was a man without a name myself.

Because of the nature of the work, the SEALs didn't want to use my real name while out on a mission. It would be too easy for someone to overhear it and then report it to the insurgents. At first I used variations that were easy for them to pronounce. Then finally one of the SEALs gave me the "code name" Johnny Walker.

Somehow it stuck. I'm not exactly sure how or why it was first chosen; there seem to have been a number of Walkers, Johnny or otherwise, before me. It did have a couple of advantages: it was easy to remember and easy to say over the radio.

"Get Johnny Walker up here."

"Where's Johnny Walker?"

"We need Johnny to talk to the jackpot."

*Johnny Walker.* Sounded good to me.

Sometime later, I found out that the name echoed the one belonging to a fine Scotch, Johnnie Walker. It's possible that the SEALs were thinking of that originally, though at that point I don't remember having made my own acquaintance with that particular whisky. Once I did, I decided the name was a natural.

I'd drunk Scotch a few times before I started worked with the Americans, but not a lot. Even bad Scotch was very expensive in Iraq and I had no taste for it—or money to buy it. Once I started working with the SEALs, I had enough money to buy the good stuff. And I suppose it was inevitable that I would become acquainted with my "relative."

I should make clear that, while Iraq is a Muslim country and the sale of alcohol was illegal under Saddam, in fact it was always available. Stores, clubs, and restaurants throughout the country sold it before the American invasion. It actually became harder to get after Saddam was deposed, as shops selling alcohol became targets for Islamic fundamentalists of all persuasions. They bombed many liquor stores and others closed out of fear.

There were many things to learn about working with the SEALs and Americans in general. The hardest things to understand were not operational procedures—my job was never very complicated, really—but things that had to do with culture that Americans took for granted. My knowledge of American entertainment, whether it was music or film, was limited. What I did know, many of the SEALs didn't share—few were very big country music fans, at least of the classic country music I'd heard growing up. And I knew almost nothing about television. But it was all fascinating, things to learn. I became a kind of cultural sponge, soaking up whatever tidbits I could.

The same with the equipment they used. The SEALs and American soldiers in general had some interesting gear. Put on night vision gear and the entire world turns green, just as if you are in a Hollywood movie.

And since you are in a Hollywood movie, nothing is scary. Because it is fiction, not fact.

I told myself that a lot, especially in those early days. Sometimes it worked.

One unit took me to a range to familiarize me with their weapons. It was "show and shoot" for the Iraqi terp.

I was not then and am not now a gun expert. Weapons are tools to me, nothing more. But I did see that the M4 was a very nice rifle—light and easy to handle, especially compared to the AK-47s I had grown up around. When later I worked with the Iraqi troops as a liaison, I made sure to be assigned one.

The truly impressive weapons were the .50-caliber machine guns and the grenade launchers. The grenade launcher—*crazy!* I stood on the side as they demonstrated it, and tried not to cringe.

U.S. regulations prevented the SEALs from giving me a gun. But I had my own personal 7 mm pistol; I believe it came from Romania or somewhere behind the old Iron Curtain. I also had an AK-47, as did most Iraqi males.

These were my personal weapons and I wasn't supposed to take them on raids. I'm sure if I'd showed up with them during the first few weeks, the SEALs would have grabbed them out of my hands and probably beaten me with them.

Trust, they say, has to be earned. It's especially tough in a war zone, and ridiculously hard when the person who has to be trusted looks and sounds like the enemy.

But I soon had plenty of chances to prove who I was and what I believed.

## 5

# TRUST AND TREACHERY

**KNEW THE MISSION** would be unusual because it was taking place during the day, something rare for the SEALs. But when I saw the guys dressed in civilian clothes, I realized it was going to be far different and probably more dangerous than anything we'd done before.

As usual, I didn't get the full brief, just enough so I could do my job. What they did tell me was dramatic enough. The SEALs had been given intelligence that a suspect would be in a certain store at ten o'clock that day. They were going to just walk in and grab him.

The suspect was a high-ranking member of the local al-Qaeda organization. They gave me a surprisingly detailed description; ordinarily the descriptions were pretty bare, and this was another indication that the mission was unusual. I forget the suspect's name now—with maybe one or two exceptions, the names never stuck with me. They were an identity that I had to check, important for the moment, completely forgotten afterward. As for what he was accused of: aside from his being an important figure in the insurgency, I doubt I knew the actual details of his résumé at the time. In retrospect, I'm sure it was better that way; it's hard to be dispassionate about a man when you know exactly how many people he has killed.

We boarded two SUVs and headed toward the block where the shop was. I was sitting in the front passenger seat, watching to see what was going on. Besides my normal clothes, I'd put on a scarf; when we stopped I slipped it around the lower part of my face, masking myself in case there were lookouts. By now I'd grown my beard out, and if anything I probably looked like a terrorist myself.

The SEALs assigned to snatch the jackpot got out of the trucks and walked across the street. As they went in, I realized they were making a mistake—they'd accidentally gone in the wrong store.

It wasn't hard to do. All the buildings on that stretch of the block looked the same. If you weren't from Mosul and you didn't read much Arabic, it was easy to get confused.

"Hey, tell him he is wrong," I said to the driver beside me. "They went into the wrong shop."

Just then, I saw the jackpot come out of the *right* building and walk by us.

*Shit.*

We locked eyes for a moment as he picked up his pace. Even if I hadn't studied his description, I'd have known who he was from that glare.

"That's the jackpot," I said, jumping from the truck. "Hey," I shouted at him, pulling up my gun. I waved it in his direction. "Stop! Stop!"

He spun around and, seeing the gun, froze. The SEALs, finally realizing what was going on, ran over. Before he could do anything else, he was surrounded.

The SEALs weren't happy about the gun, though ultimately I didn't get in any trouble for it. They were surprised I'd jumped out of the vehicle and stopped the man—grateful, but surprised.

Terps didn't do that.

And yet I felt that was what I had to do. It was natural; to not do it would have been wrong. I was part of the team, and part of the mission to accomplish a goal, which we all shared.

Looking back, I know it was dangerous, even foolish. Not only could the jackpot have had a gun, but he could easily have had friends nearby who might have opened fire on me. And by taking an active role in stopping him, I'd made it clear to everyone on the street that I wasn't only working *for* the Americans, I was working *with* them—and was therefore a highly prized target for insurgents of every stripe.

None of that occurred to me at the time.

I questioned the jackpot back at our camp. He was surprisingly free with information, mentioning a house that was being used as a possible bomb stash. Still dressed in civilian clothes, we went back out and found the place filled with bombs, missiles, artillery shells, and even sticks of TNT. It was a veritable mother lode of destruction, enough to kill thousands of people for months. We packed as much as we could into our two SUVs, blew the rest in place, then headed to the base.

To get to the air base, we had to pass over a bridge. As we approached, we saw that an Iraqi checkpoint had been set up in the middle of the roadway. Ordinarily that wouldn't have been a problem—Americans in Humvees pretty much zipped through checkpoints.

But in this case, the SEALs were in civilian clothes and civilian vehicles. They had to stop or be fired at.

At the same time, no one trusted any checkpoint in the city, even the legitimate ones. The Iraqi army was littered with insurgents and informants. Even if they weren't traitors, the soldiers could hardly be trusted; too many were prone to panic and fire without warning.

Add in the fact that the men in the SUVs had explosives and didn't want to show their IDs—that wouldn't go over at an *American* checkpoint, let alone an Iraqi one.

I glanced at the dark-skinned SEAL who was driving. He could pass for an Iraqi, as long as he didn't open his mouth.

"I have an idea," I told him. "Let me talk." I told the others to stay in the shadows or cover their faces—they were all too white-skinned to pass as anything other than Westerners.

"Hey," I said, leaning across as we stopped. I waved my ID. "You see an American patrol?"

"Eh?" asked the guard, coming over.

"American patrol? You see them?"

"Yes, yes." The guard said he had, and we started talking. It turned out he knew one of my cousins. We spent a few long minutes catching up with nonsensical chitchat. I'm not sure what the SEALs thought of the conversation; it was fortunate that it was in Arabic.

"Very good, very good," I told the man finally. "We need to catch up to that patrol."

"Good night then," said the guard, forgetting completely that he hadn't checked the others' nonexistent IDs or looked in the trucks.

Working with the SEALs had turned me into a bit of a con man as well as an interpreter and foot soldier.


LITTLE BY LITTLE, I built up my reputation with the SEALs. The outlines of my work were always the same: Once the site was secured, the SEALs would locate the suspect. I would ask him what his name was, confirm his identity, and off we would go, back to the base.

It was the particulars that varied, small things changing in countless ways: how I talked, what we said, the questions, the answers. The look in the suspect's eyes. Sometimes there was a great deal of hate, even from a man who wasn't a suspect, a person we simply left. I had to wall the look and the emotion away and go about my business.

I'd usually talk with the suspects on the way back to camp. Sometimes I got some information the SEALs could use, an address maybe, or the name of someone that might be involved. Depending on the circumstances, I might question him for a while when we arrived, gathering more intelligence or maybe confirming what he had told me before.

Of more use were the documents and other intel the SEALs would gather at the house. We'd go through it, myself and the other interpreters, looking for local information that would help the SEALs to set up another operation.

But it was often the small, nearly indefinable things that I did that impressed the SEALs the most. I knew Mosul; they didn't. You can only get so much information from street maps and satellite photos. No intelligence briefing can explain the rhythm of a neighborhood, why the lack of people on one street is significant and not a problem on another. No computer I've ever come across can straighten out the confusion that occurs when a Westerner tries to pronounce an Arabic name. The SEALs were impressed that I could tell them that there was danger up a certain street but not down another. My mind was simply processing information as it always had. The nine-year-old boy who'd ventured out of his neighborhood to show how tough he was could have told the SEALs exactly the same thing. The slingshot expert, as foolish as he might have been, would have avoided exactly the same alley.

Not that my skills weren't advancing. My English, in particular, improved tremendously. With experience, I was able to anticipate what the SEALs wanted me to do when we were on a mission. I knew where I was supposed to be before the NCO gave the order. Explosions no longer turned my stomach.

Fear remained. No one ever loses that completely, even if they become inured to the circumstances that provoke it.

I think my real value to the SEALs had less to do with my technical skills than the way I handled myself. And that came from them. The SEALs were always very businesslike and aggressive; I tried to be the same. They were great role models. While I had no illusions that I was a SEAL, I wanted to be accepted by them. And they brought out the side of me that was both aggressive and professional.

The SEALs believe that, when doing an assault, they must act with violence of action. They attempt to move as aggressively as possible, overwhelming their opponent to minimize casualties— collateral as well as their own. I interpreted the philosophy to mean this: get the job done, get it done fast, get it done right, don't fool around. Show that you are powerful, and you are less likely to have problems.

It was something I understood in my bones. If you need to arrest someone, do it quickly and don't give him a chance to escape or even struggle. Otherwise there can easily be complications.

The SEALs had a concept of brotherhood that went beyond anything I'd seen outside of an actual family, certainly beyond the camaraderie of a typical Iraqi military unit and even the American MPs I'd worked with. It's difficult to describe the bond between them, even with metaphors. I imagine most civilians might make a parallel to a sports team; in some ways, I guess, the connection between the SEALs reminded me of the basketball teams I'd been part of. But that's a pale comparison to the bonds they shared.

Part of it came from their shared and parallel experiences, and not just in war. Combat is such an emphatic experience that even strangers form tight bonds, but even the "new guy" SEALs I worked with were tight before they even saw their first mission. From their famously rigorous BUD/S classes to the months of training, they had common experiences to draw on. Each man knew that the man beside him had gone through that trial and come out; there was confidence in that, something that can't be underrated. Beyond that, each man had accepted as his own the unit philosophy that they all depended on each other and that the team as a whole was stronger than its individual parts. It was clear that they would do anything for each other, even and especially risk death.

Not only did I admire that philosophy and camaraderie, I wanted to be part of it. If I couldn't be a SEAL, I could be the best terp they ever had. Ultimately, I could be their Iraqi brother.

**BUT AS 2004** went on, Americans had less and less reason to trust Iraqis, especially in Mosul. Mujahideen were coming into the city, chased from other places or recruited by the small but growing insurgency network established by al-Qaeda. Meanwhile, the growing prominence of Kurds in the city antagonized people, adding to the friction and possibly helping to prime some against the new government.

Because of my work, I was in effect living on the U.S. base, spending the bulk of my time among Americans, not Iraqis. Going home only occasionally, I missed a lot of these changes. Perhaps I would have missed them if I was on the streets as well. Many things are clear only in retrospect. When you are in the middle of the woods at night you have a hard time knowing whether you are walking deeper in or heading out.

For me personally, things were better than they had been in years. I was able to support my family comfortably. I could buy small presents for the kids and Soheila. I moved them back to the area in Mosul where my family had lived before the war, not far from the house that we had to sell to help my sister. We took a house on a main road near the business area of the city. It was large enough for us to be comfortable.

Most Iraqi lives were not getting better. Former soldiers, now released from the army, found no jobs. The Americans were an easy target for hate. People who had no education were especially vulnerable to the whispers of the mujahideen. Some of what they said about the government was true enough—corruption was back, if not as bad as it had been under Saddam. Reality crushed many dreams, even simple ones of not going hungry two days in a row. And if you had no dreams to fall back on, what did you have?

AFTER ROUGHLY SIX months, Team 7's time in Iraq came to a close. They were replaced by Team 2. After only two or three weeks, they were assigned to go to Baghdad on an entirely different mission— PSD, or protective service detail, which basically meant that they were protecting important people. There was no need for me, so I wasn't invited. They started packing up to leave.

Though we'd only been together for three or four missions, the idea of their leaving still filled me with sadness. I thought that I'd never see them or any SEAL again. I knew they liked me and thought I did a good job, but I also knew that in war you have little control over the future, especially your own.

Knowing I was going to be out of work, I started thinking of what I might do next. There were still American units in Mosul, and I considered going over to the MPs and asking for my old job back. But before I had a chance to do that, a civilian came over to the compound and asked if he could arrange to borrow a car. I started talking to him, and as it turned out, the firm he worked for needed a translator, so I went to work with them.

It was a big change after going on direct actions with the SEALs. The civilians had some various ventures, mostly in the Kurdish area to the north. Their business consisted primarily of trying to help the new government, arranging for different types of support. (I was asked not to give specifics, most of which I don't know anyway.) Translating for them was always interesting, but the tempo was very different than working with the SEALs.

Still, I made some good friends and had some interesting times. One of the men, whom I'll call Pistol, was a smart, friendly business type who was always cracking me up with jokes. You could easily forget the potential for danger when you were with him.

The civilians loved to combine work with pleasure. They might have a meeting at a hotel or some other place in Kurdistan. We'd go up, have the meeting, then jump in a pool afterward and drink some beers. Not a bad line of work in a war.

Americans were still liked in Kurdistan, or at least I didn't see too much animosity toward them. But some of the people the civilians dealt with were not exactly role models. Pistol tells a funny story about meeting with a man whom he says was one of the worst human beings he ever met, the sort of guy who would brag about shooting kids for pleasure. Whether the man actually did that or not, I have no idea, but he was definitely a scary type. The civilians needed to meet with him to make sure he wouldn't interfere with the project they were working on. They were basically buying his support, though neither he nor they thought of it in quite those terms. And they certainly didn't express it that way the day they met.

Unfortunately for the Americans, they weren't used to Iraqi food, and it wasn't unusual for them to have digestive problems after a particularly spicy meal. On the day of this meeting, Pistol was experiencing something close to dysentery. As the meeting started, he was looking a bit uncomfortable. Things got worse by the minute, and sweat began curling down the sides of his head.

Still, he kept up the small talk with this guy. He was trying to get "in the vibe" as he called it—basically doing what a car salesman might do when he first meets a potential customer, trying to make a personal connection.

His face started to get a reddish tone. Then it went to purple.

"Excuse me!" he said finally, jumping up from his seat.

Pistol ran from the room, heading for a toilet. Apparently he didn't make it, because he came back a few minutes later, soaked in water. He looked like he had taken a shower with his clothes on.

Which he was still wearing, since they were the only clothes he had with him.

"I just crapped my pants," he announced as he walked in the room.

The Kurd we'd been talking to, the tough guy whom the Americans thought was at least a borderline psychopath, started to laugh.

Shitting yourself is funny in every culture.

The vibe had been made, and they concluded their deal. The venture could proceed, though you have to wonder how far it could go in Iraq if it depended on people like the Kurd not interfering.

I wasn't in a position to consider the moral implications of who the civilians, or anyone, for that matter, worked with. It's difficult to make those kinds of judgments in war; moral and ethical compromises abound. For myself, my goals were simple: feed my family and help Iraq become a better place.

Generally, the Americans had few problems. Their business seemed to go well, though I wasn't in a position to make any deep judgments. There were surprisingly few incidents that even hinted at trouble. But the exceptions were memorable.

Typically, getting past Kurdish checkpoints was a breeze. The Kurds in general liked the Americans, and the police and militia were well trained and disciplined. We'd show them our documents, maybe pass a word or two in conversation, and then be on our way.

Iraqi checkpoints were a totally different story. We could never tell, even in Mosul, whether the people stopping us could be trusted. American civilians would be very valuable hostages.

One day, coming back to Mosul from Kurdistan, we were stopped outside the city. The police at the post began giving my companions a hard time. They made us get out of the car and began peppering me with questions.

*Why are you coming back from northern Iraq? Why are you with Americans? What is their business? Where are they going? Why are they out at night?*

Even if the policemen were legitimate—I had my doubts—the animosity between Iraqis and Kurds in Mosul had been increasing, and resentment could easily become something more. No answer was safe.

"Where is your commander?" I said, eyeing the soldiers as they fiddled nervously with their weapons. "I will only talk to him."

They hemmed and hawed, but since I'd worked with the Iraqi police, I knew which names to mention and the veiled threats those names implied. Finally they pointed to a nearby building.

Meanwhile, they were holding my friends at gunpoint.

"If you hear gunfire," I told the Americans in English, "shoot and get away. Don't worry about me."

I doubt that put them at ease, especially since their weapons were either still in their holsters or back in the car. My own pistol was under my shirt.

My heart began pounding as I was led inside the small building. This wasn't the normal setup, and I couldn't quite figure out what was going on. Were these policemen just being overly zealous? Or was it a setup to kidnap the Americans? I worried that I shouldn't have left them; I berated myself for not simply crashing through the checkpoint and risking the consequences.

The officer in charge was inside, sitting in a small office. As

my fingers slid toward my gun, I realized I'd seen him before.
*Thank God!*

"Hey," I said to him with great enthusiasm. "Do you remember who I am? I worked with the American MPs."

"Oh yes, yes," he said, rising. "How are you?"

"Great, brother! How are you? It's so good to see you."

"Yes!"

"You are doing well! It's very good to see you."

"You, too."

I couldn't remember his name and didn't know him very well at all. It's even possible I was confused about remembering his face. I doubt he knew who I was either. But neither of us would admit it. We talked for a while, exactly like old friends, and I decided he was cool; his men were just being careful.

Or maybe not. Maybe they would have kidnapped us all if I hadn't pretended to be a great friend of the commander's. In any event, we went outside and they let us all go. Just another typical night in Iraq.

FAMILY LIFE WENT ON. In the summer of 2004 Soheila and I were expecting our fourth child. Pregnancy is always a perilous time, where great hope mixes with great fear, and the civil war that was beginning to consume my country didn't make things any easier for Soheila.

One day during the last third of her pregnancy, she became alarmed when she didn't feel the baby inside her. She went to a clinic to be checked out.

The doctor told her the baby had died.

You can imagine the horrible grief. And yet, despite all of the sadness, Soheila's thoughts passed to something more accepting: *God gives; God takes.*

Whatever God willed, she was willing to accept, she decided. She went home and wept, waiting for she knew not what.

That night she had a dream. In the dream, a cousin of the Prophet Muhammad came to her and told her to take his hand.

"I can't walk," she told him.

"Take my hand," he insisted.

And so she did, and they walked together among the clouds.

From that moment, Soheila *knew* that our child was alive. She didn't go back to that doctor. And there was no need: when the time came in July, she went to the hospital and our son was born, healthy and a blessing to his parents and siblings.

I wanted to name him after some friends I'd made among the Americans. Soheila vetoed that. It was a wise decision; the name would have been unconventional, to say the least. When my uncle heard the story of the dream, he suggested we name him for a cousin of the Prophet—it was a good name, and a show of our gratitude for God's will in letting him be born.

**ONE MORNING SEVERAL** weeks later, I left my house and headed to the airport, where I was supposed to meet one of the civilians I was still working with. I was driving my blue Opel, not paying all that much attention to what was around me . . . at first.

But after a mile or so, I realized there was another car behind me. It was a red Opel. Opels were not all that common in Mosul at the time, but other than that I'm not sure why it stood out. The car didn't necessarily look like it was following me, but something told me to keep an eye on it. Finally, as I took a turn to head toward the main road leading to the airport, I started studying the driver. He had a long beard, such as a deeply religious Muslim might wear, but wasn't particularly suspicious. The other man in the front was younger, but he didn't look dangerous either.

Why was I suspicious? I'm not sure. I was in the western part of the city, where most Sunnis lived; it was a relatively peaceful area. No one had made any threats against me. I was no longer working with the SEALs. In theory I should have had nothing to fear.

I hit a straightaway. The Opel sped up, looking as if it wanted to pass.

Hey, I thought, I'm not in a hurry. I'll let him pass. Maybe he has an emergency or an appointment somewhere. I slowed—but I also leaned my seat back a bit and slid so that the brace between the doors was protecting the side of my head, a little trick I had learned from the SEALs.

I glanced at my AK and its seventy-round banana magazine to my right.

No way would I need it here.

The car backed off. I wasn't sure whether to be worried or not. Neither the Opel nor the men in it had done anything that would make me think they were targeting me, or even necessarily following me.

The traffic was light, but there were other cars nearby. As I approached an intersection where the road I was on ended in a T, I decided I would make the other car pass me. I slowed and pulled toward the side, watching as the vehicle once more sped up to pass. I caught a glimpse of the man in the passenger seat.

He had on green fatigues, the sort the Iraqi army wore. He was young: early twenties at most. I saw him clearly.

Then I saw him raise a pistol and point it at me.

My foot jammed the brakes to stop. He got off a shot, maybe more as his vehicle sped forward then began skidding into a stop. I leapt from my car, AK in my hands. The Opel spun into a U-turn a few meters away, turning to come back.

I fired thirty, forty rounds, in the space of a heartbeat, all into the front of the red car.

My hands shook. My legs fell weak. The vehicle stopped dead in the road.

My bullets had blown out the front of the car. Both men were in the front, dazed, maybe wounded, possibly dead.

Not dead—the driver, a fat, middle-aged man, moved.

I ran up and put another half-dozen rounds into him.

I went to the back of the car and jerked open the cover to the gas tank. I grabbed my lighter and some paper I had in my pocket, lit it, and threw it in the gas tank. I jerked back, flinching as the fire ignited and the tank blew.

By now, people had come running over. They were all around the car. It was a large crowd. Mosul had definitely changed. I realized in that moment not only what the change was, but what it meant for me. There was only one way to get away from that mob alive.

"Those guys are working with the Americans," I said as the car burst into flames. "We've been following them for weeks."

"Good job!" said someone.

"Death to the infidels!"

"Praise Allah!"

"Death to the Americans and all who work with them!"

I got the hell out of there, quick.

# 6

# MY BROTHER, MOSUL, AND BAGHDAD

**L** **UCKILY FOR ME,** my Opel was still running. I drove away, zigging deeper into the city but staying away from my house. I called the man I was supposed to meet and told him I wasn't coming in that day, without going into the details. I drove around for a little while, making sure that I wasn't being followed. Only when I was absolutely positive that I was alone did I head back in the direction of my house. I parked several streets away and ran to the house on foot to make sure everything was okay.

I was worried that they would attack my family at the same time. Suddenly, the violence I'd seen from afar had become very real and very personal to me. For the first time I realized not just that I and my family might be in danger, but that there was a depth of hatred and sheer evil at work in Mosul and all of Iraq. Maybe it was overreaction or just paranoia on my part, but in those few minutes the men in the Opel had changed me from a person without much fear to one who thought he was surrounded entirely by enemies. It was as if my nervous system had suddenly caught fire, or was vibrating with energy that couldn't be turned off.

It had also been the moment of betrayal. I had denounced the United States and all of the men who had worked with me, the SEALs especially. I had, in a way, betrayed my brothers.

Not really. Not in anything but words. I hadn't abandoned them, left them for dead, or given them to the enemy. But in my mind, I was a traitor just the same.

Gradually, I realized that wasn't true. My words, given to people who had only hatred, were meaningless to the wider world, most especially to the SEALs.

I also realized something even more important. Rather than being paralyzed by fear, I had to act. I resolved to attack the hatred at its source. Even if my hands shook and my aim was poor, I would fight. Just as I had fought when attacked by the men in the Opel.

*Okay, motherfuckers, you had your turn and you see what you got. You got what you deserved. And anyone else that tries, they will get the same.*

**THE HOUSE WAS CLEAR**; no one was watching it, and no one had come to harm my family. I didn't tell Soheila what had happened on the way to the airport, but she knew there had been some sort of problem, and not a little one. I told my brother and my nephew, as quietly as I could, and then went out and stood guard. Two of my closest cousins came over and we discussed the situation and what to do. We tried to keep it a secret, but the very fact that we were whispering and kept to ourselves made Soheila suspicious.

Iraqi houses have what might be called in English a "reception room." This is a place where visitors can gather, a little like a living room in an American house, except that in Iraq it is generally a place for males only; we are very traditional about separating the genders.

Usually we didn't close the door to our reception room; now we did. I had many intense conversations there with my relatives and friends.

"I know something bad happened," said Soheila when I came out. "I know you were talking."

"You heard what we were saying?" I asked. "Then what are you asking?"

"I don't have to hear the words. I know something is wrong."

"No, nothing is wrong."

"You have to tell me," Soheila insisted. "Is someone trying to hurt you?"

"Oh no, you know me, nothing is going to happen," I told her. "No one will hurt me."

Soheila saw through the obvious lie. "No, you have to tell me! Tell me." She was practically screaming. "My heart is tough. Tell me!"

"Nothing will happen to me." This wasn't a lie, at least not in the way we think of lies. It was at that moment a truth I believed. I didn't think anyone could hurt me. My family, that was different. But not me.

And I had just proved it, hadn't I?

Soheila kept trying to get information out of me, but I insisted I was all right. Finally I told her I was taking care of everything and that she just had to stop worrying.

"Your job is getting you in danger," she said.

"I'm working in this job to keep you happy," I told her. "To take care of you and mom and the kids. So don't worry. Every job has some dangerous things, but in this one, I am fine. I am taking care of you. Do not worry."

I could still see the fear in her eyes. Nothing I could say, nothing I could ever say, could make it go away.

Word spread of the attack. More than one person came to me and said, "Oh, don't worry, it was not an attack. It was a warning shot."

*Bullshit.*

I can still see the motherfucker with the pistol, aiming it at me. I can still see the car turning back to shoot me. There was no warning intended. This was not a Hollywood movie. This was real life and death.

Anyone who needed proof could have found it embedded in my car. That afternoon my nephew came inside the house to talk to me. He held his fist out, then turned it over and opened his hand.

"Uncle," he said, "this was in the metal of your car."

It was a bullet from the pistol, embedded in the frame directly behind the driver's-side window.

CONFIDENT OR NOT, I decided it would be best to take a few days' vacation from Mosul. I packed Soheila and the kids in the car and we went west, visiting a village near Syria where we knew some people. In the meantime, I kept checking back with my brother and others to see what was going on. There were no other attacks, nor threats against me or the family. I guessed that the two men were either acting alone or, because of the amount of destruction, whoever had sent them wasn't sure what had happened. Maybe the gunmen had been bought off, or killed by Americans, or just chickened out and run away. Maybe they hadn't known exactly who they were after, targeting the car rather than the man.

Or maybe, I thought, the mujahideen were scared of me.

When I came back, I varied my routines, making sure that my car wasn't seen at or near any place associated with Americans. If

I had to go to the airport, for example, I would park my car some distance away and either walk or call a taxi.

I soon had proof that the mujahideen weren't afraid of me and hadn't given up targeting me for assassination.

Needing to go to the airport to meet one of the civilians, I left my car in the lot of a man I knew and had a taxi meet me on the street not far away. I went to the airport, did my business, and came back. The owner of the lot walked over as I got out of the taxi, a very concerned look on his face.

"Johnny," he said, shaking his head, "two men were asking for you today. I think they are mujahideen. You must take care, brother."

I thanked him and drove directly from the lot to a man who sold cars for a living.

"How much will you give me for my Opel?" I asked.

He named a price that was far below its value. I haggled a little, but not too much—the car was now worthless to me. Its make and color made it too easy to spot.

Instead of traveling by car, I started getting around by taxi and bumming rides with friends. Leaving my house to go to work, I might walk one way several blocks, or another way a few more blocks, or a third way—you get the idea. I varied my routes, making them seem as random as possible. And only when I was a decent distance away from my house or where I'd been dropped off last did I take out my cell phone and call for a ride. From there, I would go to another part of town, typically one where there was a lot of foot traffic. Or if I had business in the base area, I might find a family I knew who lived at a French village inside its confines; they often would give me a ride to the village, and from there another interpreter I knew would pick me up.

Or I might do something completely different. I might stop at a truck garage and hire someone to take me—or get a free ride, if it

was someone I knew. Varying my routine became a constant preoc-
cupation, second and third nature.

I went nowhere without a weapon. I had my pistol and I had an
AK. I was ready to kill. If someone had approached me in the wrong
way, if I had felt threatened by them, it was in my mind to shoot
them before they shot me. They wouldn't get a chance.

It wasn't that I had suddenly become vicious, nor was I a savage.
I didn't think in those terms, much less consider that I was operat-
ing in a primitive state. It was just simple arithmetic—them or me.
The equation had only one answer.


**MY BROTHER HAMID** was always my strongest friend and ally, a
bold man who thought of me first, then our family, then others, and
finally himself. He was a protector to Soheila and my mother when
I wasn't there. After the incident with the Opel, he stood outside
the house and yelled to anyone with ears to hear, "I am Hamid! I
am my brother's brother! Anyone with any problem with him can
come to me."

He had an AK-47 in his hand when he shouted that. No one
took him up on it. A few might have thought he was nuts, but no
one could deny that he was a loyal and courageous man.

*My brother . . .*

Hamid had gotten a job delivering bread to the Iraqi army. He'd
been warned that the mujahideen didn't like this. Like me, he didn't
care for their opinions.

On the morning of October 24, 2004, my brother went to the
bakery to pick up the bread to deliver to the army. It was around
6 A.M. He was alone. Three men drove up after he stopped and
started to put the bread into his car.

They jumped from the car, their faced covered by scarves or
some other masks.

"You are bad," they told him. "You are working with the enemy."

Hamid knew right away that he was outnumbered. But his reaction was typical—he didn't back down.

"You want to fight?" he shouted back. "Fight me fair or shut up."

The men actually turned around and walked back to the car. For a moment, it seemed as if his strong words had sent the cowards scurrying back to the rat holes where they belonged.

But that was only for a moment. The men reached into the car and pulled out assault rifles. They sprayed him with bullets; he died instantly.

I was not there, and what I am saying here comes from the many versions of the story that I have heard. Most are like this, though a few say that the people who killed him were angry not at him but at me, because I was helping the Americans. It's possible that that's true, and certainly it wouldn't have made him any less of a target. But by that time, anyone helping even the Iraqi army was considered a target by the growing insurgency.

I regret that I don't know the precise truth. I regret, too, that I was not there to save and protect him, to stand up for him, as he had done so many times for me.


**A SHORT TIME LATER,** my cell phone rang with a call from an Iraqi policeman I'd known from my earlier work. He told me my brother had been shot.

My first reaction was disbelief. That lasted only for an instant. I dropped everything and began looking to see where he had been taken. I knew in my heart, from the description, that he was already dead. Still, I drove around the city like a madman, looking for him in clinics and hospitals.

Eventually, I made my way back to the house. In the meantime, my mother and Soheila had managed to find him at one of the hospitals; there they got the bad news, that he was dead.

They brought the body home. They laid him out, a sheet covering his body.

I had to see him one last time. Hand shaking, I reached to the corner of the sheet and gingerly lifted it. He'd been shot several times; there was a large hole in his face.

*Hamid! My brother!*

As I left the room, riven with sorrow, Soheila and my mother told me to leave Mosul immediately.

"Johnny, you have to go," said my mother. "I have lost one—I don't want to lose two at the same time."

She was tearful and clutched me dearly. Soheila, standing nearby, nodded, then hugged me and tried pushing me with practically the same motion.

They wanted me to run. They wanted me safe.

But I couldn't leave. I wasn't going to abandon my brother—I had to arrange for his funeral. And I couldn't miss it either. He'd stood with me. I had to stand with him.

As is traditional, his body was washed and made ready for what in America is called a wake. People come to the house to express their condolences and offer support. We erected a tent in front of the house. The women were inside the house; the men outside. We had some snacks and things for people to eat after they paid their respects.

Needless to say, I was on guard for any more trouble. I was more than ready for trouble: I had a 9 mm pistol under my shirt, the AK hidden nearby, and two armed Iraqi friends ready to kill anyone who attacked. My cousin, my nephew, and some other friends were all on watch, ready as well.

Maybe I wished someone would try something. Then I would have had revenge, easily.

One of the people who showed up at the wake had a long face. He started talking about the mujahideen, saying they would come. I think now that he was trying to warn me, maybe only doing what in his heart he thought was best. But I didn't interpret it that way at the time.

I told him to shut up.

"Calm down, calm down," said the man, who was a neighbor.

"I will kill the people who did this," I told him. "I will kill anyone who tries to start trouble."

"Don't say that, don't say that."

"Yes," I told him. "What else would I do?"

The funeral passed without trouble.

I kissed Hamid's cheek before he was buried, a final good-bye.

**SOME PEOPLE ASK ME:** Did you get revenge for your brother?

The honest answer is this:

I wanted to. I would have loved to. I looked for his killers. I asked others to look for them. If I had found them, certainly at that time I would have had satisfaction.

But I never found out exactly who they were. Helping the SEALs, I had helped apprehend a lot of bad people, but there was no way to know if any of them were responsible for his death. There were just so many mujahideen and other criminals operating in Mosul.

I suppose in a sense, as I went on and helped bring others to justice, there was a kind of payback for me. But if so, it was empty. Whether you believe that revenge brings satisfaction or not, there was and is simply no way to substitute the action of what I felt I *should* do—help arrest and stop evil people—for what I felt I *must* do—revenge my brother.

As an American now, I am not supposed to believe in revenge. I am supposed to believe that more killing does not solve anything.

I know those things, and they are true. But that does not change how I feel. It cannot change how I love my brother, or the fact that he was killed by cowards who did not give him a fair chance to defend himself, who refused the invitation to fight fair. Instead they hid behind guns and masks.

I remember his death many times a day.

**HAMID'S MURDER WAS** the first of many in the community of people we knew. It was the most shocking, of course, since it was our blood that was spilled. But the others hit us hard as well. We came to realize how terrible things had become. The streets started to fill with bodies, literally.

Sunni insurgents launched a series of coordinated attacks in the beginning of November, starting what looks like in retrospect an all-out campaign to assert their control over the city. These were of a different sort than the IED plantings or drive-by shootings that had dominated attacks earlier. Mujahideen fighters launched a number of coordinated attacks against American units—including a sustained attack on the First Battalion, Twenty-fourth Regiment, near the Yarmuk traffic circle in western Mosul.

The insurgents used RPGs (rocket-propelled grenades) and mortars to up the firepower, provoking a response from the Americans that included large JDAM (Joint Direct Attack Munition) bombs and helicopter strikes. Police stations were attacked throughout the city, and the fanatics even managed to take control of one of the bridges over the Tigris for a short time. For several weeks, there was all-out warfare in the city, intense fighting on a scale that had not been seen earlier.

American observers have speculated quite a bit about what was going on, and where the influx of violent insurgents came from. There are theories that they fled from Fallujah and other places where the Americans were mounting operations to flush them out. Some think that Mosul's population had reached a breaking point and simply turned against the Shia and Kurd-dominated government, as well as the Americans.

From what I saw and heard, the mujahideen were mostly villagers from outside Mosul who'd been recruited to fight, persuaded with rhetoric and money. There were foreign fighters as well, influenced by al-Qaeda and maybe recruited by them. While there were people from Mosul, these two other groups swelled their ranks.

The fighters were poorly trained, barely even knowing how to use their weapons. They were ill equipped to fight in a coordinated attack. The Americans recovered, and once the U.S. soldiers showed up in force, they easily beat back their enemy.

But the insurgents were tenacious and learned quickly from their mistakes. They were never so foolish as to attack in large numbers again.

They had excellent intelligence, which gradually improved. They were able to get information from many, many people, and they had time on their side. They could wait and watch the air base or different buildings, recording what was going on, gradually building up mental databases. As their leaders gained more experience, they did a better job of planning and training. Eventually, they became practiced killers.

Killers, not warriors.

Warriors fight for the goal of peace. Warriors fight so things can be built. The insurgents fought to destroy.

The profound difference touches deep into the soul. If you are a killer and not a warrior, you have no problem using a woman or a child to get what you want. You do not worry about that person dying. The life of an innocent is nothing to you.

A warrior risks his life to protect the innocent.

When you talked with the mujahideen, as I did when I had acted as an interpreter with the SEALs, they told you that they were fighting for Islam, defending the faith against infidels. But it wasn't the real reason for most. The leaders, who were former Ba'ath Party and Fedayeen members, were fighting for revenge and dominance—they wanted the party to once again rule Iraq, and they felt they could accomplish this by chasing the Americans away and then battling the Shiites for control. Many of the al-Qaeda–inspired leaders were fighting for the same thing, though they cloaked their thinking in religious justifications.

Is it necessary for me to say that even the people who were sincerely motivated by religion were wrong? God did not tell them to kill people in His name. God is greater than that. God does not need a man to kill another man. God can strike dead whomever He chooses, if He chooses; He is all powerful.

Many of these so-called mujahideen killed other Muslims. Would God direct a believer to kill another believer?

From being with the Americans, I knew the United States wasn't out to harm Islam. It was more the opposite: what most Americans I met wanted was similar to what I wanted, peace for Iraq. I wanted to make it a secure place where I could raise my family, and so did they.

Most Americans in fact had an even simpler dream: they wanted to do their jobs and go home.

And in a way, that was my dream as well. But it started to fade as the gunfire and bombings increased.

**THE MAIN INSURGENT** organization said to be responsible for the attacks that year was Jaish Ansar al-Sunna. The words mean, roughly, the Assembly of Helpers of Sunni Muslims. While the group was affiliated with al-Qaeda, it is difficult for an outsider to untangle the actual lines of responsibility, let alone the group's own organizational chart. It was active not only in Mosul but in cities like Fallujah, Ramadi, Samarra, and Baquba. While it has been debated whether the group was more an umbrella organization or had direct control of the insurgent fighters in each instance, there is no doubt that the continuing campaign of attacks was organized and assisted at a high level.

It is said that the group later severed its ties with Ba'athist factions and al-Qaeda, supposedly over tactics that targeted civilians, which some of its leaders were said to oppose. Whether this was the case earlier is difficult to tell. I can say that civilians were killed in Mosul by men said to be operating in association with Jaish Ansar al-Sunna. Where actual responsibility lies, what the exact truth may or may not be, has for me been lost like a paper blown away by the wind. Only the results remain, and in a very real sense, only those deadly, horrible results matter.

It has been estimated that roughly two-thirds of the city was either under insurgent control or hotly contested at the campaign's peak in mid-November, before the Americans finally brought in enough troops to retake Mosul and restore an uneasy "peace." In the interim, the insurgency had killed many Iraqi policemen and others who worked with them or the Americans.

Even after the offensive was crushed, the mujahideen were still active in Mosul. On December 21, just a few days before Christmas, a man who was in the Iraqi army went into the mess tent in the U.S. Army portion of the base. As he walked amid the lunchtime crowd, the bomb that had been strapped to his body suddenly detonated. A total of twenty-two people were killed, with roughly sixty wounded. Fifteen of the men who died were American servicemen; the rest were contractors and Iraqi civilians who were working for Americans.

(Initial reports claimed that the tent—which was larger than many houses—was hit by a mortar shell. There were also reports that a bomb may have been placed inside and then detonated. There are those who believe these alternative theories to be true. But most observers, as well as myself, believe it was the work of a suicide bomber.)

At the time, Iraqi army soldiers didn't have to be searched and could go into the chow hall without a hassle. That quickly changed. From that point on, force protection—a military term for security—became greatly strengthened. There were all sorts of new rules, especially when it came to Iraqis. Iraqis entering certain areas had to be searched, and often required escorts.

I was included in that provision—or would have been, had I been working at the camp. With the atmosphere changing, the civilian company no longer had any real work for me. Even if they had, I wasn't in a position to give them my full attention. I moved around, trying mostly to stay alive and keep my family safe. I stayed away from our house as much as possible, never wanting to be seen going or coming. If I was targeted, I didn't want the kids or Soheila caught in the crossfire.

Just before my brother's death, I told Soheila everything about the Opel incident, explaining to her what had happened and telling her that I was taking precautions. She wasn't exactly reassured.

"Hey, Johnny," Soheila told me. "You have to go to Syria or go to Baghdad. You have to go."

She meant that I should leave her and the kids and flee to safety for a few months. I dismissed both possibilities.

"Baghdad is not safe," I told her. "Why are you saying Baghdad?"

"It's safer than Mosul."

"Of course it's not." I was right—Baghdad had its own problems. Soheila was just making suggestions based on wishful thinking. And I certainly wasn't going to Syria. What would I do there?

Not that I was doing much in Mosul. Many nights I spent with one or another of my cousins, playing cards and sometimes drinking. The days were just as empty, perhaps more so. I wasn't working, and even if there had been work in Mosul, no one would have hired me—it would have been too dangerous. I thought eventually I would go back to work for the Americans, probably the army, though it was impossible at that point to arrange any sort of plan, realistic or otherwise.

The civilians still owed me a paycheck, and finally one day I arranged to go out to the airport and get it. As I was on my way to their office at the base, I ran into a friend who told me that the SEAL unit I'd been working with earlier in the year had returned.

I went immediately over to their compound at the airport. The unit there turned out to be a group composed of men from SEAL Team 3 and Team 5, different than the men I'd worked with before.

But they had heard of me.

"Hey, we've been looking for you," said a man whom I'll call Senior Chief White. "We need an interpreter."

"I am glad I have a reputation," I told him. "When can I start?"

"Right away" was Chief White's answer.

And so I did. The unit relocated to a new camp outside the airport. Once again they wanted me to stay with them so I would be available for their night missions. I had no objections to that: instead of being a virtual nomad, always moving and looking over my shoulder, I could stay in the safest place in Mosul.

At first glance, working with the SEALs again would seem to have increased the risks to me personally. As careful as the SEALs were, they were definitely Americans and what are known as "high-value targets" to the insurgents. But the mujahideen tended to hit weak and unprotected targets—words that certainly didn't describe the SEALs. I felt safe with them, and frankly I liked working with them for many reasons.

I still dreamed of a better Iraq. To me, the mujahideen were the biggest thing standing in the way of a better future, and the Americans offered a way of combating them.

**SOMETIMES I FANTASIZE** that if I hadn't worked with the Americans, I might have started my own antiterror group, made up of Iraqis.

A noble idea, but realistically, how far would it have gotten? I lacked many things, starting with money, equipment, and a surfeit of friends who could be trusted.

**BY NOW MY ENGLISH** was vastly improved. My pronunciation was far better. My vocabulary had also expanded, especially in one particular area: curse words.

The simplest ones are the best, in any language. I still say "fuck" a lot, too much probably, with kids around. But I use it far less than during those days with the SEALs, when it punctuated every sentence five, six, ten times. I was barely conscious of it. And at least according to the SEALs who were with me, I used it no matter whether I was talking to them or in far less appropriate situations, like talking to an officer back at the base.

During an operation, there wasn't much I had to say—a lot of communication could be done by body language, or simply pointing. The SEALs and other special operations troops do that as a matter of routine. When they are moving up to a target, the last thing they want to do is alert whoever is around that they are there, so they point and use a small set of hand signals indicating what they are about to do. These signs—putting up your hand a certain way, for example—are easily mastered no matter what your language.

My improving language skills were quite useful when questioning people for the Americans, and I started doing this more and more, with better results. At the same time, I learned the best way to ask people questions and to detect when they were lying. My ability progressed from questions like *Where is the Jackpot? Are the guns in the house?* to things that were more complex, like asking who else was involved in a terror network and ferreting out the most likely person to talk when a group was detained. The latter took wit, not force. I learned to ask indirect questions that would lead me to more information, or make suggestions that seemed innocuous but that would yield me something I could use.

I approached situations in ways that would open me up to information. If I saw kids outside a house, for example, I might strike up a conversation with them, offering them candy and talking to them as comfortably and naturally as possible. I'd get their names, maybe joke a little before getting down to business.

"Where's your father?" I might ask, mentioning the jackpot's name.

Inevitably, they'd run to him.

The jackpot located, I'd try to find different ways to chat him up, to get him to tell me what was going on. Deeper interrogation took place in other units, and was not part of my job. But every tidbit I discovered might be useful in some way or another.

**THE CAMP WAS** safe but boring. And I was used to a certain amount of freedom. Mosul was dangerous at night, but there was no reason for me to sit in the trailer like a prisoner. So one night I planned an "escape."

I was fleeing boredom, not jail, but in some ways it was the same thing. Technically it wasn't escaping—I was free to come and go as I pleased, so long as I wasn't needed and obeyed whatever security rules were in force. But it certainly *felt* like escaping, as if I were a bird or an animal pushing the bars of my cage apart and fleeing.

When darkness came, I tucked my pistol under my shirt, then arranged for a taxi to take me to a hotel in town. From there I caught another taxi, then walked until I got to my cousin's house. My success that first night led to other "escapes," and they soon became a routine: when I wasn't needed, I'd sneak out and head for his house. From there we would often go to another friend's or a club where we could drink coffee and play cards.

One night we were playing poker in a coffee shop. I always faced the windows so I could see what was coming. My attention picked up as I saw four men walk by and then enter. They were strangers, but something about the way they carried themselves made them seem dangerous.

Quietly, I pulled out my pistol and cocked back the hammer, keeping it under the table but ready to fire.

Everyone nearby must have felt the tension. Mosul was not a safe place, and the men looked like they were here for trouble.

A waiter greeted them.

"Hey guys, how are you?" he said, walking over. "What can I get for you?"

"We are looking for Johnny."

*Me.*

I glanced at my cousin to make sure he was watching what was going on, then looked back at the men. None were showing their weapons—if they wanted to shoot me, it would take at least a few seconds for them to get their guns out.

By then, I would kill them all.

"You're looking for Johnny?" asked the waiter.

"Here," I said, loudly. I stayed in my seat, gun hidden but ready. My cousin, meanwhile, had placed his hand on his own hidden weapon.

The men walked over, smiling. "We wanted to talk to you," said one. "We need a favor."

I rose, revealing my pistol. "Good," I said. "But you better be careful. I almost killed you because I don't know you."

One of the men mentioned a friend, speaking a little nervously.

He went on to explain that they weren't enemies, and needed only to make contact with the Americans to give them some information.

"I can help you," I told them. And I did. But they had aided me as well, giving me a lesson in being careful: more people than I thought were aware of my comings and goings.

It was also a lesson, maybe, in restraint.

**I NEED A VARIETY** of IDs to get around Mosul and the rest of the country without hassle. Besides your name, the standard ID card typically listed your birthday and the names of your parents. (The format of the cards changed over the years. Most notably, from 2003, they started including numbers written in Western style as well as Arabic.) The details on the cards could indicate whether you were Sunni or Shiite—if someone couldn't tell from the name alone, the stamp indicating where the card was issued would tend to give the person's background away.

Needless to say, having the wrong ID card in the wrong place was asking for trouble. I managed to have "real" IDs made that rendered my name slightly differently, one in a Sunni style and the other Shia. Besides these, I bought a variety on the black market to use to help shield my identity. Typically, I would be carrying at least two different sets of IDs that alternatively identified me as a Sunni or a Shiite, and I chose the one most appropriate to the circumstances. I'd also change my accent and even my curses to match, a trick I'd learned while interrogating subjects. (Yes, Sunnis and Shia take the names of different holy people in vain.)

IDs cost about thirty or forty dollars, American, on the black market. If I could get them, I'm sure anyone, including a terrorist, could as well.

**I HADN'T BEEN** with the SEALs more than a few weeks when they told me they were moving their operations to Baghdad and asked if I would come. It was January 2005. The elections were coming up, and their task group was one of the units selected to help ensure they could be held.

The offer presented a dilemma: Should I go with them and leave my family here, or should I stay in the city?

I didn't want to leave Soheila and the kids. But ironically, going would make my family safer. If I wasn't around, people would have no reason to look for me and no reason to watch or attack my family. It would be easy, in fact, to spread rumors that I had run away, out of fear of the mujahideen.

In short, leaving was the smartest thing to do.

I went home that night and told Soheila.

"Remember, you were asking if I would leave Mosul and go to Baghdad?" I said when the kids were asleep.

"Yes?"

"I think you are right. I will go to Baghdad. I am going to work with the Americans there."

She was happy. I didn't give my wife many details about what I was doing—I didn't even tell her the specifics of whom I was working with. And I didn't ask her to come with me.

What I didn't know at the time was that Baghdad was far worse than Mosul. It had become the most dangerous place on earth.

# 7

# BAGHDAD

BEFORE THE WAR, Baghdad was a city of more than 7 million
people. A good number of them lived in poverty and suffered
the ills of the poor everywhere: substandard houses, terrible
sanitation, poor medical care, horribly inadequate education. The
list is endless.

But it was also a city of promise. It had bustling business sectors,
wide avenues, and soaring monuments. Spread out along the Tigris,
it was second only to Cairo in population in the Middle East. Its history was second to none, not even Egypt's. Baghdad was renowned
as a center of learning in medieval times, and that tradition survived
in its five universities. Everywhere in the city there is history—the
ancient walls; the Golden Gate Palace where the caliph lived; the
Suq al-Ghazel Minaret, older than the Sistine Chapel.

The British helped rebuild the city in the years before and after World War II, until it was a gem, or as close to a gem as possible before Saddam's reign cast the whole nation under a cloud. Even so, Baghdad remained a city of ambition, a place where young people came to make or find their fortune, a flickering flame of optimism and hope. With the government offices and the headquarters of many Iraqi businesses there, it was always a place of commerce and excitement. Poets, writers, and artists continued to be drawn by its schools and entertainment venues.

Maybe its grandeur was nothing compared to cities in the United States or Europe, but still it was a vibrant city, even after the war with Iran and the bombardment following the takeover of Kuwait. I visited occasionally as a youth and then a truck driver, and the energy vibrated in the air.

The Baghdad I drove through with the SEALs was a much different place, a land of gray walls and dulled ambitions, a place filled with rubble, trash, and sprays of gunfire. Whole blocks were closed by piles of debris. House facades had crumbled into the roadways. Checkpoints, concrete barriers, and barbed wire were everywhere. Walls were pockmarked with bullet holes. Shrapnel had chinked buildings; the sidewalks and paved streets were marked by bloodstains that would never come off.

Baghdad had become desolation itself, an eighty-square-mile cauldron of hatred and disgust.

THE HISTORICAL ROOTS of the hatred between Sunni and Shia Muslims owes something to Baghdad's time under the Ottomans, when the Sunni Turks clashed with the Shiite Iranian Safavids for dominance in the region. The Iranians conquered Baghdad during the Ottoman-Safavid War of 1623–39, but were eventually thrown back. During that war, there was a great massacre of Sunni believers by the Iranian shah, who wanted to purify the city for the Shia.

The memory of the conflict between the two branches of Islam has ebbed and flowed over the centuries since. For much of my lifetime, it remained largely dormant. There was conflict, certainly, and always debate—we Iraqis love to debate and argue, and settle the world's affairs late into the night with great emotion. But bloodshed between the two branches simply because of religion was unheard of.

As I have said, that had all changed with Saddam's overthrow. While Shiites were the majority population in Baghdad, there were a large number of Sunni as well. As various factions vied for politi cal control, divisions along religious lines were inevitable.

Elections were scheduled for the end of January 2005. They were the first free elections after the American takeover. Al-Qaeda in Iraq vowed to disrupt the elections, and the SEALs were among many American units that were ordered to help keep the peace and make the elections possible.

I joined a sniper team on the day of the vote, providing overwatch to protect a polling site. On a typical overwatch mission, the SEALs would take over a house or a building, make sure the family was secure and taken care of, then set up what is traditionally called a hide for the snipers to work from.

*Hide* probably gives most people the wrong idea of what the SEALs were doing. It typically conjures an image of a heavily camouflaged sniper perched somewhere in a jungle, his position perfectly blending in with the surroundings. The hides in Baghdad were nothing like that.

Typically in Iraq, at least in the cities and towns, one or two snipers would go to a roof of a building, accompanied by two or three other men providing security. The snipers—SEALs generally didn't use spotters, unlike other American military branches—would find a comfortable position where they could lie or sit while manning their gun and surveying the area. They sometimes attempted to camouflage where they were, or at least make it not look so obvious. But even when they did that, the nature of the war meant that after the first shot they were targets for others; their hide quickly turned into a fighting position.

Rooftops were generally used not only because they had a good vantage but they made setting up very easy. They didn't restrict the snipers or the men with them if they had to change position or move quickly.

Alternatively, the SEALs would use the top story of a building, or sometimes lower floors if the structure was very tall. When working from here, they usually used windows, although at times they would make small holes in the walls or use holes that had already been made. Any damage to the house was supposed to be covered by the U.S. or Iraqi government.

My job as the interpreter was to talk to the family of the house and reassure them that no one would be hurt and that they would receive compensation. This was a very different mission than going after a suspect. Often the people we stayed with were, if not pro-American and in favor of the new government, at least neutral. It was important to be as diplomatic as possible and treat them exactly as I would want to be treated.

Of course, they were often uncomfortable. Our presence could endanger them, not just that day but for days that followed. And they were literally our prisoners while we were there, though we did our best not to treat them that way.

More people than you might suppose were understanding and usually cooperative. There's a deep impulse in Iraqi culture to honor guests, and I think this impulse helped tremendously. More importantly, we showed the people by our behavior that we were trying to do the right thing. Our goal was to make their lives safer, and I think that they appreciated that.

The building the SEALs chose on the day of the elections was a commercial building still under construction, and my translation skills weren't needed. I spent most of my time up on the roof, watching with the SEALs as they scanned the streets near the polling site. It was a tense time, and an exciting one: democracy was a new sensation. It was the first time the people had a say in their own government in Iraq.

But the thing I remember most about that day was how cold it was. Baghdad in winter can be freezing, certainly for someone like me who is used to more temperate weather. I had to move constantly to keep myself warm.

Nothing bad happened on our watch. It was almost a letdown: a good letdown.

There was one great irony. I was helping protect people who were voting, but I didn't vote myself. I was working.

On the other hand, thinking back on the candidates, I'm not sure I would have cast a ballot for any of them anyway. That's the problem with democracy  sometimes you have to make the best choice from among bad possibilities.

Politics is not a clean deal in Iraq. You have to smile and laugh and get along when you want to do just the opposite. You have to act like a phony—or so it seems to me.

Am I too cynical?

I was not so jaded then. I was still clinging to the idea of a better Iraq. But what I saw as time went on soured me greatly.

It was on that mission that I befriended Sleepy Boy, a SEAL who earned his name because he could instantly fall asleep, no matter what the circumstances. It really was something incredible. When his watch was over, he would put his weapon down, lean to the side, and within seconds he was out. On that mission, the temperature must have been below freezing; still, he slept like a baby. Maybe he had Eskimo blood.

My most memorable time with Sleepy Boy came when he was driving a Humvee—but that came much later, and that story will have to wait.

**BACK IN MOSUL,** my wife watched the violence around her continue. While insurgents were leaving family members, especially women and children, alone, it didn't pay to take any chances. Assassinations and car bombings continued; IEDs were often planted on the nearby streets.

Soheila kept largely to herself, rarely going out, not even to see her side of the family. My brother's widow would go to the stores for food and other necessities. She wore her veil and kept her face covered so she would not be recognized—something many women in Mosul did, as much for safety as religious reasons. Any sort of display or action that seemed unreligious would very possibly be seized on as an excuse for an attack. Wearing Western-style clothes or makeup was out of the question.

Children stayed inside—mine especially. They might go to school for a few days, then stay home for many more. People would pass the word—things are not safe, there is danger today, plans are being made, etc. Many times these were just wild rumors, but who could afford to take a chance? There was plenty of killing to make even a doubter believe.

Our home's location near a main street was both a blessing and a curse. It was easy to sense the mood of things simply by counting the number of people passing on the street—if there were few people, trouble was brewing. On the other hand, it was right near the main route taken by American vehicles when they patrolled or drove to the nearby police station. That meant the mujahideen and their spies were always nearby. The street was a prime area for car bombs and other booby traps.

The school was nearby, another half blessing, half curse. For us, it meant that the kids didn't have to go far—but it also meant that the children were near IEDs.

More than once, Soheila heard an explosion outside in the direction of the school. Frantic with fear, she and my mother ran from the house to see what had happened, running all the way to the school until they saw our kids.

My children were always safe; the schools themselves were never targeted. But the bombs killed many on the streets. Soheila told me of passing freshly injured men on the street, blood still wet on their chest and legs. She ignored the smell of destruction, the mixture of burnt explosive and plastic and flesh, running as fast as she could to make sure our children were okay.

Other women did the same. They would ignore the Iraqi soldiers trying to cordon off the area and the Americans coming to investigate. They walled their emotions off, concentrating just on running, and just on their own children.

WHILE I'D BEEN the only interpreter for the task group in Mosul, the increased tempo of operations in Baghdad meant that the SEALs needed several, and so two more joined the unit soon after we arrived. Both had worked with SEALs before and knew the routine pretty well.

One of them was a man named Oliver. I liked Oliver, whose family had come from Lebanon. He was a nice man and a competent interpreter, but as the missions went on he began to get what the SEALs call "soft." He wasn't a coward, but he had trouble with the physical aspects of the job, like jumping over walls and keeping up with the SEALs. He flinched at trouble, and started moving slower and slower.

He never said he was scared and never ran away, but his declining physical abilities seemed to be proportional to the increasing danger we were in. I think the pressure accumulated on him the way scratches accumulate on a car, until all of the paint is worn off. The job took a toll, and in his case, it came to weigh him down and turn him into an old man.

The SEALs would ask him to do something, and he would do it. But he rarely showed the kind of aggressive initiative that the SEALs valued. They don't want to just *go* somewhere—they want to *run* there. They also want to be there before someone else suggests it. Oliver eventually wasn't up to that and soon got left behind, assigned to do inside work rather than going out on missions. That put a little more pressure on me, but I didn't mind.

Stress is a funny thing. I was smoking more, and drinking. Was that as a result of stress?

At the time, I didn't completely understand the concept. Without words in Arabic or English to adequately express what I was feeling, maybe I didn't understand completely what was going on inside my head. I knew I had to do my job, and I had to survive the war, and I had to worry about my wife and my children—were those things stress?

Surely, but again, it was like being in the middle of a vast jungle and trying to walk out. You focus on your goal, not on the mosquitos buzzing at your face at every step.

The three interpreters lived in a tiny house near the SEALs' quarters in their compound. When I say that the house was tiny, I mean *tiny*, even by Iraqi standards. There were two rooms, including the kitchen, which was where I slept. To make enough room for my bed, I moved out the washer and dryer that had been in the corner, snugging myself in as best I could.

The translators were not all one happy family. We got along all right for the most part, but every so often there would be friction and one or the other of us would get his nose out of joint, to use an

Here I am in Baghdad, kitted up and ready to go back out on another mission. I look tired because I was. We were running two, three, or sometimes more missions a night at that point.

Mosul before the war . . .

. . . and during the occupation. The devastation to my city after years of neglect and terror attacks was awful.

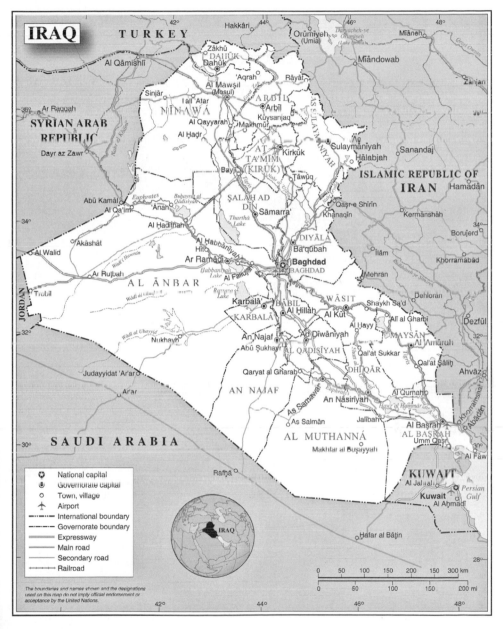

A map of Iraq. I visited nearly every important city in the country while working with American military units.

Members of SEAL Team 7 and me pose for a picture. There's a comedian in every group!

Ready to patrol. I generally wore a radio so I could communicate with the rest of the unit.

Here I am on a helo. I don't look too scared, do I?

After spending considerable time with SEAL snipers including "the Legend" Chris Kyle, I was tasked to work with a small group of Iraqi soldiers training as snipers. The truth is, I wasn't nearly as good a shot as they were, but I was very proud to help them learn.

Another photo of me getting ready for a mission, this one in Tal Afar. We made use of whatever we could find, including plastic lawn chairs.

# CERTIFICATE OF APPRECIATION

FOR PARTICIPATION IN CONTINGENCY OPERATIONS IN ORDER TO SECURE
FREEDOM & PEACE FOR THE CITIZENS OF MOSUL, IRAQ AS MEMBERS OF NSW-DET
MOSUL FROM 30 OCTOBER – 27 NOVEMBER 2005

1st BATTALION 5TH SPECIAL FORCES GROUP (A)
MOSUL, IRAQ
27 November 2005

PRESENTED TO:

JOHNNY WALKER

IN SINCERE APPRECIATION FOR YOUR OUTSTANDING SERVICE

M. RUSSELL
Lieutenant    USN
OIC NSW-DET MOSUL

MARK E. MITCHELL
LT Colonel, Special Forces
Commanding

---

# CERTIFICATE OF APPRECIATION

FOR PARTICIPATION IN CONTINGENCY OPERATIONS IN ORDER TO SECURE
FREEDOM & PEACE FOR THE CITIZENS OF FALLUJAH, IRAQ IN SUPPORT OF NSW-
DET FALLUJAH AND RCT-8 DURING DECEMBER 2005

FALLUJAH, IRAQ
29 DECEMBER 2005

PRESENTED TO:

Johny Walker

IN SINCERE APPRECIATION FOR YOUR OUTSTANDING SERVICE

M. C. MARTIN
LCDR    USN
Commanding

---

# Order of the Spur

Be it Known That

Mr. Walker, Johnny

With carbine and saber in hand, having followed the Cavalry Guidon
onto the battlefields of Iraq to free the Iraqi people and the world
from tyranny and terrorism, and having demonstrated the skill, fitness,
dash, discipline, cunning, and aggressiveness of a United States
Cavalry Trooper is hereby entered onto the rolls of the

## ORDER OF THE SPUR

and shall be given all rights associated with Fiddler's Green.
Additionally, this Trooper is awarded a pair of Cavalry Spurs which
will be worn at all Cavalry formations and Cavalry functions.

Given for Meritorious Service in support of Operation Iraqi Freedom III

Ordered this 20th day of September, 2005 by

## 3d U.S. Cavalry

XVII Regimental CSM

71st Colonel of the Regiment

Some of the acknowledgments I received
during the war. They helped Tatt with
my citizenship application.

## ODA 173, AOB 170, 3rd BATTALION
## 1st SPECIAL FORCES GROUP (AIRBORNE)

*Be It known that this*

### CERTIFICATE OF APPRECIATION

*is presented to*

### JOHNNY WALKER

FOR OUTSTANDING SERVICE, THE MEN OF ODA 173, ALPHA COMPANY, 3RD BATTALION, 1ST SPECIAL FORCES GROUP (AIRBORNE), THANK YOU FOR YOUR CONTRIBUTION TO *OPERATION IRAQI FREEDOM IV,* 13 JANUARY-13 FEBRUARY 2006.

MSG LAWRENCE F. YOUNT
OPERATIONS SERGEANT

CPT JARED THOMPSON
DETACHMENT COMMANDER

---

# 2-1 CT ISOF BDE (TF RAPTOR)
### CERTIFICATE OF APPRECIATION
### PRESENTED TO

## Mr. Johnny Walker

*In Recognition of Your Valuable Contribution while working in the Joint and Combined effort to train, advise, and assist the 2-1 Counter Terrorist Iraqi Special Operations Force Brigade TF Raptor would like to show its appreciation for your outstanding service. Your participation contributed significantly to the successful accomplishments of an extremely important mission. Your efforts went above and beyond the call of duty. The results of your contribution reflects great credit upon yourself, USSOCOM, and the United States of America.*

### Presented this

*15th Day of October 2006*

Richard Meffert
Company Sergeant Major

Patrick V. Powers
MAJ, SF
Commanding

---

# Citation
*Presented to:*

Johnny Walker

## ERU BATTALION

*For your unwavering and selfless dedication during combat operations against the enemy, Baghdad, Iraq*
*From:*

## NAVAL SPECIAL WARFARE TASK UNIT-BAGHDAD,
### Camp Dublin, IRAQ

*April 20, 2007*

*Our thanks for your instrumental role in OPERATION IRAQI FREEDOM*

SENIOR CHIEF ED, U. S. Navy
SENIOR ENLISTED ADVISOR
BAGHDAD, IRAQ

MAJOR WIZ, U. S. Navy
TASK UNIT COMMANDER
BAGHDAD, IRAQ

Working on the book in 2013. Every day in America is a dream come true.

American expression. One man in particular seemed to always be rubbing me the wrong way.

I'll call him the Kurd, because that's what his ethnic background was, but this short, round fellow was actually an American citizen. The funny thing was, he seemed always to be criticizing America—not for the war, but for itself. For America being America.

There were a million things wrong with the country, he said, from traffic to shopping malls to politics and jobs, religious intolerance to taxes. I can't even list them all.

The criticisms didn't bother me much, even though much of what he said seemed petty. What irked me was his hypocrisy. He was two-faced. When he was talking with Oliver and myself, he was very down on America, talking about all of the mistakes that the United States had made and often being highly critical of the country. But then, if we were with some of the SEALs, he would say only nice things about America.

Worse was his habit of pretending to be better than me because he was an American citizen and I wasn't.

I've already mentioned that U.S. citizens were getting paid a lot more to translate than native Iraqis were. The SEALs who knew about it didn't think it was fair, and a few told me that they had protested. I appreciated their support, but unfortunately their complaints didn't change anything.

Apparently the difference in pay schedules reinforced whatever nonsense the Kurd thought about our relative worth. One day he began pestering me somehow, getting on my nerves by being a showoff and a know-it-all. Finally I lost my temper.

"I have had it," I told him. "If you keep talking that way I will beat you with my shoe! Come, we'll go outside—if you are really a man you will fight me."

"No, no, Johnny," he insisted. "I am not going outside."

"Come on!" I told him.

His face turned pale. I doubt he'd seen me so mad. He stayed put.

"Come on!" I shouted. "Now."

Some SEALs came in and tempers were defused.

I never warmed up to him in Iraq. And yet—today he and I remain friends. I talk to him often, and see him occasionally. We disagree on many things, just as we did in Iraq.

Why are we still friends? I'm not sure. Was it the shared experience of war? Is it something in my nature, or his nature, to remain friends with a person we disagree with?

It may be. For me, a disagreement does not meant that you are not my friend or brother. In fact, I expect that you will disagree at times. I expect you to stand up to me—as I will to you.

He's still king of the cranks. Always complaining, even when I know he has nothing to complain about.


**AFTER THE ELECTIONS,** our Baghdad missions primarily involved apprehending suspected insurgents in safe houses around the area. We ran operations nearly every night for long stretches. Then would come two or three days when we stayed put before going out again. I'm sure there was a certain order and pace to the operation tempo, but I wasn't privy to the planning or the thought process behind it. I just did what the SEALs said had to be done. And that meant going out.

The SEALs used a variety of vehicles in Baghdad, but most of the early missions were made using Strykers. The Stryker is an eight-wheeled armored vehicle whose bottom looks like a metal boat and whose top resembles a moving pillbox. The vehicles can fit a half-dozen men comfortably in the back; usually a lot more were crammed inside, squeezing against their battle gear and other equipment. The vehicles could take heavy abuse from guns and even most IEDs, so if you didn't get squeezed to death inside they were very safe. But the engines on the vehicles were very loud, and were a dead giveaway that Americans were on a mission in the area. So usually we would park them at a distance from the target, then go in on foot. This meant that we were exposed for a mile or more, but it gave the SEALs the element of tactical surprise, and they felt giving up the protection of the armored vehicle was an acceptable tradeoff.

Generally, the operations were in the dark of the night. Unlike Mosul, I wasn't familiar with Baghdad, and a lot of times if it weren't for the navigator I would have been as lost as the Americans. But the night had its compensations. It was easier to take insurgents by surprise, since they usually lacked infrared and other night gear. They were also generally active during the day, and so were either tired or sleeping when we moved. And at night there was less chance of random civilians wandering into a dangerous situation.

While I'd come highly recommended, I hadn't worked with this group of SEALs before and not all of them trusted me. One, a senior chief I'll call Red, was standoffish and, I sensed, suspicious. I didn't take it personally—he seemed to be that way with everyone, or at least anyone who wasn't a SEAL.

Around the time of the elections we were assigned to find a suspect at a house deep in an area controlled by insurgents. The mission went along as planned; Humvees carried the unit close to the area and we moved in slowly, carefully, the SEALs barely seeming to breathe. I was near a SEAL I'll call Dan, a friendly but serious type who was watching out for me as we walked.

After a few moments of walking, the target house came in sight. The SEALs began moving to secure the perimeter, with a small group getting ready to stage at the front door to go in. But before they were ready, someone appeared in one of the upstairs windows and began firing.

I was near the house, separated from the lead element by several yards. Bullets began flying from an AK, answered by shots from the SEALs. As I started to duck from the gunfire, Dan fell to the ground, hit.

I saw the mujahideen gunman and the gunfire clearly, but I had no weapon to fire back—the SEALs were under orders not to give me one. Instead, I turned and ran to Dan. He was too big to carry—most of the SEALs are, even for me—so I grabbed him as best I could and dragged him with me out onto the street. The AK rattled behind me, bullets crashing into the darkness and nearby buildings. I had no idea how close any of the bullets were coming, and I was absolutely not going to stop to find out.

As the SEALs near the house responded to the gunfire, I managed to get Dan back to a staging area near the Hummers. Someone came over and administered first aid—he'd been hit in the hand, not a life-threatening injury but a serious one nonetheless. All hell continued for a few minutes—gunfire, shouting.

Then, suddenly, it was quiet, as if a switch had been thrown.

"Go!" yelled one of the SEALs. "Back in the trucks."

I helped Dan into one of the vehicles and got into another as we evacuated to the base. I never found out what happened at the house, how many insurgents there had been, whether they had been killed or simply escaped. That was often the way gunfights and battles went for me—I would catch intense snippets, fractions of the whole that might be terrifying or might, if luck was with me, be completely innocuous and mundane. Occasionally later I would get the whole picture from a briefing or, more likely, from the other guys telling their fractions of the whole as we unwound. But that didn't happen that night. The gunfight had been too intense and too sudden for anyone to process yet.

What did happen was this:

One of the SEALs came over and nodded solemnly to me.

"Red never trusts anyone," he said in a tone the SEALs reserved for the most sincere moments. "But he trusts you. Thanks for helping Dan."

I don't think anyone's ever paid me a higher compliment, or I've ever felt half so honored.

**WORKING WITH THE** SEALs in Baghdad drew me closer to them than before. Maybe closer to anyone than I've ever been in my life, with the exception of my family. We lived together, we worked together, occasionally we played together. We shared a common enemy. Gradually, I came to adopt some of their likes and dislikes for music and food—and drinks. I learned more about America and the ideals that they believed in. I was still very much an Iraqi, and saw my future here, but it was in this period that I came to admire the United States not just for its military power but for its ideals. Religious tolerance. Equality under the law. Justice, freedom, the pursuit of happiness, a chance to make yourself better—these were ideals Iraq lacked.

Maybe it wouldn't, I thought, if we kept hitting the insurgents, the destroyers of dreams. Maybe with them gone there would be a chance to make my country better.

Weeks passed into months. The time went quickly; we were always working.

But it went slowly in another way—I missed my family. The hours were long without them. I kept looking for a time when I might get away, but no chance came. Soheila and I spoke by cell phone every day, often ten or more times. But there were stretches when the cell phones weren't working, either because of power blackouts or other reasons.

Those times were hard on my wife. It was bad enough that she was hearing fighting all around her. The television was filled with news reports about attacks in Baghdad: IEDs, shootings, suicide bombers. She was obsessed with my safety even more than she was with hers and the kids', but could do nothing about it.

We must have had the same conversation a hundred times:

"Tell me, tell me, are you okay?" she would ask.

"Of course I am okay, Soheila. I am a very happy person."

"Don't lie—tell me what you are doing."

"I am working. I am very safe. This is the safest place in the world."

I would tell her the same thing, with slight variations, over and over each day. I would change the subject, asking her how the kids were and what they were up to. Maybe if there was something amusing that had happened, not related to the mission, or a joke I had heard, I would share it with her. I tried to make her laugh, or at least smile a bit. I don't know that it worked. Her voice was often strained and afraid. The poet in her was hiding.

Soheila called so often some days that it was impossible for me to answer her calls right away. Then, when I finally got back to her, she would unload.

"You cannot imagine how afraid for you we are!" she would say. Her voice was somewhere between scolding and crying. And it was, of course, loud. "Myself and your mom—we can only worry! We worry! Is Johnny safe?"

I tried to calm her down and reassure her, but I doubt she was convinced. You can only do so much for someone else's fear in the best of circumstances, and Iraq was far from the best of circumstances. As confident as I was that I would be okay, it was impossible to get her to feel the same way. Soheila prayed and read the Koran, which was more comfort than I myself could give.

My relatives and friends in Mosul were watching out for her, to be sure, but there was only so much that they would be able to do if trouble came. Relatives and friends spread rumors that I had started a business in Syria, which added to the perception that I had given up on my family and run from trouble. Those rumors helped Soheila and the kids; anyone who heard them would feel it was senseless to attack them, as they no longer had any dealings with me.

But the rumors gnawed at me. Who wants to be a coward, even a pretend one?

There were still people who wanted to kill me for having worked with the Americans. Soheila continually heard gossip and vague threats, not just at me but at her as well. Some of these rumors were from well-meaning people, who only wanted to protect her. One of our family friends was said to be a member of an insurgent cell—I have no proof that in fact he was—and he often passed along warnings meant to remind her to be careful. Whether they were based on real information or not, neither Soheila nor I ever knew. Some warnings she heeded, but most were beside the point—like everyone in Mosul, like most people in all of Iraq, being careful had become the same as breathing. Neither breathing nor care would keep them alive, however, and they all knew that.

And me?

I didn't care about my own safety. To me, it was then and has always been in God's hands. What fear I had about dying, at least in those months, was the fear that if I died, my wife and children would be penniless. So I kept working, saving my money, missing my wife and kids. Until finally I missed them so much that I decided I had to go and see them in Mosul, despite all the warnings.

# 8

# THE SEEDS OF
# A DREAM

**I** **GOT UP EARLY** that morning. The weather was good: spring, edging into summer, not unbearably hot yet, not too windy. I made my way from my house on the SEAL compound into the city, walking and getting a taxi and walking until I arrived in a Shia area. There I found another taxi driver. After talking to him a bit, I asked if he'd be willing to take me to Mosul.

He would, as long as I could meet his price. It was the equivalent of somewhere between forty and sixty dollars, for a ride that in peacetime might take between five and six hours, covering some 250 miles.

"Done," I told him.

Our route was longer and not nearly as direct as the route I had routinely taken with my truck. We skirted the worst highway with its onerous checkpoints, the cabdriver's big old Caprice bucking as we flew past fields of dust where crops once grew. The sun grew warm. I talked with the driver, but only half paid attention to his words. I thought of my family, watching the road at the same time, looking for IEDs and mujahideen and bandits, all of whom were common. Bandits were a special problem, known to prey on lone cars. A man who could afford to pay sixty dollars to rent a taxi for the trip was surely a man worth kidnapping, if not killing.

There's no way to communicate what this drive was like: boring and endless, tension filled and mundane. Knives could have been pressing on every part of my skull, around my neck, at my chest and wrists—I would have been more comfortable. I smoked cigarettes (Marlboros had become my favorite), pretended to talk with the driver, and willed our destination closer.

He knew his business, which was much more than driving. When we were stopped at a checkpoint run by the militia, he used a Shia accent, smoothly talking with the guards and getting us through. He took a different tack with the army.

We were still a good distance from Mosul, some six or seven hours later, when I gave him directions to a Shia district in the city, a place not only far from my house but where I believed he would feel himself safe. I began to get hopeful; I allowed myself to think not only of what I would do when I got home, but of how it would feel to touch my children, my older son and my baby boy, my girls, princesses in their father's eye. I thought of my wife, touching her gently, watching her from across the room.

And then something was wrong with the car. We slowed abruptly. Vehicles that had been far behind came up and passed in a blur.

"What?" I asked the driver.

Had we been shot at? There'd been no sound, no explosion.

"What?" I asked again.

He didn't know. Something was wrong with the cab. Its speed kept dropping, until at last we were crawling along. We were within sight of the city, an easy target for anyone who cared to try us.

The driver kept going as best he could. Each time a car passed in either direction, I felt my breath quicken and my heart jump.

Finally, we were in Mosul. There was no greeting or fanfare— nor, thankfully, any bullets or militia. There were only familiar streets, light brown buildings, and a slight twinge of burnt metal in the air.

Home.

The driver found a garage. I got out and left him to deal with the car. It was late afternoon, but there was still plenty of light, which to me meant one thing—it was too early to go home.

I walked a little while, then found a place where I could rest for a few moments and call Soheila. I wasn't known in this part of town, and anonymity had its rewards—safety mostly.

"Hello, Johnny," she said when I called. "How are you?"

"I am coming home," I told her.

"What? When?"

"Tonight. I'm in Mosul now."

She was more worried than surprised.

"It's not safe for you!" she told me.

"You don't want to see me?"

"Johnny!"

"I will be there after dark. Leave the gate unlocked," I told her.

"Johnny, please—"

"I'll call. Make sure the gate is unlocked."

I hung up. The next few hours were infinitely long. I saw some good friends, relatives whom I could trust. But mostly I waited, fearing that night would never come, and when it did, worrying that the blackness that fell on the city wasn't black enough.

It could never be black enough to protect me, never dark enough to shield me from the assassins lurking in the city streets. Many men would have loved to make their names by killing the man who worked with the American SEALs. To them, I was their career and their future; kill me and both were assured.

Finally I could wait no longer. Wandering through town, I finally went to a place where I knew there would be a taxi. I got a ride to a block near the house, called home, then walked around, turning in different directions until I arrived at the gate.

It was unlocked.

Soheila was waiting just inside the door. I folded her against me, holding her as close as I had ever held her or any human being before or since.

**I STAYED TEN DAYS.** No one outside the house knew I was there. Even some of our closest relatives never found out.

It was good to see my family, but I'd escaped from one cage to another, and the one in Mosul was even smaller. When visitors came for Soheila or the others, I stayed upstairs in the bedroom, making myself as quiet as a rug, smoking and softly pacing back and forth, a rat in a box whose every breath might put my entire family in jeopardy. There was little to do besides smoking and drinking the whiskey I had brought with me. I spent most of the hours in the room wishing time away.

Lying on the bed, staring at the ceiling, I decided the cowards would never have the courage to confront me. They knew I would kill them. Instead, they would go after my family. They would take out their hate on the innocent, as criminal bullies always do. I resolved to do everything I could to protect them; if it meant feeding the rumors that I was a coward, so be it.

My visit was both long and short—long because of the hours spent alone waiting, and short because we had precious little time together. I was needed back in Baghdad for work, and though I delayed as long as I could, after a week I knew not only that I had to go back but that I wanted to. My family didn't want me to leave, but they also knew that my going would make them safer.

When I left, I told them all not to worry about me. I would be fine.

"I am not the person who decides my age. God will," I told Soheila and my mother. Both were in tears. "And God plans to keep me alive for a very long time. I have a lot of work. And a lot of dreams."

My mother began to sob uncontrollably. I steeled my heart and left.


**IN THE SPRING** of 2005, a new group from SEAL Team 7 transitioned into Baghdad, taking over operations there and "inheriting" me. And it was then that I met a man who would profoundly change my life, though neither he nor I had any hint at the time.

Like nearly all the SEALs I've talked about here, the senior chief petty officer is still on active duty, so I'll refer to him only as Chief Tatt. And like most of the other SEALs, he was about average height, on the trim side, and quick with a joke. He lives in southern California and has a California "vibe"—you wouldn't be surprised to see him on a motorcycle or a surfboard.

The leadership of the SEAL units transitioning in would spend some time with the men they were replacing, getting to know what had worked and what hadn't. It was routine during that transition for the interpreters to be discussed. I wasn't included in this talk, of course, and if I had been in this instance, my face would have turned red with embarrassment.

"Listen to what Johnny Walker tells you," the chief who was leaving told Tatt. "He knows what he's talking about. He's saved us a bunch of times."

That was the highest praise a SEAL could give anyone, let alone an interpreter.

I didn't know about it at the time, and even if I had, I probably would have been a little nervous meeting the new NCO. You never know exactly how you're going to mesh with any supervisor, and in my case, language and customs were always something of a barrier. There was plenty I didn't understand about American ways or the language itself.

Fortunately, Tatt and I got along pretty well from the start. I saw early on that he and his men were still working things out. The platoon had a lot of new guys, and while they'd gone through extensive and even brutal training, it's just not the same as the real thing. On their first mission they were very uncoordinated, moving through the house we'd been assigned to hit as if they were in slow motion.

The initial entry went well enough. The house's occupants, woken in the middle of the night, offered no resistance and the place was secured. But our jackpot was nowhere to be found.

The people in the house claimed to have no idea of who he was. I started talking to them, trying to figure out what was going on, when all of a sudden I heard a shout from upstairs.

"Johnny!" bellowed Tatt. "Tell this guy to get his hands up!"

I bounded up the stairs to find Tatt holding his weapon on a semibelligerent Iraqi who'd hopped down from the roof, where he'd been hiding. Apparently he thought the SEALs had returned downstairs and wouldn't come up again; he was eyeing the window as an escape route. Tatt, meanwhile, was trying desperately to remember the pidgin Arabic he'd memorized, and was spitting nonsensical phrases that baffled and confused the suspect.

I tuned the man up quickly, telling him to put his hands up or the SEAL was going to blast him into tiny bits. Tatt's demeanor made it clear I was telling the truth, and the jackpot complied. Then I asked him his name. I guess the Iraqi realized it was pretty obvious that he was the suspect, because he didn't play any games. We soon took him away to the authorities.

One of my most important jobs was calming the family when someone was taken away for questioning. This was usually just a matter of explaining what was going on, who wanted him and why. People tended to react better if they at least knew why their husband or whoever was wanted and where he was being taken. Calming them down made them safer—yelling and screaming tended to set everyone's nerves on edge, and in that kind of atmosphere, one wrong move could lead to a tragedy. In many cases, wives turned out to be glad that their husbands were being carted off—maybe unsurprisingly, many militants were nearly as vicious to family members as they were to supposed infidels.

Tatt's team became smoother as it got more experienced, and missions that had taken a couple of hours at the start of the deployment were down to twenty minutes within a few months, thanks to Tatt and the rest of the NCOs. I admired the SEAL chief, but it wasn't until a trip to Fallujah two or three months into the deployment that we became close friends.

The SEALs were assigned a small but important role in a large operation against a major al-Qaeda IED bomb-making cell operating in the Fallujah area. While effective, raids against one or two bomb makers were inevitably frustrating, because these insurgents rarely worked alone. When one was arrested or taken in for questioning, the rest of their cell quickly learned what had happened. Even if follow-up raids were launched—generally the next day, if not the same night—some members always escaped.

The idea this time was to scoop up a dozen or more bomb makers and their helpers in a single operation. Within minutes, an entire cluster of bomb makers would be rolled up.

It was an ambitious idea, born from the hideous toll the IEDs were taking. The bombs had turned some of the major roads in and around the city into killing fields. The main route from Habbaniya to Fallujah, known to the Americans as Route Michigan, became the deadliest highway in Iraq. IEDs powerful enough to turn over a Stryker armored vehicle were common.

Which naturally made me feel a little nervous when Tatt told me that our plan was to drive up from Habbaniya on Route Michigan to Fallujah.

The mujahideen had been defeated in a brutal, house-to-house campaign led primarily by Marines during November and December 2004. But that fight—known to the Americans as Operation Phantom Fury and to historians as the Second Battle of Fallujah—was only the fiercest of many conflicts in the city. In 2005, mujahideen were diminished but still very active. It would take another year and a half before the new government really had good control of the city. By then, much of it would be rubble.

We were assigned to take down two houses very close to each other just outside the city. Our main target, said to live in one of the homes, was an Islamic teacher who was issuing the cell's fatwas—interpretations of Islamic law that, in this case, allowed Americans to be killed. Through these proclamations, he was controlling when and where the bombs would be laid.

The al-Qaeda insurgents were usually led by a cell leader who was in charge of the military operations. But a mufti—technically, the Sunni scholar or imam who issues the fatwa—who interpreted the law was critical to the operations, since he provided the formal religious reasoning or justification (if it can be called that) for the action. Their actual roles varied, but even when they were just rubber-stamping the terrorist leader's decisions, they were critical.

I suspect that the idea of providing a religious justification for killing makes little sense to Americans. But to the al-Qaeda adherents it was crucial. In their minds, the fatwas elevated their actions. Among other things, obeying a fatwa meant they were assured of going to paradise upon dying. (There are differences in the way fatwas were used by the Sunni and Shiite insurgents, as well as in general, but those subtleties aren't important here. In this case we are talking about Sunni followers of al-Qaeda.)

The SEALs were either ahead of schedule driving or there was a holdup somewhere else, because we suddenly stopped on the road well short of our target. I was sitting in the last Humvee with an EOD (explosive ordnance disposal) guy and the driver when Tatt came back to wait with us. This was a little unusual—generally the senior chief kept to himself or stayed with the more senior members of the unit.

What made it even more unusual was the fact that our Hummer was the only vehicle with no armored protection in the convoy.

"How are you?" I said when he climbed into the truck.

"Good. How are you?"

"Good."

A few minutes of awkward silence followed. I couldn't quite understand why he was there—had I done something wrong? Finally I decided to ask.

"How come you are here, Senior Chief?"

"I'm just here to sit with you."

"Oh."

"We're brothers, right?" added Chief Tatt.

"Yes."

"Okay. So if we are brothers, we sit together, right?"

"Right," I answered.

An American vehicle had been hit on the road in the vicinity a few days before. I'm sure everyone in the convoy was thinking about that as the wait dragged on. It was never a good idea to stay in one place in Iraq very long; staying along Route Michigan was certifiable insanity. Tatt or the EOD guy pulled out a ballistic blanket; we huddled in the back, the blanket draped over us.

In case you're wondering: no, it wouldn't have provided much protection if we were attacked.

"My wife is going to kill me if anything happens," said Tatt finally. "Her last words to me were 'If you get killed, I'll kick your ass.'"

No one laughed. We were probably all thinking the same thing.

I calculated that I'd be ahead if I got back with one leg intact.

Finally whatever piece of coordination we were waiting for fell into place, and we moved ahead.

We got to the suspect's house and went in without a problem. The SEALs secured the building quickly and easily; they apprehended a suspect and I was called in to determine if he was the jackpot.

I entered the room he'd been taken to and knew right off this was going to be a hard assignment. He had a determined look on his face—but he wasn't belligerent. He was reasoned and calm, not necessarily cooperative but not resisting either.

I asked his name. He gave me a false one, which of course matched his documentation.

We parried for a while. I asked him a few questions. He answered them but didn't say much else. Nothing that he did say incriminated him in any way. He was so good I couldn't help but get a feeling that he was the right person, but feelings meant nothing in the end—without real proof, he could not be taken in.

We talked a little more without getting anywhere. Interestingly, he didn't try talking me into hating the Americans or even question my religious beliefs. His answers were bland.

Finally I left the room and went to see his wife and children. They volunteered an identity that matched what he had said.

Not sure what else to do, I told them that I knew they were lying.

At first they stuck to his story. In the meantime, the SEALs who had been searching the house for evidence brought me some papers. These were in the jackpot's name—and yet the family still maintained the man we had apprehended wasn't the man we were seeking.

"Listen," I told them. "You have to tell us the truth, or we will take all of you. That is the way it will be."

It was a bluff. They didn't suddenly change their story or renounce him, but the tones in their voices changed. I could tell from their reactions that they knew I was right, that he wasn't who he claimed to be.

"Are you going to cooperate?"

His wife didn't say anything, nor did the children.

"Well then," I told them loudly. "Then we will take you all in."

I stomped over to the suspect and told him that I was taking the entire family in.

"Everyone comes," I told him. "Your wife and your kids. If you are going to lie to me—"

"Leave my family," he said finally. "I am who you are looking for. Just leave them alone."

We did.

The SEALs raided the other house nearby and picked up another suspect. By this time there were people in the street, loudly demanding to know what was going on; we could hear gunfire in the distance. We packed our jackpots up quickly and hustled out of there, driving to a base on the other side of the city.

It was the first time I'd seen the city since just before the war, when I'd taken a cement-truck load down from Mosul. Looking at the destruction, I couldn't help but think what might have been if the city worked with the Americans rather than fought them.

The war had turned me into a strangely optimistic person on the one hand—I could sense so much potential in my country, in my fellow Iraqis, and in mankind in general. But on the other hand it had made me deeply sad, stressed by the waste and sheer lunacy of the hatred I saw and experienced.

Iraq made no sense. The people had complained bitterly about Saddam. Now he was gone. But instead of working with the country that had freed them, instead of building Iraq into a great land, people fought like suicidal monsters.

**THE RAID NETTED** most of the key people in the terrorist cell. The IED attacks stopped for roughly a week following the operation. That was considered an extraordinary success at that point in the war: the residents and the people trying to protect them had less insanity to deal with for a few days.

We returned to Baghdad and a full slate of new missions, our workload gradually increasing. We worked hard; when we got a day off we partied hard—or just slept, which sometimes was even better. One night after a mission, Chief Tatt started joking with me. He had a wry sense of humor that snuck up on you; it matched his easygoing attitude. We joked about many things—women, drinking. It was the usual SEAL humor, not much different from what you would expect to hear in a locker room.

All of a sudden, Tatt turned serious.

"Would you like to go to America?" he asked.

I thought he meant as a tourist and said something about how I'd love to see the sights someday.

"Live there," he said, correcting me. "Would you like to become an American citizen?"

"I'm an Iraqi," I answered, or something along those lines.

"It may not be safe for you here. Or for your family." Tatt explained that another American unit, an Army Special Forces A Team, had recently helped get an interpreter out of the country because his life was threatened. I told him I didn't feel that was necessary in my case; I had no fear about my fate, or my safety.

"I'm fine. I'm an Iraqi. I have my friends."

"Are you sure?" asked Tatt.

"I'm going to finish this," I told him. "Iraq is going to get better."

"Roger that."

Tatt didn't say what he thought of my optimism. We went back to joking.

He didn't bring it up again during the rest of his deployment. Even so, the seed of something had been planted. I was still an Iraqi, and still in my mind I believed Iraq could be a better place. But everything I'd seen over the past few months, and everything I heard from Soheila, was working to erode that hope. A better Iraq looked more and more like a fantasy. I wasn't working on a dream; I was living in the middle of a nightmare.

AT TIMES, THE SEALs were used as a kind of special resource, helping other American or Iraqi units that were taking heavy casualties. One of those times was in al-Dora, a neighborhood in southern Baghdad that had once been home to many Iraqi Christians but by this point was infested with Sunni extremists. A U.S. National Guard unit had been assigned to the area, and while they were fine soldiers, they lacked the special training and resources the SEALs had. The SEALs started doing sniper overwatch missions and running patrols, aiming to disrupt the mujahideen networks that were giving the other Americans such a hard time. At the same time, they targeted the deadliest of the insurgent cell leaders. I think we only captured a few people on the raids, but the effect was out of proportion—not used to being hassled on their own turf, the mujahideen would lay low for several days after a SEAL operation, giving the men in the National Guard unit a temporary but very welcome respite.

In April, we were assigned to help patrol the area surrounding Abu Ghraib, the huge prison twenty miles west of Baghdad. If Americans have heard of the place at all, it's because of the torture incidents that allegedly took place there in 2003 and 2004. By the time we were assigned there, the scandal had passed; Abu Ghraib was famous for something else: a spectacular breakout that began when a truck loaded with explosives detonated near the outer wall. The attack came April 2; a hundred or more al-Qaeda insurgents hit the walls of the prison hoping to spark a mass escape. They suffered heavy casualties. While they failed to achieve their objective—the prisoners who breached the interior fence were recaptured—the attack involved complex planning rarely seen in Iraq, with coordinated shellings and ambushes at a number of bases and highways.

Even after the attackers had been beaten back, the route from Baghdad to Abu Ghraib was a veritable highway of hell. Ambushes and IED attacks were common. The SEALs decided to scout it to see if they might be able to ambush the mujahideen planting IEDs. Tatt and I drove through the area with a member of the army unit assigned to the area. We'd just started out when Tatt pointed to some round holes in the Hummer's interior.

"Dude, what's that?" he asked the sergeant who was our guide.

"Oh, we were in Sadr City a while back and an IED went off," said the sergeant nonchalantly. "Ball bearings went through."

He added that they had killed the man where Tatt was sitting.

"That's nothing," continued the driver. He pointed to a ramp on the highway. "See that? We hit an IED on that ramp and flipped over the other day. Killed the turret gunner."

If these stories hadn't been enough to impress me, the fact that several fresh IEDs had been set up along the highway on the route home to Baghdad did. One of them was truly remarkable—made of several large artillery shells arranged together, the SEALs called it a "teepee" because it reminded them of an Indian tent. Bomb units defused the devices, but it was impossible not to think about either the brazenness of the terrorists who'd planted them in broad daylight, or the implications of having failed to spot them.

The next day I went out with another SEAL who headed the unit's snipers. He's still in the navy, so we'll call him Tommy German to protect his identity.

Tommy German looked at everything with a sniper's eye. Like a lot of SEALs, he was able to mentally render a complicated battlefield into good places and bad places with just a glance. He wanted to be in the good places; he wanted the bad guys to be in the bad places. Some of this was pretty obvious. It was better to be in a high spot than a low one. But other aspects were, and remain, a mystery to me. I just learned to accept that he saw the world differently than I did. He always got good results.

I was observant myself, though of different things. After taking our survey that afternoon, we stopped in a settlement near the prison as a group of American soldiers swept through, looking for the terrorist who had just planted a bomb. The soldiers could detect certain types of explosive on a person's skin with the help of a special device. As we watched them work their way down the street, I noticed a man watching from the distance. He eyed the patrol, then moved quickly away. He was dressed differently than others, and it was clear that he was out of place.

"That's the guy they want," I told Tommy German, pointing.

"How do you know?"

"Just from the way he looked at them and turned around. You better tell them. He's getting away."

Tommy German called over to one of the soldiers, and they ran and caught up with the man. Sure enough, he tested positive for explosives.

BACK IN BAGHDAD, we started getting missions that took us farther from home. Whether that was because things had calmed down in Baghdad or become more heated elsewhere, I'm really not sure. I doubt it. It was probably more that the SEALs had been recognized as a valuable resource, and everyone wanted to use them.

Whatever the reason, it was around this time that I experienced another first—riding in a helicopter.

Our mission was in the south, near Basra, and like most of our missions, it was to take place at night. We were looking for a man named Abdullah, a Shiite who'd been organizing resistance in the area.

All of that was utterly routine—aside from the fact that to get there we had to fly. I'd never been in a helicopter. Given that I had once wanted to be a pilot, I wasn't intimidated or even very anxious.

Until one of the SEALs came up to me with a very serious face and asked, "What is your blood type?"

I had no idea what he was asking.

"What's your blood type?" he repeated.

"Which?"

"Blood type."

I thought it was a joke. "You want to know my blood?"

"Yes. What type is it?"

"Iraqi."

That didn't seem to be a reasonable answer. I thought maybe I would say "Scotch"—but his voice had turned so serious that it was clear he wasn't in the mood for a joke.

"No, no, your blood type. Not your nationality."

I just shook my head. "Red blood." I had no idea what he was talking about.

He explained, *almost* patiently, that blood has different types, and if you are injured, the doctors need to know which one to use to replace what you've lost. The explanation helped a bit, though I still didn't know the answer and had to take a simple test. But the process made me wonder: Did helicopters crash so often that people were always needing blood transfusions?

We drove out to the airstrip at dusk, where an MH-53 was waiting. The fifty-three, as it is known to the SEALs, is a large helicopter with a single overhead rotor, often used by special operations forces as a transport. It looks like a grasshopper on steroids, with big blisters in the front over gear, a pipe for aerial refueling that looks like a jousting spear, and extra fuel tanks that look like bombs to the uninitiated—which would definitely include me. There are door gunners with big machine guns, but it's a transport rather than an attack helicopter. Still, it looks pretty ferocious.

And a little too heavy to get off the ground, until those big overhead rotors get angry.

And that night they sounded *very* pissed off.

Probably sensing that I was a little apprehensive, the SEALs had me sit up near the pilot against the bulkhead, which put quite a lot of the helicopter between me and the door. The ride itself was uneventful—I just sat and hoped the big-ass helicopter wouldn't shake my brains out of my head. My eyes were closed for a good portion of the ride.

Then, just before we were supposed to land, my legs fell numb.

I couldn't wake them for anything. I don't know whether it was nerves or just the fact that I was sitting on them wrong, but they were so numb that I stumbled when I got up. I managed to get out of the helicopter, but just barely, falling face-first to the ground as the fifty-three shuddered and shook above me.

The choppers kick up a tornado when they take off, and I found myself pelted by waves of grit, stones, and violent wind. I got up, fell down again, stumbled to my feet and collapsed yet again, this time into a shallow mud hole. When I got up I was blind—the night vision glasses the SEALs had given me to wear were covered with a sheen of mud.

I finally managed to push the gear off my face and run up toward the house, which was a few dozen meters away. My radio was buzzing.

"Where's Johnny!" someone was shouting. "Where the *hell* is Johnny Walker?"

"Here, here," I answered, trying to get my discombobulated gear back into place. I think they may have thought I didn't get off the helo.

"Johnny, come on," said one of the SEALs. "We need you inside."

By the time I got myself together, the SEALs had already cleared the house. I was a mess, covered with mud and dirt, my long beard embedded with muck.

About a half-dozen men had been found in the house. They all had IDs—and none of them read Abdullah, the name of our jackpot. Rather than denying knowing him, the men told the SEALs that Abdullah was supposed to have come to the house that night, but had never arrived.

Right, I thought, looking them over. I had no hard intelligence beyond the man's name, but it seemed pretty obvious that these guys were lying. Their stories were very well polished, and they didn't look me or anyone else straight in the eye as they gave them.

I considered what I might do. My goal was to find the jackpot, but I was sure that if I asked who in the room was named Abdullah, I'd be greeted with silence, then a host of denials. So I watched them for a while, getting a feel for how they interacted. It soon became obvious that they were all stealing glances at one individual.

Abdullah?

I had the men taken out to talk to me individually, asking general questions, going over things they'd already said. I spoke in low, confidential tones, and tried to be as casual and friendly as possible.

I spoke to two or three men, then had the man they'd all been glancing at brought over.

"Hey, what's up, Abdullah?" I said in Arabic. "How they are treating you? Are you okay?"

"I am fine," he said. "Nothing is up."

His smile drained quickly as he realized he'd just given himself away by answering to his name.

"Jackpot," I told the SEALs who'd brought him in.

So at least my helicopter ride was not for nothing.

**I LEARNED OVER** time that there are many, many ways to get information from an enemy. Often the best way is to use simple questions that seem to have nothing to do with anything—working someone's name into a sentence as I did with Abdullah, for example, and then watching the response. In many cases the suspects we apprehended were prepared for difficult questioning and were on their guard to be asked about explosives and other things. But answering a greeting? That was not something they had prepared for. Saying hello was something they had done all their lives. It was nothing to worry about—was it?

I wasn't able to get information from everyone, and not every mission the SEALs staged was a success. Many times we would go out and find that the intelligence that we'd gotten was bad or incomplete. At times when we found a suspect accused of being an insurgent, the information and accusation turned out to be false. A lot of that depended on where the intelligence had come from. American sources were by far the best, probably because they had already been vetted or developed from intelligence from another suspect.

Ironically, Iraqi sources, which should have been the best, were often way off. Part of the reason was that people quickly learned that, as in the Saddam Hussein years, they could make trouble for enemies by claiming they were up to no good. If they were convincing enough, they could inconvenience the person and often do even worse harm.

There were several missions where we would look for IED parts in a building, only to find none. A thorough search could turn a house practically upside down. While that didn't necessarily mean the man who owned the house wasn't an insurgent—he might have moved the material before we arrived—in many cases it was clear he'd been set up. I felt bad, but there was little I could do beyond apologizing. This was the nature of the war I found myself in. Vague rumors had the power of a television newscast, and small vendettas and jealousies could be settled by getting someone in trouble with the authorities.

I was disappointed when we went through a mission only to find that there was no jackpot, no hidden cache of weapons, no success. It didn't seem to bother the SEALs, though—they gauged their missions by how well they performed, not by the value of the intelligence their orders were based on. For them, the important thing was doing their job as well they possibly could.

As the op tempo—the frequency and speed of our missions—increased, I found myself worrying more and more about what might go wrong. The closer we got to the start, the more I tensed. It was as if my hands and arms and legs and feet were all attached by a string to my heart. My heart beat faster, pulling the imaginary string taut, until every part of my body was ready to snap.

One day I came out of the house to get ready for an operation planned for Baghdad later in the evening. I saw Bry, one of the senior chiefs, standing in front of a Hummer with another SEAL. They were both laughing, cigars hanging from their mouths.

They looked like they were getting ready to go to a ball game, not on a mission. They were so relaxed, in fact, that I thought the operation had been canceled and was surprised to find that it wasn't.

The mission came and went; like so many of them, I can't remember the details. The next afternoon we were going out again. A few hours before we were set to leave, I came out of my house and once again saw Bry smoking and joking with a friend. It looked like they were planning a night on the town, not a journey into the worst part of Baghdad to grab a suspected bomb maker. I smiled, shrugged, and went about my business.

The next afternoon, the same thing happened. Finally, my curiosity got the better of me.

"Hey guys," I said, walking over to them. "What is this business? Why are you smoking these things? Why are you not getting ready for the mission?"

"We *are* getting ready," said Bry.

"Chief, aren't you scared?" I asked. "You are laughing—you are not serious. It looks like you are going to an adventure, not on a mission."

"So?"

"You don't worry?"

"If we don't know what's going to happen, why should we be scared?" answered Bry. He went on to explain that good things could happen just as well as bad things. In fact, the odds were in favor of good things, since the missions were so well planned. So why be afraid? Why not be happy?

"It's more likely something will go right. Don't worry about the bad until it happens."

"Okay," I said. "Do you have a cigar for me?"

He handed one over. From that point on, I never worried about all the bad things that might happen on a mission. I didn't always smoke cigars—they are an acquired taste, I have learned—but I adopted Bry's philosophy as my own. It fit in with what I had told Soheila and with how I thought about my own safety in general.

If I don't know what is going to happen, then what is the sense of worrying about it?

**ABOUT CIGARS—THE SEALs** were smoking big, fat, and very smelly Cubans. The first time I smoked one—*whoof.* My head, my stomach, my throat—I coughed my lungs dry and felt my stomach do flips for hours. But I thought what the hell. I had to copy them. And so I tried. For days, with the same results.

It took a while for me to realize that you don't smoke cigars like you smoke cigarettes: you don't inhale, among other things.

Cigars were only one of the ways that I tried melding my personality to the SEALs'. I listened to the metal rock they listened to before missions and grew to like it. They were making me American without my really knowing it.

**IF THE FIRST HALF** of 2005 was hard for Soheila and the kids, the second half was even worse. The violence in Mosul became so great that once again I had a relative whisk them from the city.

It was arranged quickly. That evening, dressed in old clothes—very traditional ones, with no hint of Western influence and no suggestion of wealth—Soheila and the kids waited by the door for the car to arrive. When she saw it pulling up, my wife pulled up the scarf she was using as a mask, then ushered the children out, urging them to run as fast as they could to the nearby car. She held the baby in her arms.

They stayed in the home of an acquaintance near the Syrian border for several days. It was a primitive place, small and without many comforts, save the most important—it was safe.

Still, there was no question of the family staying there for very long. Life was far too primitive and restricted. Living there was like living in caveman times. After a few days, the kids began to grow restless. As soon as the atmosphere in Mosul calmed down, they returned, once more in secret.

It was neither the first nor the last time they left Mosul in fear. Over the course of the next few years, Soheila and the kids would flee and stay in the homes of acquaintances outside the city a dozen times. The pattern was always the same—a fresh outbreak of violence or threats would prompt warnings from others; relatives or friends would help them leave; they would stay away for a few days or weeks. Even today, I do not dare name the people, for fear that they might be retaliated against. And yet I owe them so much gratitude that I cannot express it in words.

I was still speaking to Soheila by phone several times a day, as much as ever. In many of these conversations, she'd mention that she wanted to move to Baghdad to be with me. She didn't know how bad Baghdad was. Nor did she realize that without a support network of friends and family nearby, she would be even more isolated and vulnerable.

One of the truly diabolic aspects of Iraq was the corruption among government and army officials. Graft was everywhere, at every level. The fact that everything was for sale meant you couldn't trust anyone. The people who were supposed to protect Iraqi citizens—the police, the soldiers, the government workers— might be easily bought off or convinced to look the other way. The Iraqi army had plenty of opportunities to get information about me; while I'd be safe on base, my family would be exposed in the city. Without family or tribal connections in Baghdad, I had no one I could trust to watch them. At least in Mosul, we had people who would protect them—including several who we believed were close enough to the insurgency to hear rumors of threats.

Still aching for my family, I arranged to meet them in Kurdistan not long after they had come back from the village. They were driven up by car; I flew up. We met at the airport, then drove to a hotel and spent the next ten days together. It was a vacation—or *almost* like a vacation, since there was never a way to completely block off the danger we were in or the fear of what might happen when the week ended and we returned to the war.

**MOST OF THE SUBJECTS** we were sent after were not particularly smart or crafty; they tended to be uneducated and brainwashed, for lack of a better word, by other extremists. But occasionally we would run into a truly intelligent insurgent, one who was not only a killer but an effective one. These were sometimes the hardest men to deal with, not so much because they were smart but because they were dedicated. They believed in what they did and were ruthless because of it. Their intelligence just made them harder to catch.

Some of them had a strange sense of honor. They saw themselves not simply as warriors of God, but as *noble* warriors of God. They were proud of what they had accomplished, even when they had killed many innocent people.

One of the strangest of these types was a man we found in the Adhamiyah area of Baghdad, which is in the northwest corner of the city. It had been an upscale area before the war; by 2005 it was a hotbed of insurgent activity.

The mission started when an Iraqi came in to give information about a bomb maker working in the area. According to this source, the man had ignited an IED on a passing American convoy a few days before. That part didn't bother the informer; it was the fact that the insurgent had ignited it while women and children were passing that sent him over the edge. Killing soldiers was one thing, killing kids another.

"Enough is enough," he told the SEAL who interviewed him. "Enough."

We took the man to the house, where we found and arrested the bomb maker. Once apprehended, this al-Qaeda associate told us of another member of his cell, a much higher-ranking insurgent who proved to be the linchpin of the local insurgency. Within hours we were at his house. To our surprise, not only did Linchpin surrender without a fight, but he began talking freely about his exploits. We brought him back to the camp and he sat with Tatt and myself bragging about everything he had done.

Linchpin spoke good English, and Tatt was able to talk to him directly. The interview went on for hours, more conversation than interrogation. His information led to more arrests and a raid on a house where a false wall led to a cache of weapons that must have included at least twenty machine guns and a host of mines. From there, we raided an apartment complex looking for some al-Qaeda members and Tunisians who'd been recruited for a suicide attack. We missed the Tunisians but must have rolled up half a dozen al-Qaeda members in the process of busting the operation. The suicide attack was thwarted, at least for the time being.

Linchpin was proud that he had been captured by the SEALs; he apparently considered them warriors worthy of his own exalted rank. He took a liking to Tatt. At least that's how I interpreted his statement to the chief as he was leaving:

"Mr. Tatt, you're an honorable man. If I ever capture you, I will put a bullet in your skull and not cut off your head."

Tatt thanked him for his consideration.

Handed over to the Iraqi government, Linchpin and five or six of his associates were tried for terrorist activities. It was said to be one of the first actual terrorist trials in the country under the new government, and it resulted in convictions. The men were sent to Abu Ghraib.

A few months later, Linchpin bribed his way out of jail; according to the rumors we've heard, he paid the equivalent of six thousand dollars.

That was the way things worked in Iraq.


BACK IN THE United States, news reports of the war caused a variety of different reactions. I had no idea that there were debates over the nature of the war, whether it should continue or not and how it should be waged. The workings of democracy were still very foreign to me and while these issues affected not just me but all Iraqis, I'm not sure what I would have made of the debate. The job in Iraq certainly wasn't finished or over; the country was a long way from being a better place.

Among the debates was one on how to help interpreters who worked with the American forces. By this point, word of how vulnerable we were had begun making its way back to the States. Even though there wasn't a lot of attention being paid to the issue in the media, some members of Congress began discussing the possibility of granting special visas and then citizenship to translators and others who had put themselves in danger by helping American forces.

For me, the issue was still moot. More and more, I'd come to see America as a place to dream about, with its riches, movies, and sports stars. But it was too distant to be anything but a dream. And it wasn't my home. I'd never thought of it as anything other than a place far away. The idea of moving there didn't seem real. So when Chief Tatt mentioned it again, I gave him the same answer I had earlier—thanks, but no thanks.

I don't know if Tatt was disappointed or whether he didn't think I understood what he was offering. Whatever it was, he let it slide.

Team 7's deployment ended in the spring of 2005. According to the commendation I later received, there were roughly 150 missions during that time—not quite one a day, but close.

I felt bad when it came time for them to leave. By now, I was secure as a SEAL interpreter, reasonably sure that I would remain with the SEALs in a job no matter which unit was rotating in. But over months of living and working together with the SEALs I formed close ties with many, and there was always a question when they left of whether I would see them again.

Honestly, I didn't expect to. Things change so quickly in war. The bonds we forged wouldn't be broken, but the opportunity of seeing friends was a constant casualty. This was especially true of the senior people, who often were given new assignments and promotions when they returned to America from Iraq.

So when I said good-bye to Chief Tatt, it was with the full knowledge I might never see him again. We shook hands, hugged each other, and stepped back, an invisible wall already rising between us.

"Good-bye, brother," I said.

"Good-bye, Johnny."

I watched him walk away, not realizing I was seeing my future striding across the tarmac with him.

## 9

# MISSIONS AND DECISIONS

**H**OW DOES A dream change from wisp to flesh? And more importantly, why?

I had never thought of living in the United States, let alone taking my family and becoming citizens there, until Chief Tatt mentioned it in 2005. There was no actual way for it to happen. I didn't even want to leave Iraq.

And yet . . .

And yet the possibility of going to America began to slip into my consciousness. The things I'd admired about America when I was younger—movies, mostly, and basketball, and music—were joined by a more mature notion: the idea of living not just in safety but in a place where I would be free.

I had never dreamed of becoming an American. Was it because I loved my life in Iraq so much? Or was it because the possibility had never occurred to me?

More the latter. Absolutely the latter: my world had revolved around Mosul. And I saw no real alternative to Iraq. When I thought about moving my family to someplace safe, I thought of other parts of the country or, occasionally, Syria or another place in the Middle East. All were equally unrealistic. Life there might have been marginally safer for us, but we would be cut off from our friends and relatives even more severely than Soheila was when she went to the villages in the west to hide. And no part of the Middle East seemed very inviting. The small amount of increased safety wasn't worth the complications and problems. How would I make a living? How would we deal with the lost contact with friends?

Despite its problems, Iraq seemed the better bet. Surely things would get better.

But as the war and devastation continued, with my own life and my family's threatened, I started to think of other possible futures. If Iraq couldn't be made safe, and if I couldn't find a place of safety within it, what should I do? Where should I store my hope?

Did I dare dream of going to America? The possibility Chief Tatt had mentioned was simply that—a possibility. If it became a reality—if someone came to me with plane tickets to get us all to the States—would I go?

No, I thought. I am an Iraqi.

But the idea kept creeping back, sneaking into my thoughts when I wasn't on guard. It tickled my old interests in all things American. A hope for the future was taking shape before I even dared consciously admit it.


**THROUGH 2005,** our targets were mostly Sunni militants, mujahideen who had been Ba'ath Party members or Fedayeen members, or men who were recruited by or somehow under the umbrella of al-Qaeda in Iraq. But as the conflict continued, the groups I worked with were assigned more and more to hit Shia radicals as well. Iraq, meanwhile, was a place of quasi–civil war, with Shia attacking Sunni and Sunni attacking Shia, and the Americans stuck in the middle. Depending on where you were, the Iraqi army and police might side with the Shia, or they might simply stand back and try not to get killed.

The pace of the missions continued to increase. The overall command tried different strategies across the country to instill peace, or at least give it a chance to grow. From my perspective, the war became a continuous run of missions, one after the other. We'd brief, we'd go out, I'd talk to the people. Hopefully we'd find the jackpot and bring him back. Then back at the base, I would interview him, trying to get more intelligence so we could go out again. These post-operation questionings became more important in this period, as the SEALs tried to develop and act on their own intelligence.

Waiting while the assault team cleared a house to make sure it was safe was always one of the worst parts of a mission for me. I wanted to be with the assaulters, the guys who went in first—I always felt that they needed me there, to talk to the people they might find inside the house, to avoid misunderstandings or just dangerous situations. But I wasn't supposed to go in until the place was "cleared"—declared safe from immediate ambush or IEDs. Usually this only took a few minutes, but those were the longest minutes of the mission for me.

At times, I'd wait near or in the garage, as quiet as I could be, listening for any clue of what was going on inside. Other times I'd be farther away, back out at the wall near the street, crouched and craning my ear to hear either the radio or the sounds around me. Every so often I'd creep up and slide inside the doorway, ready to help if needed. Some of the officers in the head shed—the SEAL slang for command or headquarters—would have had a fit if they'd found out, but whatever punishment they gave me would have been nothing compared to how I would have felt if one of my guys was hurt.

I'd wait, badly needing a cigarette. The time . . . would pass . . . v-e-r-y . . . s-l-o-w-l-y . . .

Then, finally, there'd come a shout from inside:

"Send the terp! Where's Johnny?"

I didn't think of it as running into danger. I thought of myself running to help the men who were my friends. That designation now applied to all SEALs. I'd learned that SEALs were different from other soldiers. Their toughness and their loyalty to one another made them accept each other, and they had adopted me as one of them.

Very late one night the platoon boarded a half-dozen Hummers and headed to a house intel had said was being used by al-Qaeda as a safe house. We stopped close enough to run to the house from the trucks. As the area was secured, an assault team went to the door and broke it open. They rushed inside, waking the sleeping occupants. Within moments they had cleared the house, meeting no resistance.

"Johnny!" the LPO, or lead petty officer, shouted.

I went inside. The SEALs had found the homeowner, who was already telling them loudly that he had nothing to do with the insurgency.

I don't know how much they understood, but he was fairly convincing, and I wouldn't be surprised if they thought they'd made a mistake.

I'd learned to be skeptical. With one group of SEALs watching him and another searching the house, I went to talk to the rest of the family. There were two or three kids along with his wife and his mother and father.

The adults were clearly religious. Both of the men had long beards, and the women wore very modest, traditional clothing. There were little signs around the house that the family was very observant, the same way that crosses and holy pictures would tip off a Christian family. But some of their answers didn't quite match that; they downplayed their beliefs, as if trying to indicate that religion wasn't important to them.

It might be nothing, I thought to myself. First of all, a person might be very religious—be they Shia or Sunni—and not be a member of the insurgency. And there was always the chance that my perception was merely skewed: I'd gone in looking for an insurgent, and so I might be reading innocent items as clues that I was right.

I talked to the family members for a while, then went back to the man the SEALs thought might be the jackpot. I talked to him about insurgent activity in the neighborhood. He started changing his answers, altering what he'd said earlier—again, not an indication of guilt, but enough to make me feel something was going on that I didn't know.

I left and went to the mission commander. He was ready to leave.

"I think they're hiding something," I said.

"What?"

"I don't know. It doesn't add up. Have you searched the house?"

"We didn't find anything." The chief paused. "Go ahead. Talk to him some more. We'll search the place again."

I went back inside and asked the suspect if there were weapons in the house.

"No weapons. No weapons." He held out his hands.

Most homes in Iraq had at least one weapon, often an AK-47, used for protection. That was allowed and wasn't suspicious—if anything, the opposite was true: if a man didn't have a gun, I would wonder why not. I was about to give up questioning him when a SEAL came bounding down the stairs with a Russian sniper rifle in his hand. He'd found it hidden in a closet.

Sniper rifles were not generally allowed, but occasionally there were exceptions. This might be true less than 10 percent of the time; in the rest of the cases, the gun was being used against Americans or Iraqis. I decided to play it hard; if he had an explanation he would tell me quickly.

"Well, look at this," I said, taking the gun and showing it to the man. "You said you had no gun. Do we understand each other now? You are lying to me. Do not lie—tell me the truth."

"We are both Muslims," blurted the man. "They are infidels. We are on the same side. Why are you pushing my family? Why are you persecuting me? I am trying to help my religion."

"Why are you telling me, I am Muslim?" I answered. "If you are Muslim, and you are killing people, then I am not Muslim. A religion of murderers is not my religion. We do not understand God the same way. Don't play this game with me. Tell me what else you have in this house."

"The gun belongs to a friend of my son's," said the man. "He brought it to keep it with us. I told him he shouldn't, but he didn't listen."

I was sure that was a lie as well. I kept talking to him.

Soon I saw my suspicions were right. Having found the hidden gun, the SEALs started checking the walls of the house. They soon discovered a secret panel. Behind it was a laptop computer, documents, videos, a black mask, and explosives. The man was a leader in the militia; the sniper rifle turned out to be the least of the evidence against him.

By the time we had everything out of the house, the sun was just about to rise. It had been a long night, but a successful mission—one jackpot, one safe house, and a lot of insurgent material under American control. It was a good mission.

I got better and better at spotting liars. A few minutes of conversation—a glance this way or that, a few evasive answers—and I would know. It wasn't an instant thing, ever. Anyone whose house we entered reacted initially with shock. But then as they began to relax, it was easier to judge reactions.

**ON ANOTHER MISSION,** we worked with an American army unit that was acting as the lead. Our job was to surround and secure a Sunni mosque that intelligence said was being used by a group of al-Qaeda insurgents. The soldiers would then enter and look for the ringleader of a terror cell said to be operating there.

For the SEALs, this was supposed to be an easy job, if any of these operations could be considered "easy"—I don't know if that word really applies to anything you do in a war zone. The SEALs cleared their assignments, then stood by as the lead American unit went into the mosque and began looking for their suspect.

With the situation under control, I stood outside with one of the SEAL chiefs and had a smoke. The minutes passed. We waited, and we waited.

Morning came, and we were still waiting.

Always in the back of my mind, and I would imagine in everyone else's, is the fact that time is an enemy during a mission. You start out as the hunter, searching for your target. You get to the site, you clear it, you remove threats: things go smoothly.

But the longer you stay, the more chance there is that the tables will be turned. People may see your trucks or hear some noise, or perhaps someone in the house doesn't answer a cell phone or doesn't show up at a specified time—any of a hundred things might tip off a neighbor or a comrade that you are there. That in turn might tell them to stay away. Or it might tell them to attack. We were always targets. Baghdad was filled with many enemies.

That night I milled around with the others, wasting time.

Finally, I went to the SEAL in charge and asked what was going on.

"Sorry, Johnny," he said. "They're still looking for their jackpot. They have a bunch of guys inside but can't figure out who the bad guy is."

"Fuck it," I told him. "Give me ten minutes. I will find him."

"Johnny—"

"I tell you, I will find him."

"Okay, Johnny." The chief shrugged. "I'll give it a try."

He got on the radio and talked to the person in charge of the operation inside. The army commander agreed to give me a chance and told him to bring me inside.

Maybe they were desperate, or maybe not. They certainly had nothing to lose at that point. Anyway, I went inside and found the commander.

"Okay, this business, leave it to me," I told the army commander. "You want your jackpot, and I want to go back. So let me do this."

The commander looked at me doubtfully. Finally he shrugged and told me to go ahead.

"I need support from my guys," I added, meaning the SEALs. "Just let me handle it."

"All yours," he said, or something along those lines. "It's all yours."

About twenty Iraqi men had been inside the mosque when the American units arrived. I took the IDs that had been confiscated and looked them over. It wasn't always easy to tell the real ones from the fakes, and most of the ones I looked at that night looked real. I sorted through them a few times, culling maybe a half dozen that I thought might be phony. One in particular stood out, though the name on it was nothing like the jackpot's.

I took the IDs and sorted them into an order so that I had a few of the ones I thought were good on the top. Then I went into the room where the men were all being held and started talking in my loudest, most official voice.

"Hey, everyone," I told them. "I am representing the Iraqi government. And the man with me, he is representing the American government. We apologize for what happened. We have made a mistake. We had information that you guys were building IEDs and had car bombs here."

The men in the room began to relax. They knew that there were no car bombs in the building or anywhere on the grounds nearby. They were definitely in the clear.

"We deeply apologize," I continued. "This was a mistake. The person who gave us this information will be punished. To make it up to you, we will apologize to each person individually and give you money for your trouble."

I looked at the first ID card, and called the man's name. He came up; I shook his hand and apologized.

"You will have to sign a receipt for the money," I told him, waving him toward the door where some of the other soldiers with us were waiting. "They'll give it to you there and you can be on your way."

He left, a little nervously I think, but eager to get home—and collect a reward for his trouble.

Same with the next. And the next.

Finally, I called the name of the suspect—not the name on the phony ID, but the jackpot's real name.

The man started forward, then hurriedly leaned back.

Too late. We'd found our jackpot. Or rather the army's.

He soon confessed, and we turned him over to the soldiers.

A few hours later, back at the base, I was trying to sleep in the trailer when one of the SEALs came over and pounded on my door.

"You're not going to believe this," he told me when I let him in. "They want to trade. They offered us all of their interpreters for you."

"Who?"

"The army. They think you're worth more than everyone they've ever worked with."

I guess they thought it was like American baseball, where you can trade players between teams. The SEALs thought it was a great joke. But I didn't exactly understand what was going on. Was I being moved to the army?

"I have to go?" I asked.

"No," said my friend. "We're keeping you for ourselves."

When I figured it out, I was flattered. The SEALs thought it was hilarious, and started joking that they wouldn't take me on any missions with other units; they didn't want to make them jealous or risk me being kidnapped by our own forces.

**THERE WERE DIFFERENT** groups working against the government and the Americans in Baghdad. The SEALs felt it was useful to know what group various targets were allied with and tailor their strategies accordingly, though in my opinion you couldn't rely on intelligence to get the information straight. And I usually preferred not to even know—I could make my own assessment, usually more accurately.

It wasn't that I valued spontaneity. There was simply no sense preparing based on intel that might or might not be true. It wasn't just that you were wasting your time with this information; it could easily send you into a situation with a preconceived notion that was all wrong. It was always better to work with simple information and make up a plan on the spot.

Similarly, my best tricks were the ones that came directly from the circumstances. I used different variations of the common ones—using the jackpot's real name once he was relaxed, for example, or asking kids to ID who was who.

One of the other tricks was to make people feel as if they were at ease. Ironically, one of the best ways to do that was to accuse them of being something they weren't. If they knew they could disprove it easily, they were much more likely to let their guard down in other areas.

Say, for example, we were looking for someone affiliated with a Shia militia. If I was sure the people I was talking to were Shiite—their names or clothes would often give them away—I might tell them we had information that they were with al-Qaeda. They would then set out to prove they weren't, loudly proclaiming their Shiite ties. That information could then lead to information I could use to definitely identify the person we were after. It was simple mental algebra: *Oh, he suspects that I am A,* the guy might think, *and clearly I am not. All I have to do is show him that.*

Another simple trick would be to say that I was looking for someone other than the person I wanted. For example, I might claim to be looking for Tom Jones when I was actually looking for John Doe; when the suspect proved he wasn't Tom Jones by showing me an ID saying John Doe, I had him.

It was all very devious, I know. Using children to identify suspects? Was it ethical? Was it moral?

Given the circumstances, yes on both counts. I almost never knew why the person was wanted, or what charges may have been lodged against him, but if the SEALs were being sent to apprehend him, it was a very good bet that he was suspected of having killed people. The SEALs didn't deal with low-level criminals; they were assigned to apprehend very dangerous men, bomb makers and leaders of bomb makers, snipers, mujahideen fighters: people who thought nothing of killing innocent women and children if it could advance their cause.

The phony talk about religion and morals I heard from them sometimes got to me. On one mission a man began spouting to me about how he and I were brother Muslims, and how I should protect him from the infidels.

I guess I'd been hearing this speech a lot, for finally I cut it off with a sharp retort:

"I'm not a Muslim," I told him. "I'm a Jew. And I am here for one purpose—to take you to Guantánamo. And now you've said enough so that I can do that job."

He got quiet real fast. I offered him a deal—if he told us who he was working with, rather than sending him to Guantánamo, I would have him brought to the Iraqi detention center. There he could expect to stay maybe fifteen days at the most—a short time for a terrorist who planted bombs that killed women and children, you'd have to agree.

But the only way I would do that, I said, was if he explained who he worked for.

He did so quickly. So perhaps in this case my anger was not only justified but useful.

**BACK IN MOSUL,** the pressure increased incredibly on civilians, especially Soheila. Bodies lay in the streets, family members and friends too petrified to move them for fear they would be targeted next. Barely more than a prisoner in our home, Soheila thought constantly of plans to escape. She had fantasies of moving to Kurdistan or Syria. She thought of Baghdad, which was in no way safer. She might have thought of the moon, for all the good the plans she concocted would do.

We'd talk about these ideas sometimes when she called, if she was in the mood to share and I had the time to listen. We both knew the plans were impractical and impossible. We knew no one in either place, and even imagining a future there was difficult.

The optimism we'd both shared about the future had melted away. What I saw in Baghdad every night was utterly depressing—corruption on every level, killing for the sake of killing. For Soheila, things must have been even worse: our children were easy, vulnerable targets, without bulletproof vests or SEALs nearby to protect them. No matter how upbeat and happy she tried to sound for my benefit, desperation crept into her voice every time we spoke.

I know it was much harder for her to cope than it was for me. I was surrounded by friends, and I had much more physical freedom than Soheila. My bonds with the SEALs had grown incredibly strong, and though it was dangerous, I could leave the base whenever I wanted as long as I wasn't needed on a mission. Even the fact that I went on missions made things easier for me than for my wife—I could concentrate on my job rather than the unspecified but nonetheless real danger my family faced every day. I'm sure that Soheila wasn't worried about the danger to herself so much as the danger to our children.

And me. Somehow, you always worry more about the ones you love than yourself.

I don't know if it was that worry specifically that made me decide to come to America. I don't know if it was *exactly* my concern for my children and their future. I don't know what role my worries that Soheila would be taken from me played. I don't know how much it was my disillusionment with Iraq and the new government.

I do know that, from working with the SEALs, my interest in America grew greatly. I do know that I had always admired the country, but now that feeling was something more. I do know that I had always liked the ideal of freedom, but that working with the SEALs had taught me how much deeper, and much better, that ideal really was.

All of these things contributed to an idea that now became a new dream: I wanted to be an American citizen.

I wanted my family to experience real democracy, real freedom, real justice, real opportunity.

I wanted us all to be Americans. I wanted us all to have a future.

In books and movies, there's always one special moment when the sky seems to brighten. Things happen. A person's mind changes. The clouds that have been blocking the sun part, and glorious music swirls from the heavens. The moment is highlighted in a thousand ways. It seems as if everything that has happened has led to that specific point, that great moment.

It's the moment that the great decision is made, that the final plunge of the plot is determined. It's the climactic point teachers taught you about in literature class, the crucial development that leads to Act III and the final triumph of the story.

Maybe that does happen sometimes in real life. Maybe it happens often. In any case, it didn't happen to me. I saw no burst of sunlight, heard no music. I can't pinpoint the moment, but I do know that it happened—that one day the seed planted by Chief Tatt blossomed into a dream.

Could he get me out of Iraq?

We were still in touch occasionally by phone and e-mail; I decided to ask him the next time we talked.

I'm not a shy person, but asking for help is not an easy thing, and this seemed like the most difficult request in the world.

But it was necessary.

"Do you think it might be possible to come to America?" I asked. "The way you suggested—"

"I'll get working on it right away," he told me. His voice was deep with emotion.

What I didn't realize was that he had gotten a phone call from the commander of SEAL Team 1 not long before, asking him to start working on getting me out. The commander had called Tatt at home and explained that things were really bad. The commander also arranged to send a copy of the paperwork that had been used to get another interpreter out of Iraq. That made things a lot easier for Tatt, giving him a template to copy.

I told Soheila not long afterward. "America is going to be our new home. We'll be safe."

"What?"

"Tatt is going to get us out."

"Really?"

"Yes."

"It's not a dream?"

"It is a dream. But it will be real. It will be real very soon."

Having seen what could happen in war, having lived a nightmare rather than a dream for so long, I should have known to be much more cautious, if not with my hopes, at least with my wife's emotions. But hope is water to a man dying in a desert, and at that moment we were both in grave need of something to live for.

# 10

# FATAL FRIENDLIES

**H**OPE WAXED AND WANED, but life pushed us forward, some days faster than others.

With different SEAL units rotating into Baghdad for new assignments, it was only a matter of time before I started meeting old friends.

Sleepy Boy was one.

He came back to Iraq in 2006. Like most of the other SEALs who'd seen combat before, he returned to Iraq a little sharper, a little stronger.

Some things, though, hadn't changed. He was still fun.

Not too long after he arrived, the unit was assigned to a night mission in Baghdad to raid a suspected terror cell. It was a big mission, with U.S. and Iraqi soldiers involved as well as SEALs; eight vehicles were needed to take all of the people involved in the operation. I went into the lead vehicle, a Humvee with an open back. I chose my favorite seat: the rear truck bed.

I disliked Humvees. They felt claustrophobic, especially at night. The only way to lessen that feeling was to sit in the back. That way, if I saw trouble, I'd have time to react. Being inside the cab I always felt I had less of a chance of seeing anything and less time to react if I did.

Sleepy Boy, as it happened, was at the wheel. Altogether there were seven of us in the truck, a full load. Three of us went into the back of the truck: me, the gunner, and another Iraqi.

We began flying through the Baghdad night, headed toward our destination. We'd learned from experience that driving fast was one of the best defenses against IEDs and ambushes; you didn't want to give the enemy a chance to spot you and then react. I watched from the back of the truck as the city passed by, more stage set than a place where people lived and worked. Buildings were replaced by dark shapes and shadows, random lines that loomed suddenly and then disappeared. The air was warm with the smell of garbage and the faint odor of burnt metal.

I thought briefly about the mission, briefly about the danger my family was in. I looked behind me at the convoy. I tried to push the anxious anticipation away, tried to relax as Bry had told me that afternoon a year before—it seemed like centuries ago now.

It would be an easy night, I told myself. Nothing to worry about. Fate is in God's hands, and God is merciful and just . . .

Suddenly the vehicle swerved and I was thrown against the side of the rear bed. My head went light, and I realized I was flying.

Unknown to us, cement barriers had been placed in the middle of the road where we were traveling. The blocks, meant as a security measure to control traffic, were almost invisible, even with night gear.

Sleepy Boy saw the barrier at the very last moment. He jerked the wheel and hit the brakes, trying desperately to veer out of the way. But it was too late. The Humvee's momentum took it right into the barrier. I flew forward, and then everything went blank.

**I WOKE UP** a few minutes later, lying in a ditch. My mouth, my face, my head, my shoulder—nearly every part of my body hurt.

Someone was standing over me. It was a soldier from the army unit we were working with. He said something, but I couldn't hear.

"My night vision," I muttered. "I lost my gear."

"Don't worry about it," he said. "Are you all right?"

"Yes. Help me up. The mission—"

"The mission is off. You were in a car accident."

"Yes." I struggled to get up, not exactly understanding what he was saying.

"Some of the Iraqis with us were hurt. Can you help them?"

"Where's my night vision?" I asked.

"We have it. Don't worry about it."

My head in a fog and my body thumping with pain, I made my way through the rock-studded field where I'd landed to a triage area. The two men who'd been with me in the back of the Hummer were hurt, as were several of the Iraqis in the armored vehicle behind us. I did my best to make sense of what was going on, translating for the men who were helping the Iraqis. After a few minutes, a helicopter appeared; as we began medevacing people, someone pushed me aboard the chopper. I was too exhausted and confused to resist.

We landed at a Baghdad hospital a short time later. My face was pretty battered, but I didn't realize how badly I'd been hit until I lit a cigarette to smoke.

Something is odd with this cigarette, I thought to myself as I put the cigarette in my lips.

Something was missing—my two front teeth. To this day, I haven't had them replaced.

My right shoulder was torn severely and three of my ribs were broken. But none of the injuries were life threatening, and I was starting to feel more like myself as they wheeled me into the emergency room, threw a blanket over me and then started pulling off my clothes to clean my wounds.

A nurse came and began cleaning me, sorting through the cuts and bruises on my upper body. She was gentle and soft. It had been quite a while since a woman had caressed me so carefully. I guess I wasn't too wounded at all, because one key body part sprang to action, much to my embarrassment. I grabbed at the blanket to make sure it provided maximum protection.

"Leave me for a few minutes," I told her, trying to hide my embarrassment. "Give me a minute."

"You need to get cleaned up," she insisted. If she'd noticed the problem, she didn't let on.

"Just leave me alone for a minute," I said. "Please get out."

"But—"

"Just get out!" I told her.

She left. The master chief and the XO came rushing in.

"What's wrong?" they asked. "What did she do?"

"Nothing," I said, not wanting to explain.

"You have to tell us."

"No."

"Johnny, that's an order," said the master chief. My guess is that they thought she had been cruel to me because I was an Iraqi.

"But—"

"Tell us."

I pointed at the tented blanket. They smirked and left me alone.

The nurse came back at a calmer moment. I was out for about a month with rest—the most boring time ever—before the doctors cleared me to return.

The next time I saw Sleepy Boy, he apologized profusely. I decided to joke with him the way he joked with me.

"You owe me two blondes," I told him. It was my way of telling him it wasn't his fault.

"Two?"

"My teeth are worth two."

"I'm so sorry, Johnny."

"Deal?"

I believe he agreed. But so far he hasn't paid.


THE VIOLENCE MY FAMILY and I were witnessing every day finally attracted the attention of the policy makers in America. What was reported in the media was just a small portion of what was happening on the streets of Iraq, but the stories and video made enough of an impact that people began pushing for change, saying that something had to be done.

The question was what. Some Americans wanted to pull the armed forces completely out of harm's way. I can't blame them for being concerned about their sons and daughters, their brothers and sisters, their parents. And given what I had come to feel about Iraq and the situation there, I wouldn't have been surprised if America had completely given up.

Yet, I knew America was better than that.

After debating for months, the Bush administration decided to institute a buildup that became known as the "surge." Some twenty thousand additional American troops were sent into Iraq to help defeat the insurgency. Baghdad and al-Anbar—the region that has Ramadi as its capital—received most of the media attention and a great many of the troops, but the surge was aimed throughout Iraq. The idea was to engage the insurgency and defeat it, making the rest of the country safe for Iraq's new institutions to take hold.

These weren't new ideas. The Americans had been trying to get Iraqi institutions on their feet practically since the first hour of the invasion. But the surge brought more forces into the country, and it focused their efforts and American policy.

In the meantime, more Iraq police and army officers were recruited and trained. The idea was that they would take over when the Americans left. The year 2007 became a kind of make-or-break year for Iraq. Either the surge succeeded and things got better so the troops could go home, or the surge didn't work and Americans would be so disillusioned the troops would go home anyway.

Today the general consensus is that the strategy worked. After several months of intense warfare, the number of killings, both of Americans and Iraqis, began to decline. The years 2007 and 2008 were deadly years, but they were also years when things started to get better for average Iraqis. Granted, things had been so terrible that they almost had to get better, and life for people like me who were known to be working with the United States remained utterly hazardous. But Iraqi institutions did start to revive, and daily existence became somewhat easier.

I'm not sure how much long-term impact the surge had on Iraq itself. It didn't, and couldn't, address the corruption that infected institutions from the local police forces to the highest levels of government. It couldn't make people think differently about their religious beliefs. It certainly couldn't make them think more kindly toward others, or make them realize that to have a future, you have to build, not destroy.

None of that is America's fault. Nor is it an argument that there shouldn't have been a troop surge, or that America should have given up on Iraq. Americans did their best to help the country. That's an admirable thing, a good thing.

But just because a thing is good doesn't mean it's guaranteed to be a success.

SINCE I'D STARTED working with the SEALs, my relationship with other Iraqi soldiers had often been strained. Different units had different personalities, and it's unfair to make a blanket statement based on what each unit did, let alone what one or two members of it did. Having said that, I'd be lying if I said I ever 100 percent trusted any Iraqi unit. I know most SEALs rarely trusted them either. It wasn't just because of incidents like the bombing in the mess tent at Mosul. Even "normal" interactions could turn sour—or worse.

My experiences in Tal Afar were typical. Tal Afar is located in northwestern Iraq, about forty miles due west of Mosul, and was an important city during the Ottoman Empire. The modern city has spread out around the ruins of an old Ottoman castle. The old fortress is a majestic structure, built partly into the hillside, with curving walls and impressive towers that command a view of the entire countryside beyond the brown, sand-colored buildings of the city. Standing on the stone floor of the tower lookout post, it is not hard to imagine that you are in a long-ago time.

But when I was there, Tal Afar wasn't a place for daydreams. Even though it was far north, it had a history of trouble practically since the arrival of American troops. A Sunni stronghold, it had had a population of about eighty thousand before the war; a good number had Turkish ancestors or family connections, a holdover from the days of the Ottoman Empire. There was often friction between them and Iraqis with Arab backgrounds.

While American forces had launched a major campaign against insurgents there in 2004, the terrorists were never completely vanquished. Unrest continued in 2005, when a second operation was launched by both Iraqi and U.S. forces. Initially lauded as a successful venture and an example of cooperation between the two countries, in reality the Tal Afar operations only showed how difficult it was to permanently stamp out the violence. Toward the end of

2006, a series of bombings wracked the city; the bombing campaign escalated in 2007, taking dozens of lives. Meanwhile, rocket and mortar attacks killed and wounded many Iraqi police and civilians while adding to the general chaos.

I visited Tal Afar with the SEALs three times between 2005 and 2007. Each time, we came as part of an effort to apprehend local mujahideen leaders. The castle grounds were used as a camp and lookout area—they had plenty of space and great vantage, which made the place perfect. As soon as we arrived, I took a walk to one of the towers and admired the view.

With things quiet, I took out my phone to call my wife.

We'd just started talking when I suddenly heard the distinctive sound of AK-47 rounds slashing through the air and hitting the wall nearby.

*Tshkew, thskew, thskew.*

Soheila asked what was going on.

"A wedding," I told her. "You know the people—they are celebrating. Firing into the air. They are happy."

Happy to kill me, I thought, but I didn't add that.

Hanging up with Soheila, I searched the area below for the gunmen. I finally spotted some men with rifles and called over one of our snipers. In short order, the insurgents were killed or chased off. But the fact that they were bold enough to fire on the main American camp in the middle of the city in broad daylight says something about them—and the Iraqi army unit that was allegedly providing security.

The next day, we were assigned to help an Iraqi unit clearing mujahideen from an area in the city. Their plan was to go door to door, searching and inspecting every house in a neighborhood where mujahideen were known to be operating.

We met with the commander of the Iraqi unit and discussed what they needed. The SEALs had conducted dozens of these missions themselves, and had no trouble giving the Iraqi army advice. The Iraqi commander seemed to accept it. The only caveat was that he wanted to conduct the searches and most of the sweeps himself. That wasn't a problem, and the SEALs quickly supplied a strategy.

The general idea was that the Americans would move first into a central house, where they could watch the area. Once they were ready, the Iraqis would begin their sweep, moving methodically through the neighborhood, securing and searching one or two houses at a time. Meanwhile, the SEALs would protect the Iraqis and act as lookouts.

There were a few wrinkles: the Iraqis and SEALs didn't have radios that could work together, and the Iraqi unit lacked maps or, from what I could see, any ability to make them.

I drew up a map and gave the commander my cell phone number, settling on that as a means of communication. The SEALs tried mingling with the Iraqi unit, eating dinner with them and socializing as a way of building confidence between the two units. It was a tactic I'd seen them try before with American units; it was a little thing, but in battle the outcome often depends on many little things working together.

Dawn broke. Our team went to a small house nearby and began the overwatch.

Once the house was secured and the family that lived there taken care of, I went outside and took a walk around, assuming the SEALs didn't need me to be with the family. I liked to amble around and scout the area. I had a long beard and dressed like an average Iraqi; I blended in well.

The Iraqi force was just getting into position nearby. The first house they were going to hit was next door, and by coincidence, I happened to see one of the soldiers running along the fence, his helmet loose and bouncing on his head. Whether he tripped or was just discombobulated, he hit the fence as he ran. His helmet slid so that it blocked part of his vision. It was like watching a comedy routine, except it wasn't very funny.

What happened next was even less humorous. I stood watching him in disbelief as he straightened, spotted me, then raised his gun in my direction. Before I could do or say anything, he had fired three rounds.

All missed, somehow.

I ran back inside the house, surprised to be alive. He'd fired at point-blank range, no more than a few meters away.

"What's going on?" asked one of the SEALs.

"One of the Iraqis almost killed me."

"What?"

"One of *our* Iraqis," I said, explaining what had happened. The team's ranking petty officer came over and heard the story. In the meantime, the area outside was checked; the Iraqi had moved on with the rest of his unit, which was now moving to a search a new house.

"What do you want to do?" the petty officer asked me.

"I have no more trust," I told him. "He saw me—he had to know who I was. We ate with them last night."

"And he still fired at you?"

"Yes," I said. "I have no more trust."

"Then we're done with the mission."

We went to the Iraqi commander. He didn't seem to understand how seriously we took the incident. Maybe he just didn't put that much value on human life, or at least mine. But he was finally convinced to call the soldier over to talk.

"Hey, buddy," I told the man. "Do you know you almost killed me?"

"Oh, sorry about that," he said, shrugging. His tone was just a hair less polite than what you might say to someone who bumped into you outside a movie.

Our NCOs closed the operation down.

THAT WAS OUR last experience with *that* unit, but it was far from our last "interesting" experience with the Iraqi army or other forces, whether in Tal Afar or anywhere else. As the war went on, we dealt with them more and more. The quality varied greatly.

Iraqi units came in several varieties, but they could be divided into two groups, those under the Ministry of Defense—essentially the army—and those that worked for the Interior Ministry—essentially the police. The main army forces we worked with were known as ICTF or sometimes just ICF, which stood for "Iraqi Counter Terrorism Force." The primary Interior Ministry force was the "ERU" or Emergency Response Unit. These units were supposed to be special operations teams modeled after Western units. It would be a stretch to say they were the Iraqi equivalent of the SEALs or even a good SWAT team back in the States, but they were better trained and equipped than units in the regular Iraqi army and police force. All were trained by Americans to some degree; in fact, we did a lot of the training ourselves, mostly by taking them into the field.

Working with the Iraqi forces was a by-product of the counterinsurgency plan implemented by General David Petraeus, which was executed in coordination with the surge. The first phases of the plan called for tactics very dear to the SEALs—violence of action against the terrorists. The many missions against suspected terrorists, the arrests, the gunfights—all were aimed at doing serious damage to the insurgency. As the attrition mounted, Iraq's institutions were supposed to have space to revive themselves. American forces would eventually be phased out, replaced by Iraqis.

The middle space, where Iraqis were trained up to take over, was the most difficult one. It wasn't just that the soldiers needed to be taught how to do tasks like searching a building or securing a marketplace; the Americans had to trust them. As my encounter in Tal Afar showed, that wasn't always easy or possible.

As the war went on, I generally found the ICTF more dependable. Their intel tended to be a little more reliable, though nowhere near the level that the SEALs had received and used earlier in the war. More importantly, they were more professional when going after their targets. To them, it didn't matter whether the person they were seeking was Sunni or Shia. The ICTF's composition was mixed; it was a majority Sunni, but there were also a good number of Shia and Kurds in the ranks. I think the fact that they had all worked together may have helped make them more neutral; if they were going after a bad guy, they didn't care what his religious beliefs or alliances were.

The ERU units were usually a stark contrast. There was definitely a link between the Interior Ministry and the Shia militias—I visited the ministry building in Baghdad one day and saw a militia flag prominently displayed on one of the floors. The ERU members were predominantly Shia, and rarely if ever went after Shiite targets. That didn't mean that they might not do good work otherwise, but it did make them very hard to trust unilaterally.

The quality of the units throughout the country also depended a great deal on how much experience each individual member had, how long they'd worked together, and of course how good the officer corps was. I remember working with an ICTF officer who was so naive he tried to set up an observation post in the middle of farm land, where he would not only be easily spotted but quickly surrounded. I aborted that mission myself, simply by standing outside the small building he'd picked: I was seen and we had to leave. I'm not sure what might have happened otherwise.

It was during this time that I formed one of my closest friendships with a SEAL, a chief still on active duty whom I'll call the Quiet Man. The name is an allusion to the John Wayne movie—a favorite of mine—but more importantly, it described the chief's manner. He was a calm person, with a quiet manner even when the shit hit the fan.

The Quiet Man was the sort of fellow you can picture walking upright through a fire with long, measured steps, his feet untouched and his stride unhurried. He was extremely fair skinned, so he couldn't pass as an Iraqi, yet he often found himself running around in Baghdad on various errands dressed much like a civilian, driving in a pickup truck with no external security. Worried that he would get into trouble—he would have been a valuable target—I used to argue with him to take me along. He just waved me off. The most he'd let me do was fix his scarf so his white face wouldn't be so obvious.

Obviously, he knew what he was doing, because he was never attacked. But I worried about him like I worried about my wife and kids.

I'd first met the Quiet Man back in 2004, when he was coordinating interpreters for the task group I was assigned to. He'd impressed me then, not only for his combat skills but for his ability to deal with the various personalities and egos. At one point, he had ten interpreters answering to him; there was a lot of what he calls "man drama" between them—present company excepted, of course. Petty squabbles and jealousies always seemed to calm when he came into the room, and he had a way of making all the silliness disappear when he reminded you of the mission and why you were there.

Now the Quiet Man was back for his third tour in Iraq. He'd seen the arc of the entire war, as the pendulum swung from American control to Iraqi. The Quiet Man was an excellent choice to work with the Iraqi units, whether they were ICTF or ERU; he was wary, very familiar with Iraqis, and unflappable. We soon became good friends.

One of the biggest problems for the Quiet Man and the rest of the SEALs was navigating the different politics of the Iraqi groups. That was a problem for me, as well, though I at least had the advantage of knowing who was who and being able to sort the different prejudices. Dealing with the ERU could be particularly treacherous, not because they were out to kill Americans, but because they tended to view any Sunni as a permissible target. Subsequently, their intelligence was often bad.

I remember one night we went to three houses in a row without finding anything the ERU intelligence promised; worse, their men practically destroyed the houses while searching for a nonexistent weapons cache. Needless to say, that didn't win any points with either the occupants or their neighbors, who undoubtedly got a full report the next day—and for weeks to come.

We'd apologize—profusely—to the people when the intel turned bad, and pay them for damages, but there was little else to be done. It got so bad that for a while I think sources at the Defense and Interior Ministries had to be targeting each other back and forth in their own little power game. We'd go to a house and find that the owner's son was in the army, or a policeman. Under other circumstances it might have been hilarious, but here it could have easily been a matter of life or death.

There were other problems. One night we went on a raid with the ICTF. It was a good arrest; we ended up with a jackpot who was implicated in earlier attacks. But one thing seemed odd—we couldn't find his cell phone after he surrendered.

That was highly unusual; just about everyone had a cell phone in Iraq. We were discussing this back at the camp when someone—I assume one of the sources—announced that he had his phone number and called it.

A phone rang in a nearby room where the ICTF soldiers had gathered.

"Oh, I forgot I found it," said the man, turning it over.

Looting gradually diminished as the war went on, not so much because the Iraqi soldiers became more honest, but because the SEALs started checking their rooms more carefully and running inspections.

With the Iraqis taking the lead, my services were even more in demand. There was a stretch through 2006 and 2007, and even into 2008, when I and some of the other interpreters would run three or more missions a night, working with different teams. We'd get back from an operation and jump into another vehicle with the next group; come back and do it again.

Truthfully, I loved the excitement and the adrenaline; even better, I felt that I was getting a lot done and making a difference.

But in retrospect, it was taking a physical toll. I was smoking a lot and collapsing into sleep whenever my work was done.

It wasn't just me. A truck flipped over early in 2008, killing a number of Iraqi soldiers who'd been working with us. That was followed by another accident with a Humvee. In both cases, fatigue was cited as a possible—though not the main—reason for the accident. The powers that be decided the mission pace had gotten too heavy and started ordering breaks and a lighter tempo. I don't think anyone complained.

**IN 2007, WE WERE** to get a man known to us as Nassar Farhan. Farhan was considered a very high ranking Shia cell leader. I've long since forgotten the names of most of the men we were assigned to arrest, but somehow his has stayed with me. It's not because he was more evil than any of the other men we encountered—not one of them was a great humanitarian, and most were mass murderers by any sane standard. But we were looking for him for so long that it was almost like an obsession. Intel would come in and lead nowhere. He was always "on the radar"—an Americanism it took me a while to understand—but we never found him in the flesh. How many leads we chased down, how many rumors were heard and checked—the total must be in the hundreds.

One day an American army unit contacted the SEALs and told us they thought they had apprehended an individual on our list of suspects we were assigned to apprehend. They'd stopped a car in Baghdad with six men who'd raised their suspicions—why I'm not sure, though the number alone was probably a factor. One of them, they seemed to think, was Nassar Farhan.

My boss at the time was a chief petty officer I'll call the Bishop. He was friendly, quiet, and extremely low key—if you saw him on the street in the States, you would never expect that he was a SEAL. Mess with him and you'd find out real quick that you'd made a serious mistake. His hands were fast, whether there was a weapon in them or not. His only real drawback in Iraq was his light features, which made it impossible for him to pass as anything other than a Westerner.

The Bishop had me and some of the men in the platoon board a Stryker and drive over for a look. The ride took quite a while, and with every passing moment, I felt the tension build. Were we really going to find Nassar Farhan? We'd been chasing him for so long, it didn't seem possible.

And it wasn't. None of the suspects looked anything like the description we'd been given for Nassar Farhan. And none of the names on the IDs were Nassar's.

Nonetheless, I started interviewing them one by one. The IDs they'd presented *all* looked fake, but each man stuck to the stories they'd given the army unit. I was carrying an old photo of Nassar taken many years before—it was so old that he had a tie on. Maybe one of the men looked like an aged version of him, but it was anything but a close match.

The Bishop was inclined to release the men. While they were certainly suspicious, there was no evidence against them, and the names they had given weren't known to be the names of any insurgents.

While he was discussing the situation with the soldiers, I noticed that one of the Iraqis seemed to be a little nervous. Was he scared that something would happen to him? Or was he afraid that some secret he was trying to hide would come out?

I persuaded the Bishop to let me talk to the man before any decision was made on whether the group should be released. Then I marched into the room where they were being held and pointed sharply at the nervous Iraqi.

"You, come with me," I said sharply. I led him out to the Stryker.

Inside the back of the truck, I asked him what kind of work he had done before the war.

He didn't answer. Instead, he told me he was a member of the Iraqi Special Forces.

I didn't believe him until he mentioned the name of a sergeant major whom I knew. Either he *was* with the Special Forces or he had very good information on them.

"So what are you doing with the bad guys in there?" I asked.

"I don't know that they are bad."

"Do you know what they do? They kill women and children."

We talked for a while, without getting anywhere, until finally he asked, "What do you want to know?"

"You know what I want," I said. "Information on these men. Don't ask me stupid questions. Tell me what I need to know so I can release you."

He hemmed and hawed a little bit, but I could tell he wanted to talk.

"I can let you go," I told him. "But only if you give me information."

"Okay," said the other man finally. "One person inside—he is a cell leader."

"Who is he?"

"His name is Nassar Farhan."

He described the man I'd noticed, but I wasn't convinced, even though no one had mentioned Nassar to the Iraqis. I acted as if I didn't know who Nassar was. I asked a few more questions, then told my new "friend" that I would take him back inside.

"I thought you were going to release me," he said.

"First, let's find out if you are lying."

"But—"

I assured him that the others wouldn't know he'd given him up, and that everything would be all right . . . if he hadn't lied.

"He'll never admit it," said the man. "Never."

"We'll see."

Back inside, I called the man whom my friend had just identified as Nassar and took him into the Stryker.

"What's your name?" I asked.

"I gave you my real name," he said.

"I didn't say it was not real," I told him. "What is it?"

He gave a little smirk and repeated the name that matched the ID.

"Okay," I told him. "You want to play games? We will play a game. If I win, you will be hooked. If you win, I will release you. Deal?"

He pretended not to understand.

"If you answer correctly, then you will be released," I told him. "Otherwise, you will be a prisoner. Deal?"

"I am telling you the truth."

"Then you have nothing to fear. Deal?"

"Deal."

I had him blindfolded, and placed a SEAL next to him. Then I brought the Iraqi who'd claimed to work with the Special Forces in.

"Hey, I have a question I forgot to ask you," I said to him. "Nassar Farhan—can you describe him to me?"

"Yes." He proceeded to give practically a centimeter-by-centimeter description of the man I'd had blindfolded.

"What he is involved in?" I asked.

"Kidnapping, killing . . ." He recited a litany of terrorist activities.

"Thank you," I said, dismissing him. The SEAL brought him back inside.

"So what do you think?" I asked Nasser, removing the blindfold.

"No, no," he said. "He is the bad guy." He proceeded to implicate the man who'd just been talking in a number of terrorist crimes.

"Right now, I have to take both of you," I told Nassar. "But I can make you a witness against him. What do you think, Nassar?"

"Okay. I will do it."

"So your name *is* Nassar," I said, as matter-of-factly as I could.

I thought I'd get an argument, but instead he started talking freely. He told us the names of several other insurgents, including one whom he answered to. He also told us about targets. He was a jackpot of a jackpot.

The Iraqi who said he was in the Iraqi Special Forces hadn't been lying about that. He had trained in Iran and then been returned specifically to infiltrate the special operations unit. Needless to say, he didn't rejoin his unit. I believe a total of six people were arrested because of that one night.

I have no idea what happened to them after they were arrested. Once turned over to the Iraqi government, they might be put on trial, or they might even be released. I'd never know.

**A DIRECT CONNECTION** to Iran was not uncommon among the Shia insurgents and militia. While it was never emphasized in the media, Iran was actively training men and giving support and supplies to various Shia groups. Moqtada al-Sadr, the head of the so-called Mahdi Army, was only the most famous.

Al-Sadr had a complex and contentious history in Iraq, vehemently opposing Americans on the one hand and trying to become a power in the government on the other. To give you just a taste of his story: He incited protests in Najaf—a city holy to the Shia—in April 2007, pushed followers to kill Americans, then declared a truce later that summer. The following year, his followers waged open war against the British in Basra, another Shiite stronghold. By 2011, Sadr had made peace with the Shia-dominated government—not a bad idea, as by then he controlled a large bloc of votes in parliament.

It wasn't hard to get the feeling that people's lives were being sacrificed for whatever political agenda Sadr and others were pressing for. For some leaders, religion was just something to be used to advance their own agendas. That doesn't mean that all people who were religious were naive or cynical, or that someone might not be truly religious and ambitious, but it was hard not to question motivations or feel that the whole process was at its core corrupt.

**AT ONE POINT** in 2007, we went south to Basra with one of the Iraqi ICTF units. It was a mission I remember not so much because of what we did in Basra but for how we got there—via a C-130 aircraft flown by Iraqi pilots.

In fact, we were the first troops they ever transported, a fact they were extremely proud of: so proud, in fact, that they waded through the crowded plane to tell us.

I was sitting on the rear ramp near the Quiet Man. If you've ever seen the interior of a C-130, the ubiquitous cargo aircraft used by militaries all over the world, you know I wasn't sitting back there by choice—there were so many Iraqis with us that that was the only spot I could find. When I heard what the pilots were saying, I nearly bolted from the plane.

At least that's the way the Quiet Man tells the story.

Truthfully, I was nervous to begin with, and didn't care to hear any pilot saying anything about being brand-new on the job. But the flight went off without a hitch.

It's not true that my eyes were closed the entire time—I know I had them open for at least a few seconds during the flight.

The British met us at the airport, and for some reason they turned our arrival into a celebration. The ICTF soldiers were treated to a catered dinner, the sort of buffet you would see at a wedding feast. When it was over, we went out and made a routine arrest at a mosque; the Brits' preparation must have been more elaborate than the actual operation.

The Iraqi troops did a number of operations in Basra, especially in the Hayyaniya district. Any action that was deemed "culturally sensitive"—like raiding a mosque—now required the presence of Iraqi units and generally had them in the lead, at least in theory.

That didn't mean they went smoothly, or with no resistance. I was with an ICTF unit one night when a suspect decided he was going to try using me as a punching bag. I didn't take too kindly to that; I coldcocked him, punching him so hard he fell unconscious. I was worried for a few moments until I saw that he was breathing.

The British were good to work with, especially when they fed us, but they did have some odd ways. They followed regulations a lot more carefully than most Americans, even if those rules didn't make much sense. I still remember standing with them in a chow line when an alert siren rang outside. The SEALs and I looked at each other as the Brits all dove to the floor. Apparently they had standing orders to take cover whenever that alarm went off, even though it went off a lot.

We moved ahead and got food while the others waited for the all-clear. It wasn't a bad rule, in retrospect.

We'd come to the city that day for a mission on the western side of town, in a packed district of low-slung yellow and tan buildings that dotted a landscape of empty lots. Those sites had been houses just a few years before; destroyed by fighting and insurgent attacks, they'd been bulldozed away to improve security as well as the view.

The view wasn't much. Basra is a dry, hot town near Kuwait. Much of the surrounding area is desert, and the streets were arid, the air fetid. Barriers had been built by the British on some of the roads to slow traffic down. Along others there were small bushes that were supposed to add a little green.

Our target was an insurgent cell leader who had been directing local operations. We found him without any trouble and brought him back to the base. But when we got there, he began playing games. He stopped cooperating and made it clear that he wasn't going to help either the Americans or the British.

And then he started in on me.

"You are a Muslim," he told me, playing the religion card. "Why are you working with the infidels?"

"Give me one reason you call yourself Muslim," I countered. "The word means peaceful. But you are killing people. Where is peace?"

"No. You don't understand Islam. Those guys took over our country."

"Why would they do that?" I answered. "They don't need it. They came to release us from Saddam."

"You don't understand. No, no, no. This is a conspiracy from multiple countries to destroy our country and religion."

"When we fail, we blame conspiracies," I told him. "But it is our failure."

He kept insisting that I didn't understand. The world was out to get Iraq and to destroy Islam.

We spoke for a while. It was a typically frustrating conversation. The man was not well educated and fell back on a very simple formula. He started with what he considered a basic truth: the world is conspiring against Iraq and Islam. Because of that, he said, we must destroy our enemies. That was his entire argument, and I suppose the whole scope of his worldview. He could reason from A to B, but not get to C or D, let alone examine the premise of A. And no amount of logic could convince him he was wrong.

Even if he had been more intelligent, there was too much at stake for him to examine his beliefs, let alone change them. For imagine what would happen if he did: his inevitable conclusion would be that he was a murderer. And few people want to face that.

The man was depressingly typical of the suspects we captured as time went on, but it is hard to stereotype them all. More educated people made more sophisticated arguments. They usually cited American mistakes.

"The Americans killed this, the Americans killed that," they would say when talking to me. "What is your answer?"

"You are right," would be my answer. "They have made mistakes. It's war. There are always mistakes. But what are we doing to help our country? How are we fixing ourselves so that we don't need dictators or help from the outside?"

People who were educated and yet still joined the insurgency were the most frustrating to me. They had real potential to help Iraq—they were exactly the people that a struggling country needs—but they were destroying it instead. I told more than one, "Why are you not fighting with your pen instead of an AK? With your education and science—you can make a tremendous community and country."

These discussions and arguments had no effect on them, much less on the entire situation in Iraq. They were between two men, or at most three or four. Even if I had changed their views—and I don't believe that I ever did—there were still thousands and thousands of others who remained unconvinced.

**MENTIONING THE BRITISH** reminds me of a story that illustrates how far my command of English had come. American English, I should say.

Or maybe SEAL English.

The British commander of Nasiriya—I believe he was a colonel—asked to see me while we were in the area. When we met, he prompted me to tell him what was going on with the local population. He wanted to know what sort of things I had heard from talking to suspects and people on the street (hatred for anyone who wasn't part of their group), whether it differed from elsewhere in Iraq (not really), and in general what I thought the mood of the people was (ugly).

I talked to him the way I talked with the SEALs. It wasn't a conscious thing, but apparently I must have mixed in a lot of four-letter words as I spoke.

"Thank you for your briefing," said the colonel when I was done. "But I do believe that if you could not say the word 'fuck,' your speeches would be only half as long."

I laughed. He was probably right.

"The SEALs taught you very well," he added.


**NASIRIYA HAD BEEN** the scene of some nasty fighting during the very early days of the war. It was also the area where Jessica Lynch was taken prisoner and later rescued by U.S. personnel. Since that time, it had been comparatively quiet—not a safe haven by any means, but nowhere near as bad as Baghdad or Mosul or many other cities where sizable populations of Sunni as well as Shia made for a volatile mix and plenty of targets.

The Iraqi ICTF unit we were working with was assigned to pull security for a unit of U.S. Army Rangers who'd been given a tip about a house that was being used to store IEDs. The Rangers planned to go into the house, wake up its owner, and search it. The house was surrounded by a wall; to set up their assault, they had to climb over it. I went over to them as they discussed what they were doing and suggested that they might want me along, since they had no translator.

"Oh, no, we're good," said one of the Rangers. "We're ready to rock."

"Then take me with you."

"We don't need you. Thanks."

"If you climbed a wall in my yard in the middle of the night and I saw you, I would shoot," I told them. "So I think maybe—"

"No, no. We're good, we're good," he insisted.

So I stood back and watched. The first soldier went over—and was shot by the owner of the house, who thought he was being robbed.

As soon as he was shot, I started to the wall. I saw someone taking aim and firing from the third floor of the house. I pulled my rifle up—because we were working with the Iraqi forces, I had permission to carry a gun—and laid into the building, firing to chase him back. Then I lowered my aim to the second floor, hoping to keep him from getting downstairs. I changed magazines like a madman, running through practically every bullet I'd brought with me—enough so that the video image we saw later from a UAV overhead painted my gun bright white.

The Ranger was rescued, and since he wasn't hurt too badly, I suppose the story does have something of a happy or at least not terribly sad ending. But the intelligence that had taken them to the house turned out to be bad: the Iraqi was a traffic officer; he'd fired because he thought he was being attacked by insurgents.

The bad information had probably been passed along by someone hoping to cause him grief, which obviously they succeeded in doing. The whole mess was straightened out without further loss of life, fortunately.

Even among ourselves, you could never be too careful about information or a source—sometimes the people you least suspected were guilty.

We had a translator who wanted to do a good job in the worst way, or so he claimed. He started copying everything I did, from the way I talked to the way I walked, from how I dressed to how I cursed.

We were brothers, don't you know?

In his mind, maybe. He was what the kids these days call a "try hard"—he tried hard, but too hard, to make an impression. He started developing sources on his own time, trying to find insurgents in Baghdad. Then he brought the "intel" he developed to the SEAL commanders, suggesting that they authorize missions.

The problem was, his information was generally about Sunni insurgents, and we were assigned to hunt Shia.

Around that same time we got information about a cell in east Baghdad that worked out of a house. The mission was planned, and we took a source with us to the house. There were several people in the house when we got there. They seemed bewildered, but offered no resistance, insisting there had been a mistake.

Admittedly, this was what nearly everyone said when we arrived. A mujahideen cell leader would not, as a general rule, admit who he was when first confronted. So initially the SEALs weren't surprised or convinced. They called the source in and asked him to confirm that they had captured the right plotters.

He poked his head in the room, then poked it out.

"Those are the men," he said.

The glimpse around the room couldn't have lasted more than two seconds, if that. His response seemed much too quick to me, so I went up and found my boss. The SEAL team chief also felt something wasn't right—the men had protested too logically, and the source seemed too dismissive of the SEALs' concerns.

"I have an idea," I told him. "Wait until I try it, then we'll know."

The chief—he's still on active duty so we'll call him Bear—gave me a strange look, but he trusted me and didn't object when I went inside. A few minutes later, I came out dressed in one of the men's clothes. They were traditional Iraqi clothes—loose-fitting pants, baggy shirt—very different than the fatigues I'd been in.

Bear was amused, but hid his smile as he walked me over to the informer. With every step, our act intensified—I was his prisoner, and he was determined to take me in and hand me over to the authorities.

"We found another," said Bear, pushing me in front of the informer. "Is he one of them?"

"Yes, yes, he's bad, he's bad, he's bad," said the informer, shaking his head and scowling in my direction before quickly turning away.

Bear ended up having everyone released. Needless to say, we never worked with that informer again.

# 11

# FRIENDS, NEIGHBORS, AND SNIPERS

**M**ATCHING WITS WITH bad guys on missions was always interesting. Equally challenging, but very different, were missions where I accompanied SEAL sniper teams as they did overwatches in various areas.

I started doing sniper missions very early on—I'd accompanied a team in Mosul for the elections—and eventually came to specialize in them. They were not only challenging but long, generally running up to twenty-four hours. Most terps tried to avoid them, but that was exactly why I liked them.

On an overwatch mission, a team of SEAL snipers would set up a position where they could watch a specific area. Usually this meant going on the roof of a house, which in Iraq were mostly flat and nearly always used as a patio would be used in America. From the roof, the snipers would watch an area while a unit patrolled, searched, or went into a house to make an arrest. Or they might keep an eye on a place where there had been trouble—say an area where IEDs were being planted, or a government building that was believed to be targeted by bombers.

While the number of people assigned to the mission varied, usually there would be one or two snipers in the house, along with two or three men providing security. More SEALs might be used initially when the house was selected, just to make sure there was no trouble, and at various points, different Iraqi units and their members joined us. For the most part, though, overwatches were conducted by a small subset of the entire platoon. That meant there was less firepower immediately available if something went wrong—or if things went *right* and the snipers themselves were targeted.

While there were operations where the SEALs used unoccupied buildings, this wasn't possible in many cases. The houses had to be selected based on tactical criteria—in the simplest terms, the snipers needed a position where they had a good view of the surroundings and were well positioned to protect the ground troops or civilians in the area. That generally meant going into someone's home.

Unlike missions where we were sent to arrest someone, there were no forced entries to these houses. We basically showed up and knocked on the door. You didn't get to volunteer your house, and generally it wasn't an assignment you could refuse either. That made the situation more than a little delicate. While the family would be compensated for their trouble, no amount of money really could make up for what was, under even the best of circumstances, a huge inconvenience.

The *worst* circumstance could be dire catastrophe. There was *always* a possibility that the snipers and therefore the house would become targets. And in Iraq, being a target could easily mean obliteration.

With the exception of Dan, no one was injured on any of the missions that I was on. The families were always well protected, and the damage to their homes minimal. That was probably as much a function of luck as the precautions the SEALs took, but the SEALs very generously gave me credit as well. A few, including my friend Chris Kyle, say I helped save many lives. I'm grateful that they think that.

The Americans usually did their best to protect the inhabitants and make them comfortable, but uninvited houseguests are never truly welcome. My job was to be a diplomat as well as a translator. I would tell the family as much as I could about what was going on; while there were always limits, I would never lie to them. I'd be honest about the fact that we were a serious inconvenience.

I can't remember anyone trying to force the SEALs out or actively resisting—the SEALs were all heavily armed and there would have been no sense. But the reception wasn't as negative as you might imagine. Most people accepted the SEALs' presence, at least grudgingly; many even claimed to understand that the SEALs were trying to keep people safe, including the family in the house. Every so often a person actually welcomed them, if only out of curiosity.

As I started to get used to the missions, I got better at finding ways of putting people at ease. More than once I acted as a grocer and chef, going out to the marketplace to pick up some food and coming back to cook. Buying the family food—we never used their money—was one way of making a bond with them. It also let me scout the area discreetly. Going out also tended to make it less obvious that Americans were in the house—no activity at a home early in the day was a dead giveaway that something was up, and it wasn't smart to broadcast that fact to the insurgents until absolutely necessary.

A few times I took a family member out with me. I had my pistol under my clothes and watched the person closely, but by 2005 and 2006, when the overwatches really picked up, I'd become a pretty good judge of character. It was easy to tell which side the people were on within the first few minutes of our arrival.

But even if the family opposed the American intervention and the new government, my immediate goal was to make them feel safe while we were there. Once in a while, that worked so well that they didn't want us to leave.

Small kindnesses paid big dividends. Iraq was still wracked by wrenching poverty and shortages. People lacked a lot of the basic necessities, and helping them out won many over. This didn't take much; one family we stayed with had no gas for their heater or stove. We called back to the camp and at night had a truck deliver propane to them. The old lady whose house it was wouldn't let us go when we were scheduled to.

"If you leave now," she told the SEAL in charge of the operation, "I will run out of the house screaming that the Americans are here, and you will have a lot of trouble."

He called the head shed and told them we had to stay for another twenty-four hours.

I learned that it was a good idea for the family and at least some of the Americans to eat together. This was another part of the personal diplomacy, another little step in helping build some trust. There was a larger purpose to it, beyond calming the occupants of the house. If fighting an insurgency is all about winning over hearts and minds, it can be best done on a one-to-one basis, one family at a time. Showing people that the Americans were on their side—proving that they wanted to make them safe, not take over the country—and that they weren't monsters contributed to the overall war effort.

None of this was a usual part of an interpreter's job, and at first I caught some grief because of things like going out of the house with the people to shop. After a while, though, the SEALs' supervisors came to see that what I was doing was helping them a great deal. If the people inside the house were not unhappy, they were much easier to watch—and there was much less need to be wary of them. If the mood inside the house was calm, the snipers could do their job without interruption. And so the snipers started asking that I go along all the time. I was happy to oblige.

**I'D LONG AGO** passed the stage of being a "regular" interpreter. It wasn't part of a conscious plan. A lot of it was just self-preservation: I simply didn't want myself or the people I was with to be targets, or at least more vulnerable targets than necessary. But it was also an outgrowth of my personality. I couldn't sit inside a house without doing something. I had to move, I had to *act*. If I was capable of doing something, I felt I should do it.

I had to be involved in the fight.

It was one thing to win over the snipers and the noncommissioned officers in charge of the units and quite another to win over the officers, who tended to be much more cautious, or maybe just more observant of the rules and regulations.

I remember a conversation with someone in the head shed who told me, point-blank, not to leave a house once I was in it.

"You don't own me," I told him. "I am Iraqi. I have to do what I have to do."

"Johnny, how are we going to save you if something happens?" asked the officer, trying to reason with me. "We have a responsibility to protect you, but you're making it difficult."

"I know what I am doing. I know the risks. You don't have to protect me."

We argued for a while, and I'm not sure that I ever really convinced him—but I continued to go out. Gradually he stopped questioning me. When people came to understand that I took care of business, they stopped bugging me.

Or maybe I just heard them less and less.

**I CAN'T MENTION** SEAL snipers without mentioning my friend Chris Kyle, who in a lot of ways is the reason I wrote this book. I happen to be mentioned, in disguise, in his book, *American Sniper,* and it was Chris who urged that this book be written. I owe him, and all of his SEAL friends, a very large debt of gratitude.

I worked with him for only a short while when he was deployed with Team 3 in Baghdad. I liked him immediately and we became great friends. He was very humble and respectful, easygoing and friendly. We came from very different backgrounds and religions, but there was never any friction because of it. He did his best to teach me a few things about bolt rifles, long-range shooting, and hunting as we passed the time between missions.

His Texas accent was hard to understand, though.

"Speak English!" I told him constantly.

He'd just laugh and make his Texas drawl even deeper. He was a great jokester and a fun person; his death still grieves me. I was lucky to see him not long before he was killed, and I still treasure that memory.

**THE EXAMPLE OF** Chris and other snipers was very much in my mind when the SEALs began training a group of Iraqi soldiers to perform overwatch as snipers.

The SEAL unit's XO—the executive officer, or second in charge—asked that I get involved. I was reluctant. Having seen other Iraqi army units in action, I barely trusted these guys, and I must admit to some prejudice about the Iraqis' fighting abilities. But gradually the dozen or so men won me over with a good work ethic and sincerity.

I didn't teach them anything about weapons, of course, but I shared everything I knew about dealing with the families and strategies for gathering intel. I worked with the SEALs to make their exercises more realistic, booby-trapping targets and adding extra difficulties to the exercises.

I have to admit that I was proud of the Iraqi group when they "graduated" from the training sessions and began going out on missions with the SEALs. They weren't SEALs, but they were probably the most professional group of non-American soldiers I worked with in Iraq.


**BACK IN THE STATES,** Tatt was working on getting us out. Congress had passed the law making it easier for Iraqis who'd worked with the Americans to emigrate; it provided special immigrant visas which were supposed to be in plentiful supply. Tatt was excited when he reviewed the requirements. Not only did I qualify for the program, but the law allowed for a large number of immigrants and streamlined the approval process.

At least it was supposed to. The paperwork proved as daunting as ever. Ironically, the easiest part was getting recommendations from the many officers and others I'd worked with. Men I barely remembered came forward to help Tatt, writing testimonials that made my eyes tear. They cited hundreds of missions I'd gone on, and talked about life-and-death situations that I barely remembered.

It was the "routine" part of the documentation that became the barrier. Asking for a birth certificate in America is commonplace. In Iraq, it's unusual. Our record-keeping traditions are, should we say, very different from those in America.

Consistent spelling of names from one document to another is the exception rather than the rule. Spelling proved an Achilles' heel, as several times the process of reviewing my application came to a complete halt as the spelling of a name on one record didn't match the spelling on another. Tatt worked furiously to try to sort things out. Especially frustrating for him were the "normal" bureaucratic delays—it could take months for the State Department, say, to answer a simple inquiry. Their answer might contain another question. Several times he felt as if he was going back to square one.

The SEALs have an incredible informal network, both inside and outside the service; Tatt called in favors at the Pentagon and elsewhere as he put the package together. But the wheels of government moved at glacier pace, and while everyone agreed getting me out was a priority, he began to fear it would never happen.

Fortunately, Tatt didn't share his despair with me. He continued to check in, using e-mail and occasional phone calls. He was optimistic about the process and our hopes—probably more so than he had a right to be. I passed those feelings on to Soheila, who by now was in need of every piece of optimism she could get. If things had calmed down in Mosul, she didn't see it. She spoke constantly of escaping, desperation in her voice.

Another person might have given up at that point, collapsed into a weeping, paralyzed shell. Soheila wasn't like that; she was a fighter, a survivor. But the pressure of the war had clearly become too intense. I ached to help her, but all I could do was repeat optimistic lines about how we would soon be free and in America.

*Lines,* not *lies.* I certainly believed them, for I had no other choice—if I didn't believe we would be safe and free one day, I would have collapsed into a weepy, paralyzed person myself. I forced myself to be optimistic when I talked with her.

Optimism is a precious commodity in wartime, and for all the cigarettes and booze I consumed at what for me was a record pace, I found little to boost my mood for real. Only work, and being around the SEALs, made me feel whole; only my SEAL brothers made me feel there was hope for the future.

IF I'D BEEN tempted to dismiss Soheila's concerns for her safety, a short trip I made back to Mosul more than demonstrated that they were real.

We were working with an Iraqi unit that was assigned to strike an insurgent base inside an apartment complex. Because of the situation, the SEALs didn't need me as a translator or a liaison; instead, they assigned me to scout the area, then basically watch their backs during the operation. They gave me a radio and sent me out. I walked the area, surveying the complex and then finding a good vantage point to watch for enemy reinforcements. At least from my perspective, it turned out to be an easy operation; the insurgents had gotten cocky and were mostly off guard. I stayed in my vantage point, isolated and safe, filing routine reports throughout the day.

It was the walk through the nearby streets that was hard. Rubble lay in small piles next to the hulls of buildings, landslides ignited by nearby explosives. Bodies were cut up and littered the street—heads separated from torsos. The gore was incredible, even to someone who'd witnessed years of combat.

The block where I'd grown up?

It was far from the apartment complex, and in no way close to the American installations. But it, too, had been wracked by war. The neat if humble apartments and buildings I remembered were now either completely destroyed or, worse, battered from IEDs and other explosions nearby. My old home had been destroyed; the street looked like an abandoned battlefield, which I suppose it was.

The men who did this were supposedly working for God, but how can that be? If you are working for God, why would you harm those he created?

Separating a man's head from his body—what do children think when they see that? What is the effect on wives and sisters, daughters and friends?

Is that the reaction God wanted?

I know what I felt. I didn't think that the murderers were men of God. I knew they were savages and devils. Their violence had achieved the opposite of what they intended.

Certainly people were afraid. But the murderers never spoke of that as a goal. They cloaked their evil in lofty lies about Paradise and protecting our religion.

There was a lot of hatred in the city, but people were not entirely blind to the true nature of what was going on, and what the people who were targeting Americans were really like.

During my short time in Mosul, I heard comments like this:

*"Your son was captured by the Americans? Oh, that's good luck—they will not kill him."*

*"The government? Too bad—they are corrupt. You are going to pay a lot of money to get him back."*

*"Al-Qaeda? Oh . . . they are corrupt, and he is going to die."*

The physical danger that people lived in was terrible. Even those who were spared direct pain suffered. I would imagine that the things the children saw will have a deep effect on them for the rest of their lives. My children, I am sure, were affected. But there was nothing I or anyone else could do to shelter them from the horrors as long as they stayed in the city. Evil always loomed nearby, and there were much worse things than simply seeing a body in the street.

**SOME WEEKS LATER,** Soheila was inside our house with the rest of the family when she heard several cars screech to a stop on the street. She and our sister-in-law quickly put the children to bed, then ran out into the hallway. Our house had a little vestibule, separating the outside door from another inner door. The space was small, but psychologically it was large, an important barrier to the outside.

The yelling from the cars in front made it clear that the men who'd driven up were mujahideen. They were searching for someone who had the same name as one of the children inside.

"Where is his house?" shouted one. "We must find him."

"Search the houses!"

Soheila put her body against the door. So did my sister-in-law. They started praying, saying the words a Muslim uses when burying the dead.

"Where is he?!"

The men outside were so close, Soheila could hear them charging the bolts on their AKs.

"If they come into the house, we will attack them and take their weapons," she whispered to my sister-in-law. "We will fight them. We will not let them take the kids."

The women waited. The men rushed into a house nearby and came out with someone who was put into the trunk of a car.

"Where's the other house!" demanded the mujahideen. "The other one we need to get. Where?"

Someone answered. There were more shouts, and then the sound of men getting into cars and driving off.

Both women collapsed onto the floor when the cars were gone, their bodies shaking. When finally they were able to get up, Soheila called me and told me what had happened. I immediately called a relative, who drove them to a safe house in a village far away. They stayed for two weeks before coming home.


**IMPRESSED BY MY** work with the Iraqi troops, a major with the ICTF invited me to go to share a few drinks one night. We went out and after a round or so, he asked what my plans for the future were.

I was noncommittal, a very valid response in Iraq.

"Why don't you come to work with us here?" he asked, disappointed that I hadn't jumped at the chance. "We will make you an officer, find you a house on the base—it will be a good life."

He made it sound very attractive, but I wasn't tempted. If I didn't make it to America, I knew I was already doing what I wanted to do—work with the SEALs. I wasn't going to give that up for anyone or anything.

Several other offers followed; I had a chance to work with other American military units as well as Iraqi. But I always turned them down. You don't leave the best.

**THE MISSIONS CONTINUED,** one blurring into the next. From Mosul we went to Fallujah, then to Basra, and from there to Nasiriya.

Or was it the other way around? Did we go to all or any of these places?

In my memories, this time is a never-ending panorama of violence, of arrests, of people proclaiming to believe in God yet acting against His wishes. I remember snatches of conversations, but not their meanings. I remember my heart pounding, but can't picture exactly why. I remember running, but now don't know if it was real or a piece of a dream.

My reputation among the militia grew, just as it had among the al-Qaeda terrorists. One of my SEAL friends, Mikey U, says there was a fifty-thousand-dollar bounty on my head. I don't doubt it. By this time I was well known among the insurgents we targeted. Their bounty didn't matter. I'd come to hate them even more than they hated me, and I had plenty of reason.

Mikey U was with Team 10 at the time. He was a great warrior and one of those people whom you know you can completely trust the first time they look you in the eye. While he was in Iraq, he coordinated the work with the ERU, and we worked closely while he was there. The platoon did upwards of eighty or ninety operations during the roughly six months they were in Baghdad. A good number were bloody, with militia members trying to ambush or directly fight the SEALs and other units wherever they operated, and the SEALs seeking out the worst of the groups for apprehension.

The SEALs weren't permitted in certain areas or places, although sometimes the restrictions could seem very arbitrary. At one point while I was with Mikey U, we were assigned to look for a man working with the Shia militia. We ended up on a building right next to a mosque. It was so close that a person could literally step across from one roof to the other without any fear of falling.

I *could* do that. The SEALs couldn't—they weren't allowed on mosque grounds.

We were up on the house roof, looking for our jackpot, when I spotted a man not far away on the mosque's roof. I walked over, alone. The man stood looking at me. He was obviously our jackpot; it was far too late for anyone to be on the roof unless they had just hopped over to escape our search.

"What are you doing?" I asked.

He said something inane and innocuous.

"We are looking for Muhammad," I told him.

"Muhammad? That is not me."

"Who are you?" I asked.

He said his name—which, unfortunately for him, was the name of the man we were looking for.

"Prove it," I said. "Let me see."

He crossed to my roof, thinking he was free.

"I lied about who we were looking for," I told him, repeating his full name and grabbing him. "You are coming with us."

He came along quietly, knowing he had given himself away.

**I DON'T WANT** to leave you with the impression that every mission we had was successful or that things always went according to plan. In fact, things probably never went 100 percent as intended, and although we usually succeeded, there were plenty of frustrations and wasted nights.

One of our best and most elaborate plans, in fact, came to nothing. This was another mission with the Quiet Man, who could be quite clever when it came to designing operations.

The snipers were working in a Baghdad neighborhood but for some reason weren't seeing any action. Apparently the bad guys somehow knew when they were coming and had enough sense to stay away. So the Quiet Man and I discussed the situation and came up with what in retrospect seems like a pretty obvious idea: make the bad guys come to us.

How?

The insurgents had a habit of ambushing Humvees and other vehicles hit by IEDs or disabled in some way. I suggested that we fake an incident and pick them off when they came.

One night just after twelve, a Humvee drove through an iffy Baghdad neighborhood and was disabled by a bomb. The wounded victims crawled into a nearby house. They were easy pickings; no American backup was nearby.

The men, in fact, were playacting. We'd taken over the house they'd crawled to several hours before and were hiding inside, waiting for them. The explosion, the wounds—everything was fake.

Three or four cars showed up a few minutes later, spun around the area, then took off. This was typical insurgent procedure. So was the arrival of children several minutes after that. You see, the insurgents didn't want to expose themselves to danger, but had no compunction about sending kids. The children went through the Humvee, found the house where the men had gone to, then ran off.

Within seconds, the cars were back. The street flooded with men with AKs. Other men took out their cell phones and began calling for reinforcements.

But just as they were about to storm the house—and before we had fired—a single police car arrived. The man took a look around and began yelling at the others to leave.

The crowd of mujahideen took off. Our operation was a dud.

Was it just a coincidence that the cop arrived? Was he a good guy who had singlehandedly saved (he thought) some wounded Americans? A hero who risked his life against a dozen or more killers?

Or was he a member of the militia who'd somehow been tipped off or who otherwise guessed that the incident was staged?

We never found out. Either possibility—and maybe a few more—makes sense. In any event, the elaborate ruse went for naught. Days' worth of preparation had been wasted.

That was Iraq.


ONE TRIP ESPECIALLY stands out from the fog of these years, a mission to Diyala Province. We were working with a unit of Army Rangers, trying to secure a terror cell led by a man the Americans called "the Prince."

If he had some actual claim to royalty, it was never explained to me. More likely it was just a nickname or a code name they had invented to describe his role in the insurgency.

Diyala is in the northeast of Iraq, bordering on Iran. By this time in the war, Iran was contributing quite a bit to the violence, arming and advising Shia militia and other terrorists almost openly.

Iran's influence made things in Iraq considerably worse than they might have been—but I am getting away from my story.

The target building was rather large, and the plan to go in was worked out carefully by the SEALs, who would make the actual assault while the Rangers pulled security outside. Since we were anticipating meeting several people and hoped not to have to use our weapons, I was one of the first people in.

We got in without a problem—the main door was neither locked nor guarded, if I'm remembering right—and started moving down the hall. I noticed a dozen or more shoes outside one of the rooms at the far end and pointed it out to one of the SEALs.

"You should check that room," I told him.

"Not yet," he grunted. "We have to do it according to our plan. First we get these rooms."

"Do what you want," I told him. "There are a lot of sandals there. That means there a lot of people inside the room."

"But this is our plan."

You can't argue with a SEAL once he has his mind made up. The SEALs worked their way cautiously down the hall, secured the rest of the building, and only then discovered that everyone was inside the room I'd pointed out.

Given how quickly they moved, it wasn't that big a deal. Still . . .

There were a dozen or so men in the room. None offered any resistance. We'd brought two other terps along for the mission so they could gain experience; both were relatively new. After making sure everything was under control, I left them to interview the men and went outside to get a smoke.

I found one of the Ranger sergeants in front of the building and started talking. Our conversation hadn't gotten very far when suddenly we heard someone walking down the street. The sergeant raised his gun, and I raised mine.

Two men approached from the shadows. They had weapons

strung on their bodies; one carried a rocket-propelled grenade launcher, its distinctive shape like a miniature minaret looming over his head.

"Stop!" I yelled. "Stop, stop."

The men started to run—toward us. Their guns swung forward.

"Stop!" I repeated.

They were no more than a dozen yards away, clearly hostile. The sergeant fired, and I fired. Both men fell.

I walked over quickly with the Ranger. The men had grenades arranged on their chests; he theorized that they had planned on blowing themselves up once they got inside the building.

We pulled the bodies aside and resumed our watch, not talking now. This was one of those times when minutes and danger built together, where every second seemed to increase the potential for danger. Tension wrapped itself around my neck, stinging my muscles numb.

I went back inside the building, wondering why we were still here. The SEAL in charge told me that no one had admitted anything. He wasn't going to leave without figuring out whether the men were innocent or not. The two terps hadn't had much success in getting them to say anything beyond the names on their IDs.

Often the key to finding out what was going on was to find the first weak link; once one person talked, other mouths began to open. I had the men blindfolded and taken out to the garden in the back. I approached each one, pausing to ask a question or two. What I was *really* doing was looking for that weak link, touching them gently, invading their space. Their reactions told me a lot—a calm man who didn't move would be harder to break, while a man who jerked back when I tapped his shoulder was a much better bet.

I found one who practically jumped out of his skin when I spoke to him.

The starting point.

"He comes with me," I said.

We went through to the front of the building. The bodies of the men the sergeant and I had killed were still lying nearby.

"Take his blindfold off," I told the SEALs who were guarding him. I didn't give him a chance to thank me before continuing. "You see those guys? We shot them because they didn't cooperate with us."

A lie, yes, but a useful one. The man shook.

"I don't want you to be the third one," I continued. "I know you have a family. You want to go back to them, and I don't blame you."

"Yes, yes," he stuttered.

"Which one is the Prince?"

"Oh, you know. Let me think. Let me think. Can I get a drink of water?"

Once anyone made a request, I knew they would cooperate. The trick was to make sure that what they said was the truth, not what they thought I wanted to hear.

I got him the water, and he thought for a while, and then agreed to help. He told me which of the men inside was the Prince.

The problem was that I couldn't trust what he said. He was too fearful, too worried that I would do something to him. So I came up with another little ruse. I went back into the garden and had everyone's blindfold removed, except for the man my informant had fingered as the Prince.

"Thank you. We have the Prince now," I announced, starting to lead him away.

The others hung their heads, dispirited—if I'd been wrong, there would have been relief, at least from one of them.

We took the blindfolded Prince aside and began questioning him again. By now he realized we weren't going to accept his lies and leave, and he gave himself up, admitting who he was. As so often happened, that admission led immediately to more information about the cell he'd run. He gave us other names and intel, all of which led to other arrests.

**FEAR AND NERVOUSNESS** were often important indicators, sometimes of truth, sometimes of lies—and always of the great danger that loomed at every corner. Back in Baghdad, we were assigned to help get information on a local al-Qaeda cell. An informant had been found who claimed to know where one of the al-Qaeda operatives was holed up; he agreed to take us to the safe house.

The SEALs were joined by an American observer, an officer who'd apparently come to see how they were doing things. I can't recall now what his name or rank was; he was definitely an officer but not directly connected with the SEAL command.

I went over the mission with our informant before we started, asking him about where we were going and what else he knew. The area was in a place where al-Qaeda operated, and the suspect was on the list of people we were supposed to be looking for. But there was something a bit off about what the informant told us. What he was saying didn't quite fit with the map of the area where he said we would find the jackpot.

The way he talked made it clear he was *very* nervous. That wasn't necessarily unusual—there was always good reason to be nervous in Iraq—but I became suspicious. Was he worried that he would be killed? Or was he leading us to an ambush and was afraid I would figure it out?

I talked it over with the platoon leaders. Admittedly, my doubts were vague; I was working with emotion, not science. With no specific reason to stop the operation, the SEALs decided to proceed, mapping out a plan that would minimize our exposure if things went sour.

We boarded Strykers and drove to the general vicinity of the house the informant had marked. When we got out, I told the NCO in charge that I would take the informer and go a little ahead on foot to scout; they should follow at a safe distance. Anyone watching would think that we were two Iraqis not connected with the American force; this way we would find the target house and make sure there was no ambush without exposing the SEALs.

The informant and I walked down a narrow street, heading for the house he'd identified. His nervousness increased by the step. His breathing became less and less regular, and I'm sure his heart was pounding hard enough to leave his chest. It was late at night; the only light we had to guide us came from the moon and stars. He glanced around continually as we went, as if either he was unsure where he was or he expected something to come out of the shadows.

Big difference, but I couldn't tell which it might be.

We reached an intersection and he paused, examining each way or maybe debating internally before deciding how to turn. After five more minutes of walking, he stopped in front of a house.

"This is it," he said.

I glanced at the place. It looked nothing like the house he had described back at the base.

"Are you sure?" I asked.

"No," he admitted.

"No?"

"No . . . I . . . uh, I think I am wrong," he confessed. "I'm sure I am wrong. This is not it."

"Where then?"

"It must be this way."

We started walking again. He stopped in front of another house, but his body language made it clear he was just as tentative as before.

"This isn't the house," I told him.

"No . . ."

"Where *is* the house?"

"I—it's, uh . . ."

"Is there a house?"

"Yes . . . I . . . no . . . uh . . ."

I grabbed him and threw him against the wall. Then I pulled out my pistol and held it to his neck.

"I'll kill you on the spot if you take us to an ambush," I threatened. I pushed the pistol into his neck. The SEALs were too far away to see what was going on, and I wasn't about to communicate this over the radio. "I have no trouble shooting you," I told him. "Take us to the target's house right now. Now!"

"Yes, yes, I will."

I radioed back that we'd been a little confused but were now straightened out and they should keep following us. The informant took me to a house a short distance away. He seemed to have calmed a bit, as if seeing the gun had flipped a switch for him.

For good or ill, I couldn't be sure.

The place he took me to was quiet and unlit. I could tell it was abandoned—the garage was wide open, unusual in Baghdad.

"I need an EOD guy to check the house," I told the SEALs.

The explosives expert was called in and the house searched for booby traps as the area was secured.

Standard operating procedure called for the homes on both sides of the house to be evacuated, but in this case I suspected that we were being watched—I still thought in the back of my mind that this was a setup. If the families were taken outside, they might be targeted, so I told the SEALs to leave the families where they were and do the search with them in place. They did.

There were no booby traps and no explosives. But there were al-Qaeda documents in one of the rooms of the house, so it had been a real hiding place for them.

Why had the informant led me around in different directions? Why had he been so afraid?

The truth is, I don't know. I didn't know then, and I'll never know now. Maybe he'd gotten lost earlier, or maybe he chickened out of a plan to lead us to a trap and took us to an old safe house instead. Maybe he wanted to do the right thing, then worried that he would be killed for it.

Maybe my threat convinced him I was the greater danger. Maybe he just decided he wanted to be righteous rather than evil. I never saw him again, so I don't know what his half of the story was.

When we got back to the base, we went over to the chow hall to get something to eat before debriefing the mission. The VIP guest started arguing with the SEALs. He wasn't talking to me, but I would have had to have been deaf not to hear.

"I never heard of a terp leading a mission," he told them. "I don't understand why you're letting him lead you."

I interrupted before any of the SEALs could answer.

"Hey, buddy, let's eat," I told him. "Then you and I can talk."

He grumbled something in response, but shut up. After we finished eating, we went to do the debrief. I'm not sure what he told the SEAL commanders or what they told him, but when they were done, he came to me and told me to explain myself. It was clear he thought I had too much autonomy. He seemed to think I should translate and do nothing else.

"The source made me uneasy," I told him. "Maybe it was an ambush. Should I have sent the SEALs in? Should I have sacrificed my brothers?"

He wasn't really satisfied. For some reason, he started talking about families whose houses were next door to the target, feeling it had been a huge violation of protocol not to evacuate them.

"You wanted to take the family into the street?" I said. "There were no obvious signs of bombs. If the mujahideen were watching, they would have shot the family, then blamed it on the Americans. What do you think would have happened with the media? Or the insurgents?"

Things had become so bad in Baghdad that the insurgents would routinely punish anyone seen to cooperate with Americans—even if that cooperation was simply avoiding a bomb. That was another reason to keep disruptions to a minimum; I didn't want to hurt people by helping them.

I talked to the VIP for a while, explaining my advice and my decisions. He clearly didn't know that much about Iraq, let alone how the terrorists we were dealing with operated, or what average Iraqis thought.

I doubt I convinced him, but he at least ended the conversation by being polite.

"You have my full support," he told me.

How much that was worth I have no idea, but I guess it was better than him saying I should be court-martialed.

GETTING COURT-MARTIALED—or, more accurately, fired—was hardly the worst thing that could have happened to me. Around this time I took a trip back to Mosul to see the family. I traveled in secret, and no one knew I was there.

Or so I thought.

A few days after I arrived, I was driving in the city when I noticed a car behind me. It sped up when I sped up, slowed when I slowed—never a good sign.

I watched them in the mirror when I reached a checkpoint. There were two men in the front, both bearded, both obviously watching me.

Not against the law. But about as obvious a warning as you could find anywhere in Iraq.

I sped off. Moments later they appeared behind me.

Once more I did my trick of slowing down and speeding up, until there was absolutely no doubt in my mind that they were following me. Fortunately, the street had enough traffic and people around that the men behind me couldn't do anything.

We drove for a short while, the other car shadowing me but never falling too far behind. Finally we came to a small valley and a stretch of road that was more open. I slowed; the car sped up. As the men pulled close, I started to veer to the side, as if to get off the road and let them go ahead. Then, as they drew next to me, I pushed my car hard to left, into them. I must have caught them completely by surprise, because I managed to slap into their car. The vehicle flew off the side of the road, spinning onto the side.

I hit the gas. After driving about a half mile and making sure they weren't still behind me, curiosity got the better of me and I turned around to see what had happened. As I drove back down the road, I saw a crowd had gathered by the side. They were staring at a car, upside down, in the ditch.

I made my way home via a circuitous route and didn't stay in town very long after that.

A FEW DAYS after I left, Soheila received an envelope at home. There was a letter inside, along with a single bullet.

"We know your husband is an infidel," read the letter. "We will kill you all."

There was more along the same lines, threats and lies. The cowards didn't even have the courage to sign the letter.

Soheila immediately called me on the phone.

"Don't worry about that," I told her.

"How can I not worry? They will kill us all."

From what was said and the way it was addressed, I felt the threat was really just addressed at me, but that wasn't much comfort to my wife. She said that others had gotten exactly the same kind of letter and then been killed.

"Don't worry," I told her. "I am safe. This is just what they do, to scare you."

"Well, that they have done."


BY NOW I WAS long past the realization that I had to escape Iraq, but I'd started to wonder if we really would get to America. The more that I accepted it as my new dream—the more I wanted it—the less possible it seemed.

Waiting had become its own kind of torture. Finally I decided that I couldn't, and shouldn't, think it would happen. I wasn't going to America. It was my dream, and because of that, it would only be a dream. It would never happen. Ever.

Because if I did think it would happen, if I kept wishing for it, I would be devastated if it didn't come true. If I couldn't go to America, it would be as if I had climbed an enormous mountain, then slipped as I reached for the summit. To dream so hard and fail—it was a loss I couldn't take. I'd be shattered.

I started telling myself the opposite of what I hoped. I told myself that America was impossible.

I told myself to plan for Iraq. Iraq was the opposite of a dream, but it was all I had. I steeled myself and imagined only that dismal black pit of never-ending turmoil and desperation. I would survive it, no matter what. Whatever it took, I would be hard enough.

Soheila, meanwhile, was working on her own plan. She kept it secret from everyone—including me, even though we were talking several times a day. She thought of it all the time, working on the nuances. My wife has very vivid and important dreams, ones that present omens, but this was not simply a dream. This was a plan, and plans require action. Finally, in January 2008, with the violence of bomb blasts and assassinations ringing in her ears, Soheila made her plan reality.

# 12

# SOHEILA ESCAPES

ONE WINTER DAY in 2008, a friend of a friend came to our house in Mosul and told Soheila that she had heard people talking about her, saying they would come and kidnap her and the children.

The person had connections with the mujahideen and had a reputation for honesty. Whether it was because of that, the letter with the bullet in it, or the bloodshed she'd seen around her, Soheila decided at that moment she could no longer stay in Mosul. She had to take the kids and escape to Baghdad.

While the fact that I was in Baghdad made it the obvious place for her to go, it wasn't the only reason. Soheila had an aunt in the city; if she couldn't stay with me at the base, she would hide with her aunt. She arranged a ride with a van driver who made regular trips to the city.

She didn't mention any of this to me, and told the children and my mother only enough so they wouldn't worry—or try to talk her out of it. Early one morning after getting the warning, she took our four kids and some belongings, and piled into a white van for what should have been a six-hour drive to her aunt's house.

There were a dozen or so other people in the van, all headed to Baghdad for various personal reasons. Every seat was full. Soheila didn't know anyone else in the van. She kept to herself and told the kids to be quiet, not wanting to attract attention.

The direct route to Baghdad, the one that most vehicles would have taken before the war, was subject to so many ambushes, IEDs, and assorted mayhem that few civilians ever went that way. In fact, military convoys avoided the route as well. Instead, everyone took a circuitous route east through Kurdish-controlled territory, greatly lessening the time they were in danger.

This van did exactly that. Once free of the city, the ride became a dull drone across mostly vacant, arid land, yellow boredom sifting between the windswept sand: a very welcome boredom, punctuated by anxiety as the van approached towns and cities. Fear ebbed as the ride continued, each slow-moving minute taking them closer to Baghdad and Soheila's dream of safety.

Hours after they started out, the van came to a checkpoint south of Kirkuk. This was not unexpected; they'd already gone through several other checkpoints on the open road. But as the vehicle pulled to a stop, Soheila glanced out the window and realized that the people manning the checkpoint weren't wearing uniforms. Instead, they wore the ragtag clothes of mujahideen, their faces covered with scarves to hide their identities.

The van was quickly surrounded by fifteen men, all brandishing rifles with long banana clips of ammo.

The driver glanced to the back before opening the door.

"Guys," he told his passengers, his voice soft but breaking, "do nothing. Maybe we will die, maybe we will go on without harm. It is up to God."

Soheila told the children to put their heads down as the men walked toward the bus. "I will be okay," she told them. "Just be good. Just be quiet."

As the gunmen walked around the van, Soheila practiced what she would say when they took them out:

*Kill us all, not just one.*

Sand whipped everywhere outside. It was hot; the desert sun was unmerciful. The land was bare as far as the eye could see—except for the mujahideen.

The gunmen conferred with one another, apparently unsure what to do. Finally, one began to yell.

"Men! Out! Out! Now! Or we will kill you where you sit."

The few young men who were passengers got out; they were pushed to the ground, hands bound behind their backs.

The kids began to cry. Soheila, sure she was going to die, tried to comfort them, but it was an impossible task.

"Ssshhh," she soothed. "Sssshhh."

The gunmen kept the young men on the ground and stalked around the van, occasionally stopping to talk among themselves. Gradually it became clear to Soheila that they had made some sort of mistake; they had stopped the van searching for someone or something that clearly wasn't there. They didn't know what to do—which made things even more dangerous.

An hour passed, then a second one. No other car, no other truck came close.

Soheila waited. The easiest thing for the mujahideen to do at that point was simply to kill everyone and leave. There'd be no witnesses, no one to pursue them.

*Kill us all,* she rehearsed. *Don't leave any of us. Above all, don't leave me.*

Finally, one of the gunmen walked to the van. Soheila felt her breath melt from her lungs. She clasped the children tightly.

"Go," the man told the driver. "You are not the vehicle we want. Go."

*Go!*

*GO!*

One of the mujahideen cut the bonds off the young men, who jumped into the van. The driver hastily put the vehicle into gear and drove away.

Soheila didn't breathe until the gunmen were out of sight. She was still trembling when she got to her aunt's in Baghdad, hours later.

SOHEILA NEVER TOLD me the story while we were in Iraq—never, in fact, until we started working on the book.

Thinking of it now, I am the one trembling: I'd not realized how close I came to losing everything precious to me.

Some things, maybe, are better off unknown.

SOHEILA HAD CALLED her aunt, so she wasn't surprised to see her in Baghdad. I, on the other hand, was stunned.

"Johnny, I'm here," she told me on my cell phone.

"Yes, I am talking to you."

"No, I am here—in Baghdad."

"What?"

"At my aunt's."

"What? Where are the children?"

"They're here, too. We're not going back."

I can't lie: my first reaction was tremendous joy. I wanted to see them all.

But in the next moment, I felt incredible anger and fear.

"Why did you risk our kids' lives?" I asked, not even knowing the extent of what had happened. "You're in danger here. Serious danger."

"Less than in Mosul. You don't know."

"I know the danger. It's everywhere."

"You don't know." She was steadfast and insistent—the fabled mama lion protecting her cubs. "Johnny, we needed to get out. Mosul was not safe. Our lives were threatened."

"It is safer than Baghdad."

"No, you don't know what it is like. You don't know."

"But even if that was true—you just came. Without a plan. Without telling me!"

"I had to come!"

You can imagine the rest of the conversation.

Soheila never gave an inch. She was not going back. My anger eventually settled into acceptance, then relief, and finally action. They were here; we had to make a plan for a permanent home.

I didn't trust her relatives, who were Shia. At the time, many of the most active insurgent groups in Baghdad were Shia, and I had no idea whether there might be some family connections with those groups. I'm not now accusing them, and wasn't then. I simply had no way of knowing, and ignorance was deadly. Trusting too much, even a relative, would have been insane. As much as I wanted to see my wife and kids, it wasn't safe even to do that. My presence would endanger them.

I told Soheila to look for an apartment, and only when she found one—it took about ten days—could I go and meet her and the kids.


GRADUALLY, I CAME to see that Soheila had made the right move. Mosul was, at that time, even more dangerous than Baghdad.

Regardless of how serious the threat she had heard really was, it could not have been ignored. Soheila would have had to flee somewhere. And how many times could she continue doing that?

There was also the fact that our separation was wearing on her and the kids, pushing them to a breaking point.

Of course, there's a certain male pride in me that hurts to admit that she was right and I was wrong—that I didn't know what was best for my family, or at least couldn't make it happen. But pride is a useless thing against danger.

Baghdad, meanwhile, had become more stable. I was seeing the bad side of it every night, the devils working against peace, but my immersion in the darker side kept me from seeing the growing light. While it was far from a paradise, sections of the city were now relatively peaceful, even safe—at least as far as that word had any meaning in Iraq. Soheila and the children could have a home in the city where they didn't have to hide all the time. And where I could stay at night without having to worry about being seen or spending days getting back to the base.

The apartment she found was old and small, with just one room. Even for two people it would have been too small, and we had four children. But it was in al-Mansour, a good area of Baghdad five or six miles from the airport. And we both knew it was temporary.

Soheila spent the next days and weeks asking around about possible houses or apartments we could move to, but it was hard. I was working, and she had to spend most of her time caring for the children. My mother came for a visit and surprised me with what elsewhere would have been a commonplace suggestion.

"Your apartment is too small," she told me. "Find another place. You have to think of your kids."

She was right but her point had real significance for us: we had to move not because of violence, but because our apartment was too small.

I don't know if that will make sense to anyone who hasn't lived it, but it was an incredibly liberating realization. Finally, life was becoming more routine.

Of course, it was also a major logistical problem, since finding a new place involved quite a bit of house hunting. I was working and Soheila had her hands full with the kids. We needed help. Without telling anyone, I borrowed a car and drove back to Mosul and our old house. I pleaded with my brother's widow, my sister-in-law, to come and help.

"Come to Baghdad and be with Soheila," I begged. "Come and help her find a better place. The kids need a better house to grow up in."

She agreed, and became a great help to us. Together, the women found a house we could rent not far from the apartment. It was much newer and bigger than the apartment—not opulent or even grand, but after living in one room for two months, it felt like one of Saddam's palaces. There was even a school within walking distance—and the route was not one favored by car bombers or other terrorists.

My older kids had lost a lot of school. It's hard to estimate, but it's likely they went about half the time they might have if there had been no war. Soheila enrolled them in the local school and then started working with them so they would be ready when school started up again in August.

We had no furniture in the house to speak of when we moved in. Suddenly items started arriving from nowhere—the SEALs had decided to help us, finding and donating items. I also ended up with a car—not the BMW that I coveted, but an older Mercedes that had been confiscated by the Iraqis during a raid. It technically wasn't my car; it belonged to the unit I was working with. But I was allowed to treat it like my own, and I did so, taking care of it and driving it on my off days as well as back and forth to the base.

The area was relatively well off, and maybe because of that, the neighbors were too polite to ask probing questions like where had we come from and whom I worked for. I'm not sure what their reactions would have been—and in any event, I wasn't about to put them to the test. I didn't get close to any of the neighbors, which lessened the chances that they would find out anything about my background or circumstances.

There were many adjustments to be made. With the tempo of operations slowing down a bit, the SEALs gave me more time to be with my family. I started staying with them at night regularly. But that itself became a problem: I had to get used to sleeping with my wife again. When she would move in the middle of the night, I would wake up in shock. It was oddly disorienting and strangely comforting at the same time.

Sometimes when I woke, I didn't know where I was. My mind would race through my escape plan. *What do I take, what way do I go?*

Then I would realize I was in my own bed, with nothing to fear. I'd feel a little ashamed at the moment of panic.

**MOSUL REMAINED** a terrible place, at least for my family. My brother-in-law was killed in 2008, undoubtedly by the mujahideen, though the exact circumstances have never been made clear. He hadn't been working with the Americans, so their motivation is somewhat murky. But then, they never really need much to justify killing anyone.

**BY NOW, EAST COAST** SEAL teams had taken over in Baghdad, and I worked with a series of platoons from Teams 2, 10, 4, and 8 as they helped different Iraqi units. We were assigned missions all across the country, acting almost like specialists in a hospital might, called in to make arrests or do some other job in a particularly tough area, or make an arrest in a sensitive area—a mosque or some other region where it was best that an Iraqi force lead the way. Typically, we would stay a few days, handle an assignment or two, and then head back to Baghdad. One time we were assigned to capture a cell leader in an area near the Iranian border; we walked fifteen miles to the target house, a long walk for me, if not the SEALs.

There were also plenty of assignments in the capital. Sadr City remained a hotbed for the terrorists, and any operation there was dangerous. One time we came under fire unexpectedly. As we waited for the Quick Reaction Force—in this case, a unit with heavily armored Abrams fighting vehicles—I took a gun from one of the Iraqis and laid down covering fire so the men nearby could move back to a better-protected position. I doubt I hit any of the militiamen firing at them, but I gave them enough pause to slow their gunfire and let the others retreat.

The missions had long ago assumed a certain sameness, and yet each one was unique in its own specific way. A raid on the Mother of All Mosques—Umm al-Qura in Baghdad—yielded AKs, pistols, and media propaganda. Trips into Sadr City yielded suspects and occasional gunfights, including one with ten insurgents and another where more than twenty militiamen were arrested.

I was working with Team 10 when we were assigned to arrest an important Shia militia leader before he could leave the country. The orders and information came very late—so late, in fact, that not only did we have to try to apprehend him at the airport, but by the time we got there he had already boarded the plane.

The Americans had no authority to board the plane or even stop it from taking off. Fortunately, we were working with an Iraqi unit. I went to the security people—both Jordanian—at the gate and demanded that the man be taken off.

They weren't impressed until I told them that they would be arrested for harboring an international criminal.

"We are with the Iraqi police, and we have no hesitation to arrest you," I told them. It was a bluff—we weren't authorized to arrest anyone except for our jackpot, and certainly we wouldn't have detained the Jordanians and created an international incident. Once you were aboard a foreign plane, you were generally considered to be under that country's protection, and any strong protest by Jordan would have released the plane and its passengers immediately—not to mention got myself and the Iraqi commander in a mountain of trouble. But the Jordanian security men didn't know that, and after a quick phone call they decided that it made no sense to risk arrest for a man wanted by the Iraqi government.

The door to the plane was opened and we were allowed on. But then we had another problem—identifying the terrorist.

The physical description I had been given could have matched about half of Iraq, and I had no seating chart to identify him. The only clue I had was intelligence that he was traveling with his family.

Not much to go on.

I knew he'd have a false ID; I also knew that if I couldn't positively identify him I wouldn't be able to remove him. The Jordanians would surely ask for proof, and any delay would surely prompt them to change their minds about holding the plane and letting me take the jackpot off.

As we walked through the cabin, I got a glimpse of a man with a family I thought might be my target. But there was no way to be sure. Rather than tipping my hand, I moved to the back of the plane. There I turned around and considered the situation. At any moment I expected the Jordanians to decide to kick me off. For time's sake I had to take a rough approach. So I started back up the aisle.

As I started past the aisle where the suspect was sitting, I suddenly stopped, as if noticing the girl sitting next to him on the aisle for the first time.

"Fatimah, how are you?" I said.

"Oh, fine, uncle," she said, speaking politely out of habit.

Fatimah was the name of the suspect's daughter. He grudgingly admitted he was the man we were seeking and we took him off the plane, under arrest.

Raids against kidnapping cells specializing in taking Sunnis; raids against cells specializing in taking Shia . . .

The weight of the war wore me down. There were bizarre moments—tea with the owners of a house mistakenly identified as a terrorist haven while a gunfight loomed down the block— but even the surreal had become draining rather than energizing. There were safe islands, like the one where my family lived, but the sea surrounding them continued to roil. More depressing than the constant battles was the impression that Iraq had simply become too corrupt to cure itself. We stopped working with an ICTF unit because the soldiers just couldn't be trusted. We cut ties with ERU units that had their own agenda of targeting Sunnis at all costs.

Personally, I was done with Iraq. I was ready to go home to America.

**THE PACE OF** the missions left little time to play or even rest. But I do remember some times where we all relaxed and had a little fun. For Thanksgiving 2008, I wanted to show my appreciation to the SEAL team I was working with. I told one of my friends—Singer is not his real name, but it will do—that I would get them all dinner.

I'd met Singer back in 2006, when he was a new guy—a SEAL who had only recently joined his unit. He was a very friendly and supportive man, with a good sense of humor until the mission started; then he was all business. When I told him of my plan to get dinner for the guys, he insisted that I shouldn't pay myself. He took up a collection, and with the money the SEALs collected I was able to get four or five lambs (no turkeys though!) and a whole array of other food, better than an elaborate wedding.

They ate heartily. Then, maybe because they weren't used to Iraqi food, they all came down with stomach flu a few hours later. Singer has not let me forget that in all the time since.

**THE RELATIVE CALM** of our Baghdad neighborhood was shattered that fall when a large car bomb went off down the street a few hundred feet from our house. Aimed at Iraqi and American soldiers, the explosion destroyed a number of stores. The explosion was so severe that a piece of the door from the car that had been blown up flew all the way to our garage.

When the bomb went off, Soheila was standing in the front room. She dove to the floor as the windows shattered with the shock, then scrambled to her feet amid the broken glass and ran inside to look after the kids. They'd already thrown themselves down, huddling on the floors of the rooms, safe. It was a well-practiced precaution, but familiarity made it no less frightening.

But this was what safety looked like in Iraq; most places were a thousand times worse.

Not long after the bombing, kidnappings began in the neighborhood. This was a new development: the sons and daughters of rich people were targeted by criminals, who would take them while they were going or coming from school. It was about money, not jihad, not Islam, not God. We knew one of the victims, a child of a neighbor. The ransom they demanded was immense; though apparently the fee was always negotiated down, one million dollars was a common demand. I don't know the details, how much was paid or how it was arranged, but the child did return.

In a few cases, the police were called, but for the most part, people found it far safer to deal with the kidnappers personally, without police. The kidnappers looked at it as a business proposition. While sometimes they claimed to be warriors of God, they generally spent their money on new cars and flashy clothes. Most operated openly and without fear, much like the Mafia in American movies.

And just like in those movies, the "real" authorities could not be trusted either. The Iraqi police and the army often proved to be as corrupt as anyone.

It was common for the army to search houses for weapons, explosives, and other items that supported the insurgency; I'd helped train some of the units. In theory, they were always supposed to be acting on intelligence, visiting houses where there was a strong probability of illegal activity.

But often their intelligence was nonexistent. The real purpose had nothing to do with fighting the mujahideen or a Shia militia, and they were the ones engaged in illegal activities.

One morning at six when I was away, a squad of soldiers came and knocked on my door, waking Soheila and the kids.

"Open up!" yelled one of the soldiers. "We have to search the house for terrorists."

Soheila went to the door but hesitated. It was clear that the men were from the army—she could tell from the uniforms and the truck out on the street. She thought of mentioning that I worked with the Americans, but that was potentially dangerous. She knew from Mosul that many soldiers worked with the mujahideen or sold them information. She decided that the safest course was simply to open the door and not mention me or the Americans.

The men pushed into the house. She gathered the children in the hall and waited.

The soldiers went straight to the bedroom, searched quickly, then came out and went through the rest of the house. They returned without finding anything, as Soheila knew they wouldn't.

"Sorry, sorry," they said, returning. "We found nothing. False report. Go back to sleep."

Relieved, Soheila and the children went back inside. It didn't seem as if anything had been taken—the soldiers had been through so quickly, she was convinced they had come just to satisfy a superior that they were working—another common reason for "raids." It was possible they had picked the house simply because they knew there would be no trouble there.

Excitement over, they all fell back asleep. When they woke, they began going about their normal business, eating and then preparing to go out shopping. Soheila sent our oldest into the bedroom, where we kept our money.

"Mama!" said my daughter, returning. "The money is gone! I couldn't find it."

Soheila ran in to look for herself. All of our cash had been taken, including what remained of our life savings, which had been hidden in the closet. We'd had a kilo of gold and about ten thousand dollars, saved up from my earnings. (At the time a kilogram of gold would have been worth twenty to twenty-five thousand dollars in the United States.) Her jewelry was missing as well.

Soheila called me, and I called some American commanders and advisors to the Iraqi army. The commanders came and questioned Soheila, allegedly investigating, but it was too late—the criminals were gone. We never knew whether they had simply been masquerading as soldiers or whether they were actual soldiers who were now covering up the theft.

**BACK IN THE STATES**, Tatt was becoming more and more frustrated with the process of trying to get us a visa. Though he never told me, he started thinking of alternatives that included simply spiriting me out of the country. I'm not sure how that would have worked—I doubt he was either—but through it all he kept trying to either get the paperwork through or find a way around it. He finally enlisted the help of an immigration attorney in California who went to work on the case pro bono. Getting George the lawyer to help turned out to be one of the most important things Chief Tatt did; as he put it later, without the attorney's aid he would have "suck-started my pistol" many times. George sacrificed considerable time and worked extremely hard to help Tatt; together, they started making progress—the questions that came back were easier to answer.

I should mention that I was hardly the only interpreter or Iraqi citizen whose status was affected by the glacierlike speed of the review process. According to a story published by the McClatchy news service in March 2013, less than five thousand visas have been issued under the program, despite the fact that five times that number have been authorized. Many good men and their families are in Iraq, in the same situation we were in. Thank God and the SEALs that I was able to fit into the program.

Toward the end of 2008, Tatt forwarded me a set of forms that needed to be filled out. It was only then that I started to let myself think it was really going to happen. I stopped playing my mental games, walling myself off against disappointment. Soheila and I got passports for the kids. I bought an Xbox 360 and some video games and told the kids to play them to help them learn English. I did the same with American movies.

It wasn't just English they had to learn. They knew very little about American customs. *When do you eat? What's the music like? What clothes should you wear?* There is only so much that you can pick up from foreign broadcasts, and I would imagine that much of that is wrong. We tried to get as much information about the United States and American life as possible. It was our future, and finally a future we could believe in.

# 13

# LIVING THE DREAM

**T**HERE WERE SIGNS of progress in Iraq as 2008 came to a close and 2009 began. On January 1, the United States handed over security in Baghdad's Green Zone to Iraqi authorities—something unimaginable two years before. At the end of the month, provincial elections were held with a minimum amount of violence. In February, the new American president, Barack Obama, announced that the majority of American troops would be withdrawn from the country by August 2010.

Still, Iraq was hardly a model of peace and understanding. While the number of American troops killed in the country declined, it remained a dangerous place for translators as well as soldiers. In February, Iraqi policemen opened fire on Americans who were touring their positions, killing a U.S. soldier and an interpreter in Mosul;

three other men were wounded. The same day, an interpreter was among those killed in a firefight in Diyala Province in eastern Iraq.

We'd already made our decision and had no illusions about staying in Iraq. I could tell that conflict would continue without the Americans; it might even grow worse. So much blood and hatred had soaked into the fabric of the country that it would take years if not decades for peace to truly return. Most importantly, it was very depressing to hear people always talking not about how to build things, but how to tear them down. That was not talk for children to hear. It would not help them shape their future.

Even if hatred and greed weren't contagious, the fact that I had worked so closely with the Americans would always mark me in Iraq. Worse, it would make my family's lives that much harder, covering them with a shadow that might be impossible to escape. There were bound to be many people who hated me for working with the Americans and would hold it against them.

But life went on. I invited some of my American friends to visit us at the house. They had to sneak in—not only for our safety but theirs. Still, it felt good to host them. There is a fine tradition of hospitality in Iraq. To open one's home to a guest honors the host as well as the guest.

We also got a dog.

I don't suppose there's a father anywhere in the world who can resist the pleas of his kids for a puppy. After a spirited campaign for a pet, they finally broke me down. We ventured to a pet store, where the kids and I selected Shero. He was a male German shepherd, with maybe another breed or two mixed in somewhere back in his ancestry. A smart dog, he was a fun addition to the family . . . even if Dad ended up walking him a bit more than was promised.

**THE MONTHS PASSED.** Iraqi forces took over more and more of the operations. These were not small missions—hundreds of bad guys were rounded up, and I often found myself in the middle of the action. That was where I wanted to be. The SEALs who were acting as advisors had to forcibly keep me back at times, which to me made no sense. I was often the most experienced person in the unit, certainly more so than the Iraqis, and to me being the second or third person in the "train" as we entered the house made perfect sense. I could often defuse a bad situation with a simple phrase or two. If things were going bad, I could usually spot it before anyone else.

Gradually, I began being assigned to fewer and fewer operations. It took a while before I realized that the American commanders had started to hold me back because I was going to leave the country. That's actually a standard military practice—they protect "short-timers," but of course I had no idea.

There was plenty of danger and plenty of fanaticism still to deal with. The attitudes of the extremists remained hardened and in many ways unfathomable.

We captured a fighter at one point who told me he was sorry he hadn't died.

"Why?" I asked, though I suspected I knew the reason.

"I wanted to have lunch with Muhammad," he told me.

"Lunch?"

"I have been promised."

I thought of asking whether he had checked with the Holy Prophet's scheduler to see if he would be free. Instead, I merely asked him to explain. These sorts rarely had a sense of humor.

"I want to fight and be killed so I go to Paradise immediately, and eat with Muhammad," he said, repeating what he had said as if it were obvious. When I finally got him to elaborate a little, I learned that some so-called religious leader had promised that he would have *exactly* such a reward if he died fighting Americans.

We talked for a while, but it was a one-sided discussion, with him reciting some American mistakes as justification for his misguided martyrdom. It was clear he had been brainwashed by his so-called religious leaders until he was no more than a walking bomb.

There's no denying that America made mistakes in the war and elsewhere; certainly no nation has ever been perfect, and war by definition is an ugly, error-filled activity. The occupation, though well intentioned, had its share of mistakes and even outrages. Many of these mistakes could be used to inflame Muslims—burning Korans, for example, was a foolish and grave error, a grave sin that should have been avoided.

But the answer to such things is not hatred. You cannot protect your religion by destroying others. You have to build it, make things, show the world how great God is and how great the people who believe are. Instead of knocking down buildings, you make them.

I always believed this, in some way, from the time I was young, but the war made my beliefs stronger and more explicit. Seeing death and destruction taught me how precious humans are—how much potential we all have. If I had not witnessed so much death, I would think those thoughts were trivial and easy. But I've seen what happens when people do not value life, and I've paid dearly for that simple knowledge.

One thing always impressed me about the SEALs: they didn't care what my religion was. I could have been a Shiite Muslim or a Christian, a Buddhist or a Rastafarian, and they would have treated me the same. I know because we had translators of those faiths, and not once was religion an issue for them.

IN EARLY JUNE 2009, Tatt sent a message to one of the team members working with me:

**TELL JOHNNY TO GET READY. HE'S TRAVELING ON JULY 7.**

Really?
Really.

I couldn't believe it. But then I could. Things started moving quickly—time sped by faster than it had in a decade.

The only thing we could take with us were clothes. We started selling and giving away things discreetly, careful not to make too big a deal of things.

We stumbled when we had to figure out what to do with Shero, our dog. It was too complicated to take him with us, but giving him up was hard for the kids. We spent a lot of time trying to figure out who we would give him to, without coming to a conclusion. In the end, I decided the best thing to do was bring him back to the store we had purchased him from. It was a sad day for the dog, for the kids, and for me.

But we were going to America, escaping to live our dream.

Where, though? America was a big place, bigger than I could even imagine. Tatt and everyone else wanted to know what city we would settle in.

I'd told him and others Virginia—which of course is a state, not a city. I'd been working with Team 10, an East Coast team. They filled my ears with stories about Virginia and the rest of the East Coast, telling me how wonderful it was. With the time getting closer and our departure now *real,* we had to make genuine plans: we needed a city or town to head to.

My friends with Team 10 volunteered to look for a job for me as well as a place to live. They started putting out feelers. But as we were getting ready, Tatt suggested we might be more comfortable in southern California.

It was a much more temperate area, similar to Iraq in many ways. There was also a large Iraqi and Middle Eastern community, much larger it seemed than anywhere in Virginia. This meant that my family would have an easier time settling in. And the government and military had many installations and related businesses; there'd be plenty of opportunity for jobs.

Somewhere along the way, someone mentioned snow.

Snow?

"You can get snow in Virginia," said an Iraqi who'd moved to the States some years before. "It's not often, but it does happen."

I had seen snow in my travels during my younger days, but I didn't like it. The presence of the Iraqi community was really the decider, but if there had been any doubt, snow would have sealed it.

We managed to sell some of our furniture and gave the rest to relatives. But we kept the news that we were moving to America as quiet as we could. I thought it would be dangerous, even in the better sections of Baghdad, to admit you were close to Americans. The news might reach kidnappers, or even the mujahideen. To openly voice a dream—my dream—of someday living free in the United States would be the same as inviting death.

**JULY 7, 2009:** Neither Soheila nor I slept the entire night. At six o'clock, we looked at each other, hopeful and yet not daring to hope, then got out of bed and went to get the children.

Inside, I had mixed feelings. I wanted my family safe. I wanted a better life. I wanted freedom.

I wanted to live the dream. And I would do it. There was no going back—I burned my old papers, everything I had, every connection to the Americans, every trace of my life here: I was afraid that if I were caught with them now, on the way to the airport or in the plane, they would betray me. The Iraqi government—or worse, terrorists—would know I was trying to escape, and kill me and my family. My past was now dead. My only hope was the future.

But leaving Iraq meant that there was a good chance I would never see my mother again. Leaving Iraq meant that my sister-in-law, who had helped us so much, would be left behind. Leaving meant that my brother and sisters, our entire family, many of my Iraqi friends, the people I knew of my tribe—at best they would be very distant now. Most if not all of them would find it safer not to acknowledge my existence. Others would have to denounce me, as I had once had to denounce my American brothers, to keep from being killed.

Leaving was something I had to do. It was not simply that I had to follow my dream, or even that I had to protect my wife and give my children a better life. It was that I had to breathe, and in order to breathe, I had to walk into the future.

The future was America. Iraq was the past.

The Mosul I knew, the city I had grown up in, was gone. It had died, just as my father had died, and my grandfather, my great-grandfather, and all my ancestors. I held the city as I held them, in the shards of my memories, in the odd remembrances and the strong feelings evoked by old photographs and nostalgic songs.

Iraq itself was fading, melting into the shimmering fog of the past, its outlines fading with each moment.

I had to move forward. I had to become an immigrant.

Finally, after an interminable wait, a car pulled up outside. Soheila and I pushed each of the children out quickly, getting them in as if we were back in Mosul at the height of the war, escaping the mujahideen.

It took only a few minutes to get to the airport, though it seemed like hours. IEDs, ambushes, checkpoints—all of the fears I'd lived with for so many years haunted me now, looming at the edges of my vision, rising one last time to taunt me. I was watchful and restless, lips tight, breath shallow.

We were as safe as we could possibly be, and yet as fragile and vulnerable as a wisp of smoke in a windstorm. We were all quiet. Saying anything would have broken whatever spell protected us.

Two SEALs were waiting for us at the airport. They were all smiles. I was having trouble breathing.

As we made our way to the airplane, my mind raced in many

different directions. I tried to dismiss the fears and the paranoia about all the bad things that might happen. I tried to welcome the newness of America, and anticipate what freedom might bring. The concerns of my kids, their immediate needs for food and the restrooms, were a welcome distraction—it was easier to comfort and assure them than deal with my own uncertainties.

Then we were aboard, finding our seats. We settled in together, our own little cluster in the aircraft.

Then the plane door closed.

I looked at Soheila. We shared a moment of doubt: Were we dreaming? Was this becoming real?

All I could think of was the mission months before when we'd pulled the militia leader off the Jordanian plane. Was that going to happen now?

The passengers were in but the door was still open. What were they waiting for?

I sat in the seat, trying to remain calm—I didn't want my wife or children to know how nervous I was. They had no idea: they knew nothing of the mission, and as far as they were concerned, nothing could stop them now.

Finally, the door was closed. And yet I still could hardly breathe. It was not until the plane started to roll that I let myself believe.

*We're going to make it!*

I became weightless as the wheels left the runway. In that moment my fears fell away. Finally, reality and dream merged: we were on our way to America, on our way to safety and freedom, to the future.


**WHAT HAPPENED NEXT** will sound anticlimactic to an American; it will seem like nothing. Often it seems that way to me as well— nothing and everything. But that is the best part of being an immigrant: even things other people think of as being trivial are special.

None of us had ever been on a commercial airliner before. We didn't know what to expect, really. That may have helped keep the kids calm.

We flew into Jordan, stayed the night there, then took a flight to Chicago. A friend met us; we went straight to a hotel, exhausted by the trip and everything that had led to it.

The next morning, I found a computer in the hotel lobby and used Google to find a map of the area. I saw that there was a shopping center not far away. I gathered up my youngest son and together we set off in that direction, curious about what an American shopping center looked like.

It was strange and wonderful to be on the street with my little boy and not be thinking about IEDs or being followed or being shot, not looking over my shoulder or wondering whether I might be caught in some accidental crossfire.

I was living my dream. It had taken the better part of a decade and several thousand miles, but I was a human being again.

Son on my shoulders, I walked through the streets until we came to a Target department store. Inside, we went down the aisles filled with clothes and household goods. I hadn't seen so many things for sale under one roof ever in all my life.

I had to buy something. It was as if I needed to prove myself that this was really happening: if it was *just* a dream, the cash register would explode; I would wake back in my old reality.

Hearing the amount of the bill, counting out the dollars, getting change back—these were all things I had done thousands of times in Iraq, but here it was new. It was a strange triumph, an assertion of who I was and who I would become.

I wasn't dreaming. I was wide awake, and I was in America.

We landed in California the next day. Four or five SEALs met us at the airport in full uniform. They'd already found us a house to rent. One of their wives took my wife shopping for groceries and household staples, all with money they had pooled among themselves. Their kindness and friendship was unbelievable. It was as if they had adopted us.

Tears were in Tatt's eyes when I brought my family to his home for a barbecue a few days later. I'm sure they were in my eyes as well.

"If I were to die tomorrow, I'd die a happy man," he told me. "Because I did one good thing in my life—I got you to safety."

Chief Tatt has done many good things in his life; his courage and bravery in Iraq made him a hero by any measure you care to use. But I am honored and humbled that he thought so highly of me to think that. And I am surely grateful for the three years and countless hours he spent getting me home to America.

A few days later, I found the beach. I remember walking out to the pier and simply being amazed.

"These people know how to live!" I said aloud, so surprised and happy to see a place that looked as if it came from the pages of a fairy tale. I walked around almost dumbfounded, enjoying the sun and the easy breeze. Since that day, I've seen many fancier things and been to many elaborate parks and luxurious settings. But the beach remains a special place for me; five minutes from work, and I can remind myself of the great dream I am privileged to live.

We found schools for the kids. I won't say that it has been easy for them to adjust to their new lives, even if they all seem content and with new friends. Transitions are difficult, even when you are going from a nightmare to a dream. But they are becoming very American—my boys play the latest video games, and their English is better than mine. The girls know more about fashion than I could learn in a lifetime. I would not be surprised if you couldn't tell where they were born without quite a bit of questioning.

My accent, of course, marks me as an immigrant. And my background and religion are different from the majority. But while Muslims are sometimes regarded with suspicion in America, religion hasn't been an issue for us. Partly this is because we live in an area where there are others from the Middle East, and so while we may be a minority in the broad United States, here we are normal. But I think also that most Americans are tolerant about religion when they know a person or interact with them personally. Many simply never ask.

I haven't often felt that I have to defend Islam. Still, the defense is easy: Islam, as a religion, is not involved with killing. Extremists are the problem, not the religion. Christianity went through a period when people were burned at the stake for their beliefs. Was that because of Jesus's teachings? Or because of people who misused the religion as an excuse for themselves, their own lust for power or whatever satisfaction they got from killing?

The latter, I think. It is hard to argue otherwise.

I don't feel the need to go to the mosque very often. God is everywhere; He hears me pray wherever He is and needs no special notice. Prayer itself is not even as important as how you behave— you do as you believe, observing God's will, fulfilling it. The way you act is the way you understand religion; if you act like a killer, then you do not understand God.

But I am not a religious teacher or anything like an expert. The bottom line for me is that religion is something that comes from the heart. You can't fake God out, so don't be so foolish as to try to fake yourself out.


**WE'VE HAD MANY** joys since we came to America. Most of them are simple. Friends come over for dinner; we barbecue chicken and sometimes steak on our small propane grill. We plant flowers in the small flowerbed in front of our house. We get a new dog, and friends help us make a doghouse.

When we lived in Iraq, even before the war, Soheila and I tended not to celebrate personal dates like birthdays and wedding anniversaries. It wasn't because we didn't think they were important; I think every human being knows that those days are special. But with the difficult economy and the struggle just to stay alive, to find work, to eat, there was very little reason or means to celebrate. When you are struggling for water, you do not think too much about champagne, to borrow a saying from an American friend.

Now, though, things are different. I may not be the richest man when it comes to money, but my life here has given me much to celebrate, and I take the time with my wife and family to commemorate every personal holiday we have.

The celebrations are simple. For my most recent birthday, we went to a shopping mall and department stores—a funny way to spend a special day, you might think, until you remember the poverty we escaped from. The array of clothes, the tools, the furniture, books, toys—walking the aisles is like walking through a dreamland. Being able to buy simple necessities when you need them is a luxury I may never get used to.

And I can never eat enough birthday cake, even though I don't have much of a sweet tooth.

Soheila gave up her idea of becoming a doctor well before we got married, but she has continued to learn, and lately has been talking about going to college to study political science. She has been following elections and studying up on them. She likes to write and read—and still she writes poetry, now in English as well as Arabic.

In the meantime, she has found a job teaching Arabic.

As have I. With help from my SEAL friends, I have found a job supervising language instruction for active-duty servicemen. While language instruction is our task, our goal is not simply to give our students a few words or phrases they might use in the course of their day. We try to teach them as much as we can about the different cultures they are likely to encounter. Words are only one aspect of understanding. It is all about context—you have to know where the words are coming from if you are to truly understand them.

Though most of what I do now involves supervising others, I still work directly with students from time to time. It's a job that suits me. My experiences have taught me how important it is to share knowledge. I've learned firsthand the value of hope and the importance of passing it on, whether you are doing that with encouragement or a vision of the future.

Teaching is much more difficult than the translating I did during the war. In Iraq, the most immediate translations were of very simple concepts—go here, go there, have you seen this person, etc. Now I have to communicate technical terms, detail sentence structure, and encourage people to have long conversations. I have to talk about customs. I have come to think in English rather than Arabic. It sometimes feels as if a new room has been built in my head.

But it's a good room.

I am still getting to know the United States. There is much about the country to learn, and many places to see—Washington, New York, the Midwest. I would love to go to Iowa and see the corn growing in the vast fields, and someday I will hunt in Utah.

This has become our country. We are hungry to learn as much as we can about our new history, from the Revolution to the moon launch. But it is not because of the past that I have come to America. It is because of the future. It is because here it is possible not just to be free, but to be free with a purpose—to be free to build things, whether they are houses or buildings or companies or new lives. That should be every human being's goal: to be creative and productive, not a destroyer, not a person who tears others down or punishes the innocent for his own evil thoughts.

**LIVING THE DREAM** does not mean that you are completely protected from the past. I can't completely forget the habits I learned in war, the precautions that made me safe. If I see a car in my rearview mirror for too long, I often turn off the road I'm on and look for a different route. If a friend sneaks up on me from behind, I have been known to pull a knife from my pocket.

There were good times in Iraq, even during the war, and I try to think of them. We helped a lot of people. But sometimes when I sleep, my mind wanders back into the dark places and the fears return, unbidden.

Living the dream does not mean that you are protected always from sorrow. I miss those I've left behind, some very deeply.

**I WOKE UP** one morning in 2012 and saw Soheila standing near the bed, her eyes red. She looked as if she hadn't slept.

"What's wrong?" I asked.

She shook her head, as if she might keep it secret.

"What?" I said again, this time more gently.

"Your mother."

My mother had died the night before. Soheila had gotten the phone call while I slept; she spent the entire night in our bathroom, tears flowing. She muffled her sighs so she wouldn't wake me.

My mom was in her seventies. She was my last link to my older relatives, to the old Iraq before Saddam, before these times. Her death severed my connections to that time. Losing her was like losing my security system and a large part of my history. It's a sorrow deep within, something that follows from a distance but never leaves, even as I turn toward a hopeful future.

That future is definitely an American one. Every day there are reminders for me. Some are simple pleasures in America, where even being stopped by a policeman for a traffic ticket can remind me how much better off I am here than in Iraq.

Other reminders are tragic: as we worked on this book, an uncle and his son were both killed in an attack in Mosul. Their deaths pained me greatly. And it didn't help to know that I myself couldn't go to comfort the family, much less attend their funerals. My presence in Iraq would put many people at risk; anyone who helped me would be a marked man.

MY TIME WITH the SEALs, my days in the war, affected me in ways I don't even understand. I am reminded of a sculptor, who works scraping stone for five years, getting his sculpture just right. At the end of that five years, his hands are bent with the exertion against the stone. He has created a great work of art, but what has he done to his hands?

Iraq now has become a dark place to me, a place I saw at night, a place where I worried about my wife and children. Destiny—and the SEALs—took me from there and put me in a place of light.

If you read or watch the news, you know that Iraq is struggling. It's even worse than the reports say. There is much killing, more than is ever broadcast. Mosul especially has become a place of turmoil, with different groups vying for power and the specter of revenge as well as hate hanging over the city. Sunni versus Shia, Iraqi versus Kurd—the divisions have become sharper as time has gone.

They have taken a great toll. I am looking now at a photo of an area of the city I knew well, a residential and business area of three- and four-story houses, a place where there was once a park and a vibrant street life. Children crowded in the alleys that spread out from the main streets; there was a mosque at one side.

The mosque remains, its walls battered and stained black from fire and explosions. A good number of the other buildings are gone, their only traces rubble at the edge of immaculately bulldozed lots. Some of the surviving buildings lean, their foundations disturbed forever. Others are crumbling. If there is a building that has not been touched by the war, I can't see it through my tears.

Sometimes I wish had the power to make true changes in Iraq. These are just thoughts, not real desires: I would never become a politician, and I have no plans to run for office anywhere, in Iraq or in America. But if it were possible, if *all* dreams could become realities, then I would first impose martial law on all Iraq, stopping all conflict in the country. I would bring in American and European teachers as well as policemen. I would rebuild Baghdad. It would be a new city, rebuilt from the ground up.

Then I would go to Basra and do the same. Mosul would follow, Tal Afar—one by one, each city around the country would be replaced with a new version, rising from the ashes of the war's destruction.

I'd rebuild all of Iraq's institutions—the police, the army, universities, everything. I would start programs to send as many Iraqis as possible to live in the United States for a year or two. When they got back, they would understand the possibilities.

I'd get the money to pay for this from oil—and from ending corruption. Simply taking the money from the thieves' pockets would do a tremendous amount for the people of Iraq. Money is being siphoned off by corrupt people everywhere. Payments are even going to Iran. Stop this, and there would be plenty of money to build anything you can think of.

Five years, maybe ten, and Iraq would be an entirely different country.

It's an impossible dream—an idealist's dream, not something an immigrant should have, since an immigrant needs to be a realist.

Still, there are many realistic things that can be done to make Iraq better. Improving the schools should be a priority. Many of the worst problems in the country stem from the lack of education, a grave fault that the war has made worse. People for the most part are ignorant about many things, most especially the world outside their country's boundaries. They know little that is real about America, which fosters hatred; they know very little about other religions or even their own, which fosters intolerance. Is it any wonder that violence is the result?

**WHEN I'M ASKED** about the war, the question is sometimes really a different one: *Do you blame the Americans for stirring up the trouble?*

Was America the cause of the violence?

No. We had the seeds for this destruction within us all along, and whether it would have come out so soon or been delayed years, eventually the killing would have started; cancer will do its job later if not sooner.

Saddam was his own cancer. If we had been able to deal with him ourselves . . .

Outside influences—al-Qaeda, Shiites in Iran, the Iranian government—took advantage of our suffering and confusion after the dictator was gone. In the struggle for power, nothing was sacred, not even human life or religion. People called themselves "warriors of God" and claimed to be righteous followers of God's plan, defenders of the faith, protectors of the good. But what they did, what they *always* did, was the opposite.

God is a creator, and He wants us to celebrate what He has created. He wants us to create as well. But the people who pretended to be working in His name were not builders or creators. They didn't protect the innocent, let alone their religion.

Instead, they blew things up. They gave grenades to children, strapped bombs on women, drove explosives into marketplaces where innocents struggled to get the basic necessities of living. Instead of building a community, they tore it apart. Where once there had been many people of different faiths and different opinions living together, they brought fear and death, suspicion and evil.

It was easy. All it required was hatred.

To build a community is much harder. To make people safe and confident, to make them trust and then help each other—that is something that takes patience and a lot of sweat.

Killing people in the name of God? That is to me the biggest sin against Him. How can you dare to do that? It is God's creation—how can you blaspheme by undoing His majestic work? How could you think that God, the almighty of everything, would need *your* help to do anything?

We are not put here to be about ourselves. That is a truth I know above all others.

**ANOTHER QUESTION** I am asked is easier to answer: *Will you ever go back to Iraq?*

No.

Even if it was somehow possible to go without fear, the Iraq I knew is gone. Maybe my children will decide to visit, or their children, or their children's children. They'll be like all Americans, nostalgically looking not only at their roots but at what might have been. I hope what they see before them will be a country that has reached the greater part of its potential. I hope that they see peace where once there was war, new buildings where there were ruins, pretty homes where once there were slums.

And I hope that they realize they have made themselves a much better life in America than they ever would have had there.

**I AM AN IMMIGRANT.** Soon I will become an American citizen. It will be the next step on my journey. I will help other immigrants and other citizens.

I will have my rituals, old and new.

I am already accumulating them. On Sunday mornings I like to rise before the rest of the family. I get coffee at a local shop, then drive over to a swap meet held at an old drive-in movie theater. Tables and tents line the tired macadam. People hawk wares of all sorts, old and new, some very used, some still wrapped in plastic. I like to listen to the people as they talk and bargain; I occasionally do a bit of haggling myself. But mostly I like to walk along the aisles and look at the variety of my new country. There is a great freedom in this place—no one at the swap meet tells you where to go, or what to buy, or what to think. Every item for sale is a possibility— what use might this tool be put to? What joy might this toy bring to a child?

We are all immigrants in this place, all living a dream of possibilities, not merely wishing for a better future but doing our best, in everyday ways, to make it. It is the immigrant's dream, and it is finally a reality I can safely share.

# ACKNOWLEDGMENTS

First, to my beautiful wife: You are the love of my life, and I am so incredibly thankful to have you by my side. Your strength and support through everything were the glue that held our family together. And to my children, this is all for you—so that you have a better life. The American dream is yours; cherish it and never forget the hardships that gave you this amazing opportunity to live in freedom.

Several people helped guide me through making this book, and they deserve special thanks. I would like to thank Jay Hoffman for his endless support in many facets of this process. At William Morrow, editor Peter Hubbard believed in me and my story from the very beginning; I am thankful for his guidance along the way. I also received invaluable aid from Sharyn Rosenblum, Heidi Richter, and Cole Hager, without whom the book would never have been a success.

I would also like to express thanks to my friend Brett Harrison. Brett was a driving force behind this book, helping to make it a reality; without him this next step in my dream never would have happened.

Like many people, I owe a debt to Chris Kyle that can never be repaid. Thank you, brother.

And, Jim, thank you for your extreme patience with me. You spent so much time and an incredible amount of effort making sure my story was told accurately and in a way that honors the sacrifices made by everyone who served. Our friendship will remain for many years to come.

Suzanne, my sister, your generosity and that of the community upon our arrival in the United States will never be forgotten. My family owes you a sincere debt of gratitude.

To Tatt, Brad, Kevin, Jeff, Taco, JT, Bear, Quiet Man, Bishop, and all my SEAL brothers: A simple thank-you is not enough for changing my life and the life of my family and making my American dream exist. Your talents and sacrifices for each other and this country continue to amaze me. You have been such a big part of my life, and I am so grateful for all of it. Not all of you are in the book, but you are all in my heart. When I was away from my family, I found another one with all of you. You truly are my brothers.

—JOHNNY WALKER

A large number of active-duty SEALs and recently retired members of the military and other government agencies helped Johnny and me as we worked on the book.

As we noted earlier, we have decided not to use their names, due to their service or, in some cases, private contractor status. While it may not be front-page news in America, the war in Iraq is continuing every day, and American as well as Iraqi lives remain in great danger. We trust and hope that they will realize that we are both overwhelmingly grateful for their assistance, and that they understand that we don't want to inadvertently place them in any danger.

Besides echoing Johnny's words above, I would especially like to thank the Walker family for their hospitality and patience in the two years it took to write this book.

—JIM DEFELICE

# COLLABORATOR'S NOTE

By Jim DeFelice

One late afternoon in the spring of 2011, Chris Kyle and I were sitting in his den working on the book that became *American Sniper*. We'd been working since the early morning; it was our third or fourth day straight and we were both badly in need of a break. But neither one of us was about to admit that to the other; SEALs don't ever need breaks, and New Yorkers are too arrogantly competitive to admit to anything smacking of weakness.

The conversation began dragging, and if we weren't going to take a break we needed something to change things up a bit. So I suggested we go through a bunch of Chris's photos and free-associate a bit. We'd played with that in the past—Chris would look at each photo and describe it; I'd ask questions to fill out what he was saying.

Somewhere in the middle of this, we came upon an image of an Iraqi in full battle dress, holding an AK and grinning wildly. It was clear he wasn't a SEAL—wrong cammies and gear—but he also was clearly not a member of the Iraqi army, let alone a member of the mujahideen.

"Who's that?" I asked. I thought maybe he was a para—a CIA officer or contract employee working with the SEALs.

Not that they ever did that.

Chris laughed. "Johnny Walker," he said. "The only Iraqi I ever trusted with a gun."

That pretty much begged further explanation. During most of Chris's time in Iraq, the Iraqi army was notorious for having traitors in its midst. The SEALs—and Chris—worked with them often, and they were of course armed, but there was never a high confidence factor.

"He saved my ass a bunch of times," added Chris. "All of ours. Johnny Walker. He was a real badass."

*Badass* being the highest accolade Chris could give anyone.

"What did he do?" I asked.

"Johnny was a terp. But he was a lot more than a terp. A lot more."

*Terp,* of course, means interpreter. I was pretty intrigued by that—while interpreters played a really important role in Iraq, I'd never heard them praised by the guys who'd actually been on the ground with them. Chris Kyle calling one a badass—now *that* was something different.

I forget the rest of the conversation; it wasn't very long, and we quickly moved on. But Johnny Walker and his role as a kind of Super Terp remained with me.

Johnny appears in *American Sniper,* with a different name and his identity heavily disguised—sorry, but at that point I believed not only that his life was in danger but that if he were identified in that book the mujahideen would make a serious effort to find him. (His nationality is wrong, and there's no mention of him coming to America. I'll let you work out who he is.) Unfortunately the stories about Johnny—like the vast majority of what Chris and I talked about—were left on the cutting-room floor.

I didn't entirely forget about Johnny, but I didn't think much about him either until the summer of 2012. By then, *American Sniper* was a megahit, Chris was filming a TV show, and I was waiting for final clearance to get a double-hernia operation. One day our editor, Peter Hubbard, called me and asked if I knew who Johnny Walker was. He'd just finished talking to Chris, who'd urged him to publish Johnny's story.

"Would you write it?" Peter asked.

I'm not sure if I was under painkillers at the time—probably—but with both Chris and Peter pushing it, I would have agreed in any event.

USUALLY WHEN I collaborate on a memoir—I've done a couple of others besides *Sniper;* all were best sellers—the goal is to re-create on the page what the main "author" sounds like in person. Without boring you to death with a lot of talk about technique, the process is trickier than it may seem; vocal tics and identifiers don't always work quite right on the page. The final product is always an approximation of the subject's voice, optimized for the written word.

In Johnny's case, there was an added complication: he's not a native English speaker. Johnny speaks English fairly well, but if it were replicated in the book it would have been close to unintelligible.

I worked with him quite a bit not to just get his speaking patterns, but the thought processes behind them. Johnny is surprisingly philosophical and introspective. He has complex notions about religion and life, not all of which he can easily communicate in English. The trick was to adapt his thoughts as well as his words to easily readable prose that sounds the way he would sound if he were a native speaker. Listening to Johnny speak Arabic—a language of which I am wholly ignorant—turned out to be extremely helpful. His cadences—long and complex, and often quite emotional—supplied as much of the basis to the way this book sounds as his English. His Arabic has a very rhythmical sound, with what at least to a Westerner sounds like a heavy, recurring beat. I tried to duplicate it here by using word repetition and some formal rhetorical flourishes, which also gave the prose a little of the more formal style it would have had if rendered in his native language. At the same time, the book wouldn't sound like Johnny if it didn't have at least some of the slang he learned from Americans along the way.

Johnny and I have worked to get this book to sound as close as it can to how he talks and thinks without making it completely unapproachable to an audience raised on English. Hopefully, we've succeeded.

**THERE WERE, OF COURSE,** other problems in writing the book. The trickiest had to do with the vagaries of memory. Personal recollection of events is always an issue in a memoir; in fact, it's an issue in any nonfiction writing. It was especially an issue for Johnny. He saw so much action during the war that events often blurred together. Unlike the SEAL teams, which rotated in and out of Iraq after roughly six months of work, Johnny went essentially nonstop from 2003 until his escape to America. He was on a *lot* of missions, and a lot of them were very similar. Sorting through them was hard enough; putting them into the proper order was even tougher. We worked with several different timelines in an effort to get everything straight. In fact, while the major events in the book are presented in their proper sequence—working for the army, the SEALs, Soheila's escape from Mosul—we were never able to place a lot of other, fortunately minor, episodes. There was so much material available that in most cases we left them out. In the other instances, we've noted our uncertainty about where exactly they fit on the timeline.

We've also been purposely vague about the methods the SEALs and other units used. This isn't a book about techniques and military procedures; beyond that, we didn't want to inadvertently threaten the lives of any American in a future operation. For similar reasons of security, no SEAL on active duty is identified in the book. Most of the Iraqis aren't either. We've also left out the names and some identifying features of Johnny's children and his relatives back in Iraq. Those relatives and their acquaintances, unfortunately, remain in considerable danger.

**BY THEIR VERY NATURE**, books are always a much different experience for the writers than for the readers. When I think of this book, I think primarily of the hospitality of Johnny's family and friends, who accepted me most graciously into their lives. There were late-night barbecues, a good portion of drinking, and long arguments on politics and religion that went completely over my head because they were primarily in Arabic.

But I'll also think of Johnny and me driving in the winding hills outside of San Diego one early Sunday morning, the sky clear, the weather perfect. Suddenly a Hells Angel appeared behind us. Johnny, driving what can be best described as a four-cylinder family car, decided he wasn't going to let him pass.

He didn't. The fact that we didn't careen off into a ravine was a bonus, as far as Johnny was concerned.

Hells Angel or not, the motorcyclist eventually decided he didn't want to deal with a maniac and turned off at an intersection. Much to my relief.

"You are worried about my driving, brother?" Johnny asked as we continued on at a (slightly) more sedate pace.

"Never," I said, prying my hands off the dashboard. That was probably a bit of a lie—the gravel we'd kicked off into the ravines on both sides of the road would have filled a parking lot at Dodger Stadium, and we'd violated all of Newton's laws in the ten minutes or so we'd raced the biker.

We were both quiet for a moment.

"How you doing?" I finally asked.

"Livin' the dream, bro." He turned and gave me a big Johnny Walker grin. "Livin' the dream."